The Paraprofessional's Guide to Effective Behavioral Intervention

The Paraprofessional's Guide to Effective Behavioral Intervention is a comprehensive guide to appropriate behavioral strategies in the classroom, based on the Least Restrictive Behavioral Intervention (LRBI) and Positive Behavioral Interventions and Supports (PBIS). This highly practical book provides:

- an increased understanding of the processes underlying student behavior in the classroom, including motivation;
- a wide range of strategies for establishing and promoting positive behavior, as well as counteracting and reducing negative behaviors;
- skills related to nationally recognized standards for paraprofessional competence;
- an understanding of widely accepted principles and practices such as Response to Intervention (RtI).

Set in the context of the legal requirements for paraprofessionals to work "under the direction of a professional" (ESEA) and be "appropriately supervised" (IDEA), *The Paraprofessional's Guide to Effective Behavioral Intervention* illuminates research-based, practical strategies shown to be effective in a wide range of educational settings and which can be implemented immediately and with confidence.

Betty Y. Ashbaker is Associate Professor of Counseling Psychology and Special Education at Brigham Young University, USA.

Jill Morgan is Senior Lecturer in Education at the University of Wales Trinity Saint David, UK.

The Paraprofessional's Guide to Effective Behavioral Intervention

Betty Y. Ashbaker and Jill Morgan

Routledge
Taylor & Francis Group

NEW YORK AND LONDON

First published 2015
by Routledge
711 Third Avenue, New York, NY 10017

and by Routledge
2 Park Square, Milton Park, Abingdon, Oxon OX14 4RN

*Routledge is an imprint of the Taylor & Francis Group,
an informa business*

Library of Congress Cataloging-in-Publication Data
Ashbaker, Betty Y., 1950–
   The paraprofessional's guide to effective behavioral
intervention / by Betty Y. Ashbaker & Jill Morgan.
      pages cm
   Includes bibliographical references and index.
   1. Teachers' assistants—Handbooks, manuals, etc.   2. Behavior
modification—Handbooks, manuals, etc.   3. Classroom
management—Handbooks, manuals, etc.   4. School psychology.
I. Title.
   LB2844.1.A8A73 2015
   371.39'3—dc23
   2014031059

ISBN: 978-0-415-73918-4 (hbk)
ISBN: 978-0-415-73919-1 (pbk)
ISBN: 978-1-315-81684-5 (ebk)

Typeset in Bembo
by Apex CoVantage, LLC

To our families, teachers, and colleagues, who have taught us these lessons—by their deliberate examples and instruction—we give our thanks.

To paraprofessionals, who work so hard to help students learn—academically and behaviorally.

To Alan Hofmeister, who introduced us and started us on the path to paraprofessional supports.

Contents

Acknowledgments

Special thanks

- to Alex Masulis, our editor, who has been encouraging and supportive throughout this project,
- to Teresa Quist at Brigham Young University for assistance with formatting and other organizational work,
- and to Christopher Wells Barlow for artwork.

Introduction

This book is about behavior. Although there are many published texts on this topic, this text is specifically for paraprofessionals (teacher aides, paraeducators, classroom assistants, etc.—we know that your designated titles are numerous). This text is designed to provide you with a comprehensive guide to appropriate behavioral strategies, based on the notions of the Least Restrictive Behavioral Intervention (LRBI) and Positive Behavioral Interventions and Supports (PBIS) as recommended by the federal Office of Special Education Programs (OSEP). It also stresses the importance (as required by law) of paraprofessionals working under the direction of a qualified teacher or other professional.

Appropriate behavior is essential for all students to access learning. As a paraprofessional who supports the teaching/learning process, you need to be an expert in using strategies that promote and maintain positive, appropriate behaviors in students, and know how to deal effectively with negative behaviors, so that the focus of classrooms remains on the teaching/learning process. This is true of your work with all students, not only those who have disabilities or special needs.

This book can serve paraprofessionals in a variety of ways:

- As part of a self-directed program of study to increase your repertoire of professional skills, especially in the area of behavior; this may be on your own, in collaboration with other paraprofessionals as part of a study group, or in collaboration with your teacher or other supervisor as part of your professional development.
- As a prescribed text for a college course relating to your work as a paraprofessional—perhaps as part of an associate degree program.
- As part of a school or school district in-service or professional development training.

The book provides an overview of behavior management. It provides practical applications for common classroom situations and is based on well-researched practices and theory. Paraprofessionals will find throughout this book opportunities to stop and think about their reading and how new information applies to their work setting. These opportunities take the form of questions, statements to respond to, and a variety of forms and matrices that will enable you to consolidate your understanding of the theory and begin to apply it in practice. Occasionally they even take the form of a blank page—so that you can map your thinking and reflections in whatever form suits you best.

Take advantage of these opportunities. Reflection is considered to be an important factor in determining whether knowledge can be put to good use in practice—that is, whether the learning really has any usefulness, or whether it remains interesting theory with no connection to the real world in which you live and work. Although many theories are interesting to learn about and contemplate, as someone who works in a dynamic environment such as a classroom, the application of theory is likely to be of greatest interest and use to you. And the act of writing down your reflections is an important step in developing your thinking and understanding. Merely pondering an idea may be useful, but it is only production of some sort—speaking to someone else about our thoughts or writing them down—that forces us to focus and articulate or explain our thinking.

You may wish to consider writing a regular blog to record your thoughts about what you read. Setting up a blog is simple, and there are a variety of websites that offer free access and advice on how to begin, how to make your blog attractive to readers, and how to personalize and develop your blogging style. This type of reflective writing would also potentially provide you with more food for thought as others respond to your blog and you, in turn, respond to them. Blogging is a very common activity now; indeed, if you put the authors' names into a search engine, you'll find links to our own blogs and webpages.

Are You a Blogger?

Try setting up a blog of your own to state your views about your work as a paraprofessional and your role in managing classroom behavior. You will find that there are many other paraprofessionals who will be interested in what you have to say and pleased to have someone with whom they can discuss their ideas and behavioral challenges.

We have included—and highlighted in boxes and sidebars—results of education and other social science research so that you can understand the theory base of what we do in classrooms and, therefore, why we do what we do. We hope you will find these research tidbits of interest, but bear in mind that the research base for education is constantly being updated. With the Internet, the results of research are now generally much more accessible than they were even 10 years ago. So we would also encourage you to carry out your own investigations and track down additional research on topics that particularly interest you.

If you are reading this book as part of a college course or professional development (PD) training with your school district, you may be assigned to pursue a topic and track down relevant research. However, even if this is not the case, we recommend that you take advantage of the information that is widely available—far too much to include in a book of this size.

The purpose of behavior management systems—whatever shape they take—is first *to establish positive and appropriate behaviors*. Of course, any school-wide or classroom-based approach to behavior must also take into account the negative behaviors that inevitably occur and how they will be dealt with. However, the only way to successfully promote positive behavior is to focus on that positive behavior and use it to crowd out potential negative behaviors. This is an important concept that you will find referred to consistently throughout this book.

There are some other basic themes that also recur throughout the book and provide principles for action for paraprofessionals and teachers:

1. Positive behavior must be the first aim and focus of classroom behavior management systems.
2. We should aim to use Least Restrictive Behavioral Interventions (LRBI) and Positive Behavioral Interventions and Supports (PBIS) to reduce the focus on negative behavior and stress a focus on learning/teaching.
3. The clear link between behavior and learning.
4. The legal requirement that paraprofessionals must work under the direction of a professional.

Basic Principles

1. Positive behavior must be our first aim and focus.
2. Least Restrictive Behavioral Interventions (LRBI) and Positive Behavior Interventions and Supports (PBIS) keep our focus on learning/teaching rather than behavior.
3. The clear link between behavior and learning.
4. Working under the direction of a professional.

We will expand on each of these principles, but here are the essential elements.

1. *Positive behavior as a first aim and focus.*
When we talk of managing behavior in schools, so often the students who come to mind are those who cause us the most concern—or even aggravation! Managing behavior somehow has come to mean managing difficult or inappropriate behavior. This is a reactive stance, as that behavior has already occurred. That makes us take a step back—as if we are just waiting for students to misbehave so that we can jump in with the solution. It's a firefighting approach, but we all know that it's much better (safer and less stressful) to take precautions with small children (hide the matches, teach them the dangers of fire) rather than constantly stand ready to extinguish any fires they might accidently (or intentionally) start.

And so it is in education. In recent years educators have come to see that a pro-active approach that focuses on positive behavior is by far the more effective way to manage both appropriate and inappropriate behavior. By being proactive, we set high expectations and show that we believe students can succeed in reaching those expectations. If we can encourage positive behavior in our students, we automatically reduce inappropriate behavior. We don't ignore inappropriate behavior, but it is not our primary focus.

In this book we talk about Plan A—the proactive, planning ahead for positive behavior patterns—and then Plan B—the strategies and procedures we will use for those students whose behavior causes concern despite our best efforts.

2. *Least Restrictive Behavioral Interventions (LRBI) and Positive Behavioral Interventions and Supports (PBIS).*
We use LRBI and PBIS to reduce the focus on behavior and stress a focus on learning/teaching. **LRBI** and **PBIS** are two current, positive, and very proactive approaches to behavior management that present a solid foundation for developing your understanding and skills in relation to student behavior.

The notion of **LRBI** is an important one. Put simply, it is the idea that least is best: when we respond to inappropriate behavior we use the least complicated response or sanction—one that presents the least disturbance to the important work of teaching while sending a clear message to the student that the behavior is inappropriate and needs to stop. But this notion applies equally well to positive behavior—our response to compliant and cooperative students should likewise be just enough to let them know we've seen and approve but not enough to interrupt the flow of classroom activity.

PBIS is an approach to behavior management proposed by the federal Office of Special Education Programs (OSEP). It is based on a number of core principles, including:

- the need to intervene early on behavioral issues,
- the need to teach appropriate behavior rather than assuming students will just automatically know how to behave appropriately, and
- the need to carefully monitor students whose behavior is of concern so that we can make adjustments as necessary to the strategies in place to manage that behavior.

Although the notion of PBIS was developed by OSEP, these principles are uni-versal and apply to all students—including those with disabilities. PBIS is based on many years of research into behavior management approaches in classrooms across the USA—and in other countries. Notice that it constitutes a proactive and positive stance rather than the firefighting reactions we have already referred to that so often focus solely on the negative behaviors of the minority of our students.

3. *The clear link between behavior and learning.*
The business of the classroom is teaching and learning. Teachers are there to teach or facilitate learning; students are there to learn and respond to teaching. Effective teaching strategies help manage behavior: when material is interesting

and relevant to students and presented in an engaging way, students are much more likely to behave appropriately. Likewise, in a classroom where inappropriate behavior is kept to a minimum, the students are freed up for learning and the teacher for teaching. Teachers of course need skills in both areas, and we explore these issues further in upcoming chapters. The important concept to note here is that behavior and learning have direct and significant effects on each other. What we are aiming for is the highest possible incidence of learning and the lowest possible incidence of inappropriate behavior because the one will guarantee the other and vice versa.

4. Working under the direction of a professional.
There is an additional thread that you will find running through this book: the teacher has ultimate responsibility for all that happens in the classroom, including your work as a paraprofessional, but you need to be well informed to provide effective support for both students and teacher.

This principle speaks for itself, and this book is intended to ensure that paraprofessionals become better informed—particularly in the crucial area of behavior, which is a responsibility shared by all who work in the classroom. Our aim is to provide you with theoretical and practical knowledge that will help you with that responsibility.

This is a good point at which to pause for a moment and consider this collaborative relationship between paraprofessionals and teachers (or other qualified professionals). You may work in one of a variety of settings:

- in a general education classroom with just one teacher and with the same students all week,
- in a resource room with the special education teacher and students who attend the resource room at different times of the week and for differing amounts of time,
- in a junior high or high school where you accompany a student through different class periods and subject/curriculum areas and therefore a host of different subject specialist teachers during the course of the week,
- as a job coach, accompanying a student to a supported employment setting off the school premises for substantial portions of the week.

Whatever the specific details of your work setting, we strongly emphasize that all of your work needs to be carried out under the direction of a professional educator. If you are employed with Title I funds (or work in a Title I school-wide program), there is a specific legal obligation for this type of instructional supervision (see the box on next page). However, presumably you can understand why supervision by a professional is simply common sense as the teacher has full responsibility for the classroom—including your work, not just that of the students.

It is not the responsibility of a paraprofessional to ensure that there is a system in place for the proper supervision of his or her work. However, if you feel that you are not *actively* supervised, we challenge you to seek supervision, to find out who your supervisor is and who you should go to if you have questions about your work, pay, or assignments.

This extract is from the federal Title I requirements for paraprofessionals, mandating that paraprofessionals work under the direction of a professional educator. (No Child Left Behind (NCLB) Act of 2001, Pub. L. No. 107-110, § 115, Stat. 1425 (2002)).

Requirements of Section ESEA 1119—Paraprofessionals

- All paraprofessionals hired after January 8, 2002, hired with Title I, Part A funds or employed in a Title I, Part A schoolwide program and assisting with instruction must meet one of the following requirements prior to hire:
    1. Completed at least 2 years of study at an institution of higher education.
    2. Obtained an associate degree (or higher).
    3. Met a rigorous standard of quality and can demonstrate through a formal state approved assessment, the knowledge of, and the ability to assist in instructing, reading, writing and mathematics, or assisting in instructing and the readiness of above named subject areas, as appropriate.
- All paraprofessionals working in a Title I, Part A funded program, including a Title I, Part A schoolwide program, shall have earned a secondary school diploma or its recognized equivalent.
- Title I paraprofessionals will not be assigned a duty inconsistent with duties outlined in Section 1119.
- Paraprofessionals work under the direct supervision of a teacher—consistent with Section 1119.

Paraprofessionals should know what their precise responsibilities are for supporting behavior at all levels:

- what the school district requires,
- what the school has in terms of rules and routines,
- the rewards available to students who behave appropriately,
- the sanctions considered appropriate for students who behave inappropriately, and
- the extent to which you have authority to offer rewards and impose sanctions on students as a paraprofessional.

You should be able to state clearly what is expected of you by your supervising teacher—for several reasons:

- You need to keep within the confines of the law as one of the many facets of professionalism and to protect yourself and your school or district from involvement in legal proceedings.

- Students deserve to be taught and supported by adults who have the best possible knowledge and understanding at their disposal—not only in terms of subject matter or curriculum, but also in terms of managing the learning environment. And that includes knowing how to establish and encourage positive behavior as well as how to respond to negative behavior.
- Consistency is essential to the success of any behavior management system so that students have clear guidelines and a uniform response to behaviors no matter which staff member they are working with. Where there is a lack of consistency, the whole system of behavior management can break down. Students need to know the boundaries, and all personnel need to adhere to the same rules.

There are several aspects of consistency:

- Consistency among the adults so that students know they will get the same response no matter which adult in the classroom they go to or interact with. There should never be any doubt as to what constitutes acceptable or unacceptable behavior in the classroom, or what consequences there will be (positive or negative) for particular behaviors.
- Consistency for all students—it is the behavior that prompts the reward or sanction; whoever "does" that behavior should get the same response without favoritism. No student should be singled out for special rewards or particularly harsh sanctions just because of who he or she is.

- Consistency across time—today, tomorrow, next week; acceptable behavior is always acceptable behavior; unacceptable behavior is always unacceptable. Students should not be left to wonder whether it's okay today, even though it isn't tomorrow. Some students will always push the boundaries—even though they have already pushed them before and encountered an appropriate response—but the majority of students will try once or twice, realize that the boundaries are firmly in place, and accept that is the way things are.

Monday, Tuesday, Wednesday, Thursday, Friday

Being consistent can be tricky because not only must you be consistent—those around you must be consistent too. You have little control of the behavior of other adults with whom you work, but you can identify the inconsistencies in yourself by taking data. We talk about identifying behavior and tracking it in later chapters. One of the responsibilities you may have in the classroom may be taking data on students. There will be other responsibilities too. Let's look at the role you serve in the classroom and school.

What Is My Role?

As part of your hiring and employment process, you should have received a job description. An important point to note is the distinction between your role and that of your teacher or other supervisor. Check your job description and see if it identifies your responsibilities regarding behavior, reinforcement, and discipline. The *Audit: Behavioral Responsibilities* form on the following page can help guide you as you identify your responsibilities and limitations. Of course every job description cannot list each and every behavior issue that may arise in the classroom, so you will need to add clarification and specificity by asking your teacher and/or supervisor. But there should at least be mention of supporting behavior management in your job description, no matter what your other responsibilities are.

The *Audit* form will guide you through an audit of your responsibilities with regard to student behavior. It will also help you identify the support system that should be in place in your work setting—the people you can turn to for advice and guidance, to address your questions and concerns, and to meet professional development needs.

Everyone should have a thorough understanding of what is expected of them in their employment. The *Audit* form can help you identify these expectations. You can use it as you clarify your role with your supervisor. We will revisit this audit in Chapter 1, having you check and adjust your responses according to the new knowledge and understanding you will have gained.

The Importance of Knowing What Is Expected of You

- It keeps you within the law, protecting you, your school, and the school district.
- Students deserve support from adults who have the best possible knowledge and understanding and who can work together to facilitate student success.
- Consistency is key to effective behavior management: students need to know the boundaries, but all personnel need to adhere to the same rules.

Audit: Behavioral Responsibilities

These are my responsibilities with regard to student behavior:

-
-
-
-
-

These are things I'm <u>not</u> supposed to take responsibility for with regard to student behavior:

-
-
-

If I have questions regarding my behavioral responsibilities, these are the people I can go to:

-
-
-

If I have concerns about other paraprofessionals and their approach to student behavior, I can talk to:

-
-
-

Imagine a fence that designates the boundary of a piece of property where horses are kept to graze. That fence, if it is to keep horses in, must be secure all around the perimeter of the property so that the animal knows that those are the limits of its range of movement. If there are breaks in the enclosure, the horses will find their way out. Although a fence may seem to represent a limit to freedom, it is also a safeguard to protect the horses from getting lost, from accidents that could be caused by motor vehicles, or from other dangers to their well-being. Likewise, limits are placed on your responsibilities to safeguard you from the consequences of straying into taking actions that are beyond your legal purview.

Chapter Content

Here we present an overview of each chapter to give you a taste of what is to come so that you can see how the book fits together. The book is designed to be used either as a linear, read-and-study text or as a reference in which you can dip into the chapters in any order, according to what most interests you.

1

In Chapter 1 we present a variety of historical perspectives of behavior, looking at operant conditioning, social learning theory, and various behavioral models, including religious perspectives. These provide a number of different lenses for looking at and thinking about behavior. We provide you with prompts for examining and documenting your own attitudes and practices in relation to student behavior as well as those of the other adults in your work setting. We ask you to identify any contradictions or mismatches as well as the commonalities of approach and to consider any action you might take to enhance and contribute to positive behavior in the classroom. We also make reference to the legal basis for behavior, including professional standards for teachers and paraprofessionals in this area.

2

Chapter 2 addresses factors that impact student behavior—both positive and negative. These include internal factors such as motivation, background, and prior experiences of learning and social environments, and external factors such as work groupings, physical arrangements, routines, and other classroom or school factors. We also look at what are often called the ABCs of behavior—the interrelatedness of the antecedents (or triggers) for behavior and the consequences that follow. This includes adult behavior as an antecedent, in recognition of the relationship dynamics of the classroom. You will learn to observe behavior and take data on observable behavior.

3

Chapter 3 is about Plan A: how we can set students up for success. Setting precedents for success includes the use of rules and routines, setting clear expectations, using effective teaching methods, and the need for a whole-school approach. We also look at the need for teaching social skills, including collaborative behavior, as many of the behavioral issues in classrooms revolve around the social aspects of working together with others in a confined space. We engage you in a discussion of what constitutes acceptable/unacceptable behavior and look at the importance of helping students to *understand or internalize* behavioral expectations, not just recite or memorize them.

4

As part of the continuing discussion of a proactive approach to encouraging and maintaining positive behavior, Chapter 4 looks at rewards. The LRBI principle applies here as much as it does to our response to negative student behaviors. We also consider the important principle of choice: teaching students that they can choose the type of learning environment they work in by choosing to behave in ways that result in positive consequences and a purposeful, positive working atmosphere.

5

Chapter 5 is about having a clear Plan B: how we handle the fallback position of establishing and administering sanctions. We look at the essential characteristics of sanctions—that they be timely, appropriate in scope and focus, meaningful to the recipient student, and simple. We link classroom sanctions to the whole-school approach and revisit the notion of student choice. We also provide background information and statistics on the cost of school exclusions and the wider costs to society of school failure, with an opportunity for you to consider what some of the root causes of that failure may be.

6

In Chapter 6 we take a diversion into behavior and special needs. There are certain conditions and disabilities—in addition to the most obvious such as ADHD, Autism or Emotional Disturbance—that have a recognized and distinct impact on behavior. As we explore these and other categories of special educational needs, you will have opportunities to gain greater insight into what prompts student behavior. We also consider the extent to which inappropriate behaviors can be modified for these students and whether rewards and sanctions "work" in the same way for them as they do for students with no identified disability or special need.

7

Chapter 7 considers some of the more recent developments addressing school behavioral issues, such as Response to Intervention (RtI), Restorative Practice, Philosophy for Children (P4C), and Circle Time. These are what might be considered pastoral approaches, and their success lies in engaging individuals in discussions and activities that promote empathy and increased understanding of the consequences of their actions.

8

We use Chapter 8 to bring together the many ideas that have been presented throughout the book. We review the chapters, summarizing and drawing together recurring themes (particularly the focus on positive behaviors, the use of LRBI and PBIS, and the clear link between behavior and learning). We also provide you with opportunities to revisit and reconsider your personal philosophy and approach to behavior, reflecting on changes that may have occurred as a result of your reading and study of the material presented. Finally, we provide you with a range of prompts and suggestions for practical application of principles in your work setting.

Resources

After Chapter 8 you will find a wealth of resources:

- A Glossary of terms relating to behavior management and more general, related classroom topics.
- Useful Websites and Organizations that provide information and resources for working with students and teachers on behavioral issues.
- An Index to enable you to use this book as a reference and easily find material of interest.

We remind you that throughout the book you will find prompts for reflection on what you have read. They come in various formats to allow for differing learning preferences and a variety of perspectives. We strongly recommend that you take advantage of these opportunities to extend and consolidate your learning.

The fact that you are asked to record your thoughts and feelings about a topic or situation obliges you to think more carefully about how you can put your new knowledge and understanding to use. It should also help you retain the material longer.

You may be asked to complete these reflective exercises as part of a college course if you are reading the book as a college text, but even if you are using the book for self-study the activities can help you think through the ideas and information you read about here and apply them to your situation.

Summary

In sum, this book offers the following advantages:

- Increased awareness/understanding of the processes underlying student behavior in the classroom, including motivation, and the importance of self-efficacy.

- Knowledge of a wide range of strategies for establishing and promoting positive behavior as well as strategies for counteracting or reducing negative behavior.
- Understanding of the importance of using the least restrictive behavioral interventions—both for promoting positive behaviors and reducing negative behaviors—and of using OSEP's Positive Behavioral Interventions and Supports.
- The security (emotional and legal) of knowing the extent and limits of your own role in relation to behavior and under the direction of a professional.
- An appreciation that success has its own rewards and that the ultimate goal of behavioral strategies is to instill in students a sense of their own worth and the satisfaction of intrinsic motivation rather than always seeking extrinsic rewards.
- Understanding that the natural momentum of the effective instructional cycle draws students along with it. This not only ensures learning but also ensures engagement—an essential component of learning and a natural controller of behavior.
- Skills addressed in the book will relate to nationally recognized standards for paraprofessional competence (for example, those published by CEC).
- Research-based strategies shown to be effective in a variety of education settings, particularly those where paraprofessional support is typical.
- Practical strategies that can be implemented immediately and with confidence.
- The content is set in the context of the legal requirement for paraprofessionals to work "under the direction of a professional" (ESEA) and be "appropriately supervised" (IDEA).
- The incorporation of widely accepted principles and practices such as Response to Intervention (RtI).

Do You Realize . . . ?

1. The very large number of paraprofessionals (estimated at **1.3 million**) across the USA.
2. The diversity of paraprofessionals' roles and work settings (Title I, behavior support, in-school-suspension proctor, special education, job coach, etc.), all of which require knowledge of effective behavioral principles.
3. The legal implications of No Child Left Behind (2004), which requires that paraprofessionals be "highly qualified," leading to a substantial increase in the number of college courses for paraprofessionals, typically at the associate degree level. These are variously housed in Special Education programs, or under Early Childhood Studies or Child Development. There are now many hundreds of such courses across the USA.
4. Although some states offer systematic training for paraprofessionals, the majority do not (either as in-service or pre-service).

(Continued)

5.   Many paraprofessionals work independently with assigned students, so they have minimal opportunity to observe their supervising teacher's behavioral strategies.
6.   Paraprofessionals are often hired to work with the students who are most vulnerable and needy, both academically and emotionally.
7.   Few teachers and paraprofessionals have common planning time when the teacher might provide on-the-job training for the paraprofessional.
8.   In essence (and this is well documented): *the students with the most specialized needs (including those with behavioral disorders) typically spend the majority of their day with a paraprofessional (the least well-trained member of the classroom team), not a teacher.*

We wish you enjoyment in studying this material and the sense of satisfaction that comes from knowing that your work is based on solid principles and well-tried and tested practices.

Chapter 1

Basic Principles of Behavior

What You Will Learn

Learning Objectives:

In this chapter you will learn the basic principles of behavior. First and foremost is the essential basic principle that underpins the entire text—that the focus is on positive behavior. This essential principle supports engaging students in learning. You will learn that there is a clear link between behavior and learning and the use of reinforcement and punishment to increase appropriate behaviors.

You will gain a basic understanding of Least Restrictive Behavioral Interventions (LRBI) and Positive Behavioral Interventions and Supports (PBIS) as we focus on learning/teaching rather than behavior.

A basic understanding of the legal basis for behavior management, including professional standards for teachers and paraprofessionals, will help you know where you are recognized in this area.

Our Aim Is Positive Behavior

When we hear teachers and other school personnel talking about behavior in schools, it is amusing to note that it is most often bad or inappropriate behavior that they are referring to. The term "managing behavior" somehow has come to mean managing difficult or inappropriate behavior, and the examples that most readily come to mind are the students whose behavior is a cause for concern. However, any action can be considered a behavior—good or bad, better or worse. Practically all of our actions and mannerisms can be considered behavior.

Of greater relevance here is whether we merely react to negative behaviors that have already occurred—a defensive posture, where we are just waiting for students to misbehave so we can take corrective action and make things right—or whether we take a more proactive stance, prepare for the best rather than the worst scenario, and preempt negative behavior by concentrating our efforts on promoting positive behavior.

When confronted with negative student behavior, the old traditional schools used strategies that controlled, contained, punished, and excluded as a way to deal with students with behavior problems. Fortunately, in recent years educators have come to see that a proactive approach that focuses on positive behavior is by far the more effective way to manage both appropriate and inappropriate behavior. By being proactive, we set high expectations and show that we believe students can succeed in reaching those expectations. If we can encourage positive behavior in our students, we automatically reduce inappropriate behavior. We do not ignore inappropriate behavior, but it is not our primary focus.

Traditional schools used strategies that **controlled,**
contained,
punished,
excluded.
In recent years educators have come to see that a proactive approach that focuses on positive behavior is by far the more effective way.

What Is the Link Between Behavior and Learning?

In the Introduction we talked about the classroom as a place where the primary business is—or should be—teaching and learning. The role of the teacher—and you share this role as a paraprofessional—is to teach; students come to school to learn. You will already know that there are a wide variety of different methods available to teachers (and we will discuss this further in Chapter 3), but the most effective methods are those that present relevant and interesting material geared to the students' individual abilities. This type of teaching is much more likely to engage students and promote on-task behavior.

Engaging Students in Learning

To consider student behavior in the classroom without looking at instructional activities would be a grave error. Students must have something to engage in if they are to also have appropriate behavior. Take, for example, a student who is often out of his seat, moving away from his desk, and roaming about the classroom. A teacher or paraprofessional could have him sit in his chair to practice sitting.

But what will he do to enhance his learning while he is sitting? To merely practice sitting on a chair serves no purpose. Learning requires having something to do—such as completing a math assignment, reading a book, writing, or drawing. It makes sense to see if he can remain seated while solving math problems, for example, and writing the answers. But this is something of a chicken-and-egg situation: Which comes first—the good sitting or the engagement with the task? The math task gives him a reason for sitting and also enables him to engage with the task. But if the task is uninspiring or has no relevance for the student, he has no incentive to sit and engage with it.

On the other hand, when a learning activity is by its very nature engaging—or presented in an engaging way—the student will want to sit and engage with it. Solve the issue of engaging work, and you solve the issue of sitting.

Source: iStock #1129083

It also is sensible to include the student in setting goals for this type of engagement. "Tom, I'm going to see if you can stay in your seat while you complete these math problems. How long do you think you can remain seated?" (Student gives an estimate of 10 minutes.) "Yes, I think 10 minutes is a reasonable goal. Would you like me to set the timer?" Research studies have shown that students are more likely to achieve their learning and/or behavior goals if they participate in developing them. They also put more effort into achieving those goals and show more interest.

The Goldilocks Principle

Teaching and learning activities are the reason for school. Yet, if the learning activity is too difficult or too easy, the student can quickly become bored or frustrated and disengage from the activity—and be likely to leave the activity, get out of the chair, and move about the room. We could think of this as the Goldilocks Principle.

If you're familiar with the fairy tale, you'll know that when Goldilocks visited the house belonging to the family of three bears, she tried the stools, the beds, and the porridge. Father Bear's bed was too hard, his stool was too high, and his porridge was too hot. Mother Bear's bed was too soft, her stool was too short, and her porridge was too cold. But Baby Bear's bed was "just right"—as were his stool and his porridge. And why were they just right? They were just right because Baby Bear's needs and preferences matched Goldilocks's needs and preferences. So too with our students—the learning activities we present for them must meet their abilities (or needs) and preferences to be engaging. Too difficult, and the student will quickly disengage. But likewise, if the activity is too simple and lacks challenge, students will quickly become disinterested.

Easy? Difficult?

How do you know if the activity is too easy or too difficult for the student? One of the best ways to find the answer to that question is to ask the student about the assignment. Pose questions such as, "Can you show me where you are on the assignment?" "What will you do next?" "Do you need help in figuring out that answer?" Through these types of questions, the student can show you what he is doing, where he is in the process, and what he plans to do next. Careful observation and listening to the answers to these questions provide you with a means to identify where and how he is challenged by the concepts—if he is flying through the work because it is too easy, or whether or not he is stumped.

Work Is Too Easy

Some students may complain to you or the teacher that the work is simple, easy, or stupid. These are warning signs that signal you should closely observe how the student tackles the activity. You will note that the work is too easy if the student rushes through the assignment—finishing it accurately and much more quickly than most of the other students.

When work is below the students' achievement level they may engage for a while, but if it continues to be too easy they disengage and find other things to do. This lack of interest in starting or completing the assignment often leads to daydreaming, to getting out of the chair and moving about the classroom, and potentially to more generally disruptive behaviors.

Work Is Too Difficult

Determining that the work is too difficult is not always as easy to spot. The student may not be willing to tell you it is too hard for him, to avoid potential embarrassment. He may, however, say, "This assignment is stupid," or "I just don't like it." Close observation may show that he dives into the assignments with enthusiasm but quickly becomes discouraged. He may drop his pencil and get out of the chair to move away from the work, thus escaping the activity. Other unwanted behaviors may follow, such as interrupting or teasing neighbors who are working. The student is no longer engaged in learning and his classmates are stopped from learning, too.

Paramount to appropriate behavior is to have engaging learning activities for students. If you identify the activities that are too difficult for the student—or too easy—consult with the teacher for the guidance that can be given to remedy the situation.

Just Right!

When the work is not too difficult and not so simple that the students feel they are wasting time, they will engage in learning.

Source: iStock #3950338

Make sure the student understands each assignment (what to do), how it is to be done (e.g., handwritten), and the expectation for achievement (e.g., at least 80% correct). Verify that he has the prerequisite skills leading up to this assignment. For example, in order to find the coordinates on a map, a student must first have the prerequisite skills of knowing latitude and longitude. These proactive measures will help to facilitate student engagement and ensure that tasks set are "just right."

Verify students have the prerequisite skills, then
Teach students
- What to do.
- How it is to be done.
- The expectation for achievement.

Behavior Theory—What Makes It Happen?

In this section we briefly take you through some historical perspectives of behavior, so that you can better understand how ideas have developed—in a variety of different fields of study—and how they have influenced what we do in schools today. As you read about the different perspectives, take note of those that you recognize as being part of the different behavioral approaches you've experienced.

An American psychologist named B. F. Skinner developed a theory of behavior from studying animals such as pigeons and rats. He placed pigeons and rats in special boxes that had buttons in them. If the animal pressed the button, the animal received food. Skinner found that an animal that was rewarded with food became much more likely to push the button again. He also found that giving the animals something they didn't like made them less likely to push the button. This research continued and became the basis for his theory of behavior, known as **Operant Conditioning**.

B. F. Skinner had based his work on the experiments of Pavlov, who had observed what he referred to as a **"conditioned" response** in animals. Pavlov is well known for his experiment with dogs. When he consistently rang a bell before feeding a dog, the dog soon began to anticipate the food and salivate just on hearing the bell—even if food wasn't then produced. Pavlov measured the amount of saliva the dog produced and was able to "condition" the salivating response of the dog using a number of different noises and objects. That is, under a particular condition (the bell or other noise, or even the appearance of the lab assistant who fed the dog), the dog produced saliva because he anticipated food once he heard the bell or saw the lab assistant. This was a natural, physiological behavior—a spontaneous response—in the dog, and we must bear in mind that neither Pavlov nor Skinner was thinking in terms of education or classrooms. They were more interested in behavior as a general concept.

Before we go on to consider Skinner's Operant Conditioning as it relates to education, can you think of ways in which students are "conditioned" to behave in certain ways, just because of what they see and hear? Take a moment to think about this. You'll find some examples in the nearby box. We've left a couple of lines for you to add other actions and responses.

Conditioned Responses in Students

When:	This Is What They Do:
Students hear the bell for the end of recess . . .	they move toward the school door or line up.
The school bus stops at the school door . . .	the students get off the bus.
_____	_____
_____	_____

The theory of Operant Conditioning focuses on making behaviors more or less likely to reoccur. Essentially, when a person does something (the behavior), he or she receives a consequence. The consequence is whatever happens immediately after the behavior is performed. If the consequence is some form of reward—known as **reinforcement**—then the person will be more likely to repeat that behavior at some time in the future. If the behavior is followed immediately by a consequence that is undesirable, known in Operant Conditioning as a **punishment**, then the person will be less likely to repeat that behavior in the future.

Reinforcement and Punishment

If you think about how parents and teachers discipline their children, how businesses treat their employees, or how you respond when a friend does something nice (or unpleasant) to you, you will see reinforcement and punishment taking place. A mother may give her son a hug when he cleans his room without her asking. A teacher gives grades for good or bad work. Businesses may give good employees raises in pay or other incentives, and you thank your friends and return a favor when they help you. A student who makes his friends laugh when he or she tells a joke in class may continue to make jokes more and more frequently. Sometimes reinforcements and punishments may be counter-intuitive. Children who throw a tantrum to get out of a difficult or unpleasant task, such as eating a food they greatly dislike, may feel like that was a good reward, even if they were punished, and may begin throwing tantrums more often just to avoid that unpleasant food or task. The price of being punished was worth the end result of avoiding the disliked food.

How to Improve Behavior—Positive Reinforcement and Positive Punishment

Psychologists who study Operant Conditioning techniques identify four basic ways to reinforce or punish behavior:

1. **Positive reinforcement**
2. **Positive punishment**
3. **Negative reinforcement**
4. **Negative punishment**

Let's look at each of these. As we already mentioned, a behavior can be reinforced to make it more likely. A behavior can be reinforced by *adding* reinforcement, or by *taking away* something difficult. Likewise, a behavior can be discouraged by the administration of a punishment, which can involve giving the person something they *don't like,* or by *taking away* something they do like. When a reinforcement or punishment involves adding something new to the person or animal, this is called **positive reinforcement** or **positive punishment**. If the behavior is reinforced or punished by taking something away, this is called **negative reinforcement** or **negative punishment**.

Please note that the words "positive" and "negative" are not used here in the same way that people usually use them. In Operant Conditioning, positive does not mean that it was good, fun, or uplifting. It means something was added. And negative does not mean that it was boring, saddening, or disgusting, but that it was taken away (think + and − in math, rather than like and dislike). It is also important to remember that taking away something doesn't necessarily mean the person is being punished. If you had a bad headache and you decided to *take some aspirin* (the behavior) and the headache goes away, you would be more likely to take aspirin next time you had a headache. This would be a negative reinforcement, because something was taken away (−), and it's likely that next time you get a headache you'll take aspirin again. Also, in Operant Conditioning a positive consequence isn't always reinforcement. If a child tries to pet a skunk and is given a large helping of skunk spray as a consequence, she will be less likely to pet a skunk again. This is an example of positive punishment because something was added (+) but the effect was to reduce the likelihood of the behavior happening again.

Credit: Christopher Wells Barlow

Parents and teachers often use all four forms of reinforcement and punishment. From studying Operant Conditioning techniques, psychological researchers have found that **positive reinforcement is the most effective way to change behavior**—that is, adding something that will increase the likelihood of the behavior being repeated. Reinforcing a person's behavior with praise, food, or money will encourage him or her to continue that behavior. Taking away or reducing chores or other undesirable things as a reward is also effective. This is sometimes called **escape**. Negative reinforcement is also very effective. These methods will give you the most long lasting results, as well as immediate results, most of the time. If punishment must be used, negative punishment is preferable to positive punishment. In other words, taking away privileges will be more effective than yelling at a child.

Most to Least Effective Methods of Operant Conditioning

Most Effective			Least Effective
Positive Reinforcement	Negative Reinforcement	Negative Punishment	Positive Punishment
Adding something to encourage the behavior	Taking away something to encourage the behavior	Taking something away to discourage the behavior	Adding something to discourage the behavior
e.g., giving praise	e.g., relieving a child of chores because they've been helpful to someone else	e.g., taking away a privilege (computer time or time with friends) because the child ignored his mother when she called him in for dinner	e.g., sending the student to the principal because he used bad language to the teacher

Grandma's Rule—Premack Principle

An important aspect of Operant Conditioning is placing the reinforcement *immediately after* the behavior. If you give students the reinforcement and then expect them to perform a difficult task, they may not be very willing. Also, if you want students to do something difficult and they want to do something much more fun, you can tell them that the fun activity will happen only when the difficult activity is completed. This is called the **Premack Principle**. For example, Grandmother said, "Eat your vegetables and then you can have dessert." This Premack Principle is as easy to remember as Grandma's Rule.

Using Variety in What You Do—Differential Reinforcement

You may ask, "So if I want my child/student/other person to stop doing some annoying or unhealthy behavior, do I need to use punishment?" Not necessarily. A simple method can be used to eliminate behaviors using what is called **differential reinforcement**. Differential reinforcement involves reinforcing the behaviors you want, not punishing the behaviors you don't.

There are different kinds of differential reinforcement.

1. You can reinforce a behavior that is incompatible with the behavior you want to get rid of. For example, if you want a child to stop picking his nose, you can provide reinforcement whenever he puts his hands in his pockets or gets and uses a tissue.
2. Another type of differential reinforcement is to reinforce a behavior other than the behavior you want to get rid of (also known as the target behavior). An example of this would be reinforcing students when they are quiet, when they are working hard, or when they are standing in line, but not reinforcing

students when they are talking out of turn (i.e., ignoring them). This is a useful example for the classroom, because we do often add something to this type of situation. When a student is talking, what do we often add? Our attention. We say something to the student, or give him or her a look that sends the message that we've noticed and don't approve. But ignoring that student adds nothing to the situation, so we are not reinforcing the talking out of turn. Students will quickly learn what behaviors get them reinforcement and they will typically stop displaying the behaviors that do not.

Extinction—Another Word for "Stop It"

Differential reinforcement can be very effective and is preferable and more effective long term than punishment. But there are situations that warrant positive punishment. If a person is putting himself, herself, or someone else in danger and that behavior needs to be discouraged very quickly to prevent an incident, positive punishment may be needed. Police use positive punishment when a person is dangerous, but soon follow it with negative punishment, such as taking away his or her freedom with handcuffs and jail time.

Credit: Christopher Wells Barlow

Let's add a word of warning here. When attempting to stop a behavior with negative punishments such as ignoring the person or taking away privileges he or she enjoys, you can expect a sudden increase in the target behavior soon after implementing the new consequence. This is called an extinction burst. Extinction refers to a behavior that was targeted and stopped. This goes with the old saying that "things get worse before they get better." A student who is used to throwing tantrums to escape from difficult tasks may try throwing even bigger tantrums when the parent or teacher all of a sudden starts ignoring him or refusing to reinforce his behavior by giving in. But the student will eventually give up in all but the most extreme cases. Just be aware that changing behaviors that have been reinforced for long periods of time can be very difficult. So just be patient and hang in there.

Going Back to Goldilocks

Lastly, the things that are reinforcing for one person may not be reinforcing for another. Reinforcement and punishment are very individual matters. One child may work harder on homework for a sticker, while another child thinks stickers are no reason to perform such a difficult task. How difficult or undesirable the behavior is, or how desirable the reinforcement is, will determine how much reinforcement is needed. Different levels and schedules of reinforcement may be needed, depending on the age and development level of the person. In general, younger children need reinforcement immediately and often in order for them to make the connection between the behavior and the consequence. Giving a 2-year-old a piece of chocolate on Friday for something he or she did on Sunday will not get you results and reinforce the behavior because the child probably doesn't remember anything about it, nor would he or she understand whatever explanation the parent gave. But adults will work for a month if they know that a nice paycheck will be waiting for them.

Researchers have also found that varying the number of times the behavior must be performed before reinforcement is given, as well as varying the amount of reinforcement, are the strongest ways to reinforce someone's behavior. A good example of this is a slot machine. People paying to play will play and play, not knowing when they will be rewarded or if they will be rewarded at all. And occasionally they may be rewarded by winning a few coins, but they will continue pulling the lever, hoping for a big payout. Casinos make enormous profits based on this hope.

Does It Work?

If you decide to use Operant Conditioning techniques to change behavior in yourself or others, you must consider whether you will reinforce or punish, and whether you will use positive or negative consequences. You will need to select the reinforcement or punishment that will be most effective for the person, while avoiding unnecessary physical or emotional discomfort, as well as decide how often you will reinforce or punish the behavior. Also, be sure to show respect for the person's dignity. Ask yourself, "Is encouraging or discouraging this behavior in my own/the person's best interests?" "Is it the most effective and least obtrusive method possible?" These are important questions to consider before attempting to change someone's behavior. We will revisit rewards in Chapter 4 and sanctions in Chapter 5, where you will have more opportunities to consider how Operant Conditioning translates into everyday classroom practices and strategies.

 Test Your Knowledge

Meanwhile, see if you can determine what type of reinforcement is used in the following examples.

Example One. You have most likely observed a mother chatting on the phone while her child is attempting to get Mother's attention. When the child becomes noisy—thus interrupting the phone conversation—Mother will briefly stop talking to the friend and tell the child to be quiet. As Mother goes back to her conversation, you observe that the child's behavior becomes louder and more disturbing; the cycle continues with Mom stopping to rebuke the child again and again. We hear Mother say, "I can't talk on the phone without my child disrupting me." What type of reinforcement was this?

Answer: Mother shushing the child is much more rewarding for the child than being ignored altogether. In this case the child finds more pleasure in getting Mother's negative attention. So this is an example of positive reinforcement—the mother's attention (added to the situation) is making it more likely that the child repeats the behavior.

Example Two. In one classroom, a paraprofessional counted the number of times a student named Konrad shouted answers without raising his hand. The data showed that the teacher did not call on Konrad when his hand was up, but if he shouted out the answer she said, "Konrad, raise your hand before giving answers." This occurred 10 times in a 20-minute period. When the paraprofessional and teacher went over the data, the teacher could see that Konrad caught her attention for behavior that was not appropriate and that did not follow the rules. Is this an example of reinforcement or punishment?

Answer: Again, this is reinforcement—for Konrad, bad or negative attention was better than no attention at all, so he kept repeating the behavior!

Observational Learning—Learning by Watching

This discussion of shaping behavior by using the principles of reinforcement and punishment has been about deliberately trying to change behavior based on B. F. Skinner's theory of Operant Conditioning. A rather different theory of behavior change was proposed by Albert Bandura, a Canadian psychologist. It has come to be known as Social Learning Theory.

Albert Bandura studied the way people and animals learn. He noted that learning could occur vicariously by a person simply observing another person performing a behavior, noting the consequences, and modifying his or her own behavior in a future similar situation. He referred to this change in behavior as "observational learning," and his research clearly documented children's tendency to imitate adult models. The results of multiple studies carried out by Bandura and his colleagues in the early 1960s showed that a model's behavior is more influential when:

- the behavior is seen as having positive consequences;
- the model is liked, respected, and perceived positively;
- the observer thinks there are similarities between the model and himself; and
- the observer is rewarded for paying attention to the model's behavior.

Teachers apply the concept of observational learning when they praise a student for raising her hand before answering a question. The teacher may praise the "model" student in an effort to get other students (who want to be like the model student) to do what the model student did. The teacher is smiling and positive and will say something like, "I really like it when you raise your hand and wait for me to call on you before you answer the question." This happens quickly, without breaking the rhythm of the classroom learning, but is explicit enough to help all the students understand the desired behavior.

On the other end of the spectrum is the fact that observational learning can take place in a negative way. Students may respect the classroom "bully" and want to be more like him. They may find it rewarding to get negative attention by doing the things that the bully does. One of the experiments that Albert Bandura is well known for is the Bobo doll experiment, which involved young children (preschool to kindergarten age). There were variations to the experiment but this is the basic scenario:

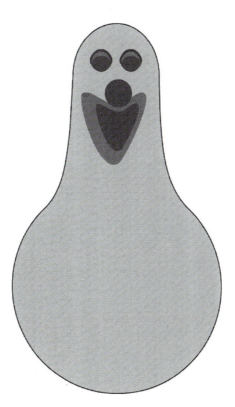

Credit: Christopher Wells Barlow

Each child was shown a short film that featured an adult and a Bobo doll (a tall, inflatable doll shaped like a ten-pin bowling pin, with sand or water in its base so that it returns to an upright position if it is knocked down). For no apparent reason, the adult would beat the Bobo doll, yelling at it and screaming. When the children were later given a Bobo doll to play with, they would beat the doll in the same way as the adult in the film clip.

Bandura referred to this as observational learning because there had been no direct teaching involved in order to change the children's behavior, and it appeared to contradict the idea that behavior is shaped by reinforcement or rewards. He varied the experiment in that the adults in the film were sometimes given candy after they had beaten the doll, sometimes reprimanded, and sometimes received neither candy nor a reprimand. The extent of the aggression shown by the children varied according to which version of the film they were shown; however, in all cases the children's behavior mirrored the aggression shown by the adult in the film.

Bandura's experiments have been criticized for a variety of reasons, but now, 50 years later, the same issues are being discussed as children are exposed to violence on television and aggressive video games that reward players with points for killing and other sorts of violence. Several carefully controlled studies in recent years have shown an increase in the likelihood that those who watch or participate in violent games, television shows, and movies will be more aggressive in their own behavior. Bandura's experiments suggested that this would be much more noticeable in boys than in girls, particularly if the model was male.

Early School Environments: Spare the Rod

In the early days of education in the United States, school personnel handled misbehavior of students in a reactive, punitive, and punishment-oriented manner (since we're no longer discussing Operant Conditioning, we're now using the word "punishment" with its common negative connotation). It was common for parents and teachers to use a cane or yardstick (a long wooden measurement instrument) as a form of punishment for the slightest act of disobedience. They argued that this extreme form of punishment would deter student offenses. In schools, because the punishment was given out in public (and in the full view of peers), the belief was that public embarrassment would further shame the offender into obedience. It was, of course, also intended as a deterrent for other students, making it clear what the consequences would be if they behaved in a similar manner. A punishment that was lesser in physical pain may have been greater in emotional taxation—the student was required to sit in the corner of the classroom wearing a large triangular hat with the large letters "DUNCE" (or sometimes just the letter "D") written on it. Offenses were often minimal—failure to raise a hand, forgetting to return homework, reading a word incorrectly—but punishments were severe. Parents and educators took their guidance from the Holy Bible:

> "He who spareth the rod hateth his son: but he that loveth him chasteneth him betimes" (Proverbs 13:24) and "Withhold not correction from a child: for if thou beatest him with the rod, he shall not die. Thou shalt beat him with the rod, and thou shalt deliver his soul from hell." (Proverbs 23:13–14)

In the eyes of the student, harsh, cruel, and unjust punishment often did not match the minor offenses. The obvious injustices caused resentment in students and supported the justification for bullying. Instead of helping a student learn from his errors and repent, the opposite often happened. Students became resentful and unwilling to attend school.

The thoughts of Viktor E. Frankl, a psychiatrist and survivor of the Nazi prison camps during the Second World War, are instructive here. Frankl wrote about his experiences as a concentration camp inmate. He noted his feelings of injustice at receiving sharp blows to the head for no real reason. He writes, "At such a moment it is not the physical pain which hurts the most (and this applies to adults as much as to punished children); it is the mental agony caused by the injustice, the unreasonableness of it all. Strangely enough a blow which does not even find its mark can, under certain circumstances, hurt more than one that finds its mark."

In more recent decades, school punishments evolved away from beatings but nevertheless included punitive management techniques often resulting in detention, reprimands, referrals to the office, and time taken away from group activities. School personnel focused on the inappropriate behaviors displayed by students before looking toward the antecedents, the events that precede the inappropriate behaviors. Together with rewards for appropriate behavior, this type of behavior management has been referred to as "carrot or stick."

Today's School Environments: Positive Focus

Today educators use more positive reactions to problem behaviors, which bring more positive effects. Proactive, preventative measures include effective classroom instruction, expectations for classroom rules that are explicitly taught, and social skills instruction that is designed to increase student success in the school environment. Effective schools strive to prevent behavior problems rather than just relying on consequences to deter the recurrence of the problem behavior. Positive intervention involves increasing positive interactions with students and teaching skills that produce competencies. Additionally, in noting the connection between learning and behavior, researchers theorize that academic and behavioral problems spring from two issues:

1. The student is not receiving instruction on his or her ability level, thus causing the avoidance and behavior problems seen in the classroom.
2. The student has behaviors that inhibit academic functioning, putting his or her achievement behind that of peers.

This takes us back to the earlier discussion of which comes first—the behavior or the engaging and motivating teaching? Looking at the issue from the negative viewpoint: Which comes first, the problem behavior or the lack of academic achievement? It may be difficult to analyze exactly where the problem behavior begins, but as one of the adults in the classroom, you share the responsibility for providing the best possible environment for learning, one that promotes appropriate behavior so that everyone's efforts can focus more fully on learning, a natural support for continuing appropriate behavior.

Positive Behavioral Interventions and Supports

Today's schools use what are often referred to as Least Restrictive Behavioral Interventions (LRBI) and Positive Behavioral Interventions and Supports (PBIS) to reduce the focus on behavior and stress a focus on learning/teaching. The notion of LRBI is an important one. Put simply, it is the idea that least is best: when we respond to inappropriate behavior we use the least complicated response or sanction—one that presents the least disturbance to the important work of teaching, while sending a clear message to the student that the behavior is inappropriate and needs to stop.

We have already briefly referred to PBIS, which is an approach to behavior management proposed by the federal Office of Special Education Programs (OSEP). It is based on these core principles:

- the need to intervene early on behavioral issues,
- the need to teach appropriate behavior rather than assuming students will know how to behave appropriately, and
- the need to carefully monitor students whose behavior is of concern so that we can make adjustments as necessary to the strategies in place to manage that behavior.

Where Are Paraprofessionals in All This?

To this point in the chapter the main focus has been on engaging students in learning through the use of a variety of theoretical models or approaches in the classroom. We have discussed behavior theory and reinforcement or punishment. Today schools most frequently use PBIS to prevent behavior problems and to address those that arise. One of the most common and essential of those positive supports is the establishment of rules. Rules must be established to manage the construals, or beliefs, that students bring to schools. You also come to the school setting with beliefs that are already established. In this section we look at students' construals and rule-setting procedures to provide support for learning among all who enter the school with different interpretations of the way they should behave.

Construals and Rules

In the area of social psychology, researchers study what are called "construals." **Construals** are how individuals perceive, comprehend, and interpret the world around them. They study how people's behavior or action is similar or different. These influence the nature of individual experience, including cognition, emotion, and motivation.

Paraprofessionals and other teaching staff who have experience in the schools recognize this concept. They see the influence of experience on students' thinking, emotions, and motivation to learn. The nature of students' experience may lead to lower learning rates. For example, some students may have been well trained by parents to use manners and are quick to say "thank you" and "please may I?" They may defer to other children and avoid conflict at all costs. Conversely, some students have been taught to stand up for themselves, push ahead, and take what they believe is rightfully theirs. They may be quick to push other students aside and to refuse to get in a line with the other students. Some of them may be bullies—intimidating the other students. The conflict appears when students from different construals come together in one school or classroom. School administrators and teachers set school and classroom rules to manage these diverse groups and their different construals.

Establishing Rules

Rules help students to understand the behavior that is expected. Rules must be explicitly identified and taught to the students. All school personnel must know, understand, and enforce the rules. It is vital that everyone maintain consistency in applying and enforcing those rules.

As a paraprofessional, you are not often in a position to decide the school-wide or classroom policies or rules regarding discipline. Therefore, it is important that you identify what the school expects of you in terms of reinforcing/rewarding students and meting out punishments. Now is an excellent time to learn the school policies. You have an opportunity to interpret your own construals—or what you believe—about behavior and the way students should behave while on the school premises and in the classroom. Some teaching staff may believe that it is important to be strong and forceful when rules are violated. Others prefer to avoid problems by ignoring them.

Under the direct supervision of a qualified teacher, paraprofessionals can provide support and assist with positive, preventative interventions while working with students. Preventative methods to be utilized include setting rules for the small group of students you are assigned to work with. You can show students how to follow classroom rules, reward students, help to build a positive classroom environment, give positive and corrective feedback, redirect students to a more appropriate behavior, reinforce replacement behaviors, reteach social skills, and give praise and offer external rewards. You may not set school rules but you certainly can influence the extent to which students abide by those rules. We will discuss this in greater depth in Chapter 3.

In the Introduction we provided you with a form for auditing your responsibilities in relation to behavior (*Audit: Behavioral Responsibilities*). Having examined some of the approaches to behavior that have been prevalent in classrooms across the decades, this would be a good point at which to examine and document your own attitudes and practices in relation to student behavior as well as those of the other adults in your work setting. You will see a form for this on the next page. We ask you to identify any contradictions or mismatches as well as the commonalities between your approach and that of your teacher (or other school authorities). Then we ask you to consider any action you might take to enhance and contribute to positive behavior in the classroom in light of what you have written on the form.

Construals and Contradictions

How would you describe or characterize your approach to behavior? (What do you think is most important when it comes to managing student behavior? How do you deal with inappropriate behavior? What about the students who are always "good"—what do you think should be done for them?)

How would you describe or characterize your teacher's approach to behavior? (What are his or her priorities when it comes to managing behavior? How does he or she deal with inappropriate behavior? What does he or she do for the students who are always "good"?)

Use a highlighter or colored felt-tip pen to show where you and your teacher have the same approach to different aspects of behavior; use a different colored highlighter or pen to show where you differ in your approach.

What do you think should be done about the differences in approach? Take a moment to consider this, and briefly record your thoughts.

Legal Framework

Here we make reference to the legal basis for managing behavior. In the United States there are regulations that apply to the behavior of students in the schools. Two federal laws affecting education are No Child Left Behind (NCLB) and Individuals with Disabilities Education Act (IDEA). Both regulate the training and educational requirements of new and existing paraprofessionals. First, we look at NCLB, which is also referred to as the Elementary and Secondary Education Act (ESEA). As referred to in the Introduction, under this act any newly hired paraprofessionals working in Title I programs must have completed one of the following: two years of study at an institution of higher education, an associate degree, or passed a state or local assessment to show they meet a standard of quality.

According to NCLB, 2001, all paraprofessionals must demonstrate a "knowledge of, and the ability to assist in instructing, reading, writing, and mathematics; or knowledge of, and the ability to assist in instructing, reading readiness, writing readiness, and mathematics readiness, as appropriate" (PL 107–110 § 1119, p. 115). Further, NCLB specifies that paraprofessionals working under Title I may not provide instruction to students unless supervised by a teacher, but they may provide assistance with classroom management (US Department of Education, Office of Elementary and Secondary Education, 2002). It is noteworthy that the US Department of Education recognized paraprofessionals and specifically mentioned the important role you take in assisting in both instruction and classroom management.

For the purposes of Title I, Part A, a paraprofessional is an employee who provides instructional support in a program supported with Title I, Part A funds. This includes paraprofessionals who:

- provide one-to-one tutoring if such tutoring is scheduled at a time when a student would not otherwise receive instruction from a teacher,
- assist with classroom management, such as organizing instructional and other materials,
- provide instructional assistance in a computer laboratory,
- conduct parental involvement activities,
- provide support in a library or media center,
- act as a translator, or
- provide instructional support services under the direct supervision of a teacher [Title I, section 1119(g)(2)].

Individuals who work in food services, cafeteria or playground supervision, personal care services, noninstructional computer assistance, and similar positions are **not** considered paraprofessionals under Title I.

Requirements

Earlier we discussed NCLB and the requirements for paraprofessionals. We look now at another important law, the IDEA of 2004, which states that paraprofessionals who are "appropriately trained and supervised" can assist in the provision of special education services to children with disabilities (20 U.S.C. 1412(a)(14)). IDEA also specifies that paraprofessionals should receive in-service and preservice training to ensure that those providing services to children have the necessary skills and knowledge to meet student needs.

Another US federal law addresses school violence. This law is called the "Zero Tolerance" Law. According to data from the US Department of Education and the Center for Safe and Responsive Schools, at least 75% of schools report having zero tolerance policies for such serious offenses as bringing firearms or other weapons, alcohol, drugs, or tobacco into the schools, or being violent. This law will be discussed in more detail in Chapter 5 along with its implications for students.

Some Facts About Paraprofessionals

There is a clear need to provide information to paraprofessionals as, according to the Study of Personnel Needs in Special Education (SPeNSE, 2003), paraprofessionals in the United States today spend at least 10% of their time doing *each* of the following activities:

- Providing instructional support in small groups.
- Providing one-to-one instruction.
- Modifying materials.
- Implementing behavior plans.
- Monitoring hallways, study halls.
- Meeting with teachers.
- Collecting data on individuals with exceptional learning needs.
- Providing personal care assistance.

The qualified special education paraprofessional performs tasks prescribed and supervised by a fully licensed special education professional. Qualified paraprofessionals deliver individualized services to individuals with exceptional learning needs in a wide variety of settings, including general education classes, community-based functional learning sites, and just about everywhere that an individual with special education needs can be found. Paraprofessionals bring a wide variety of backgrounds and experience to their jobs.

In the United States, 29% of paraprofessionals have high school diplomas, 38% have completed some college, and 32% hold an associate degree or higher. Paraprofessionals with college experience have demonstrated increased confidence in collaborating and communicating with teachers. The majority of paraprofessionals are supervised by special education teachers and overwhelmingly report that they feel supported by their special education supervisors.

To ensure that paraprofessionals have the required skills for their expanded roles, the Council for Exceptional Children (CEC), in collaboration with the National Resource Center for Paraprofessionals, validated the specialty set of standards for paraprofessionals who serve individuals with exceptionalities. These are the knowledge and skills that all paraprofessionals serving individuals with exceptionalities should possess. Details can be found at the CEC website.

CEC Paraprofessional Professional Development Standards

The CEC is the largest association in the USA dedicated to children with special needs. CEC has recognized the increasingly critical role of paraprofessionals in special education service delivery. The organization notes that for more than 50 years paraprofessionals have helped special educators provide important services to individuals with exceptional learning conditions. Historically, paraprofessionals have provided services ranging from clerical tasks to assisting with individualized functional living tasks. CEC recognizes that paraprofessionals today have become an essential part of the special education team in delivering individualized services and serving prominent roles in the instruction of individuals with exceptional learning needs at all ages. CEC has developed the CEC standards for paraprofessional preparation. You may wish to consult these standards as a means of comparing your own knowledge and skills in relation to behavior against a nationally recognized set of standards. Standards such as these can also form a good basis for identifying areas in which you feel you could enhance your skills and knowledge and for setting goals for your own professional development.

Summary

This chapter has covered the basic principles of behavior that focus on being positive with students and providing support for appropriate behavior as a basic means of preventing problem behaviors. When carefully inspected, the link between students being actively engaged in learning and students behaving appropriately becomes obvious. Students who are motivated to learn will act out less frequently. However, bad behavior must also be dealt with, often for the safety of others, and when that happens the interventions must be the least restrictive possible. Some of this is regulated by law so this is important to know. Specific approaches to negative behavior will be the topic for a later chapter in this book.

Learning Outcomes

By now, after completing this chapter, you have most likely met the learning outcomes. Your goal is to always focus on supporting positive behavior.

- You know that you should strive to use positive behavior support to engage students in learning.
- You can explain that there is a clear link between behavior and learning. If the work is too difficult or repeatedly too easy, the student will "escape" from the activity by withdrawing, and he often acts out.
- You can demonstrate how praise and other forms of positive reinforcement can increase the good behaviors you wish to see in the classroom. And you know that severe punishment that was used in the early days of our schools has not proven effective but has caused students to be rebellious.
- Along with your knowledge of reinforcement and punishment, you have learned your role in your school assignment.

- You can briefly explain Least Restrictive Behavioral Interventions (LRBI) and Positive Behavioral Interventions and Supports (PBIS) that focus on learning/teaching rather than behavior.
- You can explain a basic understanding of the status of paraprofessionals described in the law and noted in professional standards.

Looking Ahead

In the next chapters, you will learn about internal and external factors and will be encouraged to take realistic looks at which of these factors are within your control and/or responsibility. You will also give consideration to your own behavior and how it impacts both positively and negatively on student behavior.

Bibliography

Bandura, A., & Shunk, D.H. (1981). Cultivating competence, self-efficacy, and intrinsic interest through proximal self-motivation. *Journal of Personality and Social Psychology, 41,* 586–598.

Council for Exceptional Children (CEC). (2004). *Parability: The CEC paraeducator standards workbook.* Arlington, VA: Council for Exceptional Children.

Frankl, V. (2006). *Man's search for meaning.* Boston, MA: Beacon Press, pp. 23–24.

Gerrig, R. J., & Zimbardo, P. G. (2005). *Psychology and life.* Upper Saddle River, NJ: Pearson Education.

Individuals with Disabilities Education Improvement Act (IDEA) of 2004, 20 U.S.C. 1412(a)(14). The IDEA regulations can be found at Assistance to the States for the Education of Children with Disabilities, 34 C.R.F. §§300.1–300.818 (2013).

NASP Resources. Zero tolerance and alternative strategies: A fact sheet for educators and policymakers. Available at www.nasponline.org/resources/factsheets/zt_fs.aspx.

National Dissemination Center for Children and Youth with Disabilities. http://nichcy.org/.

No Child Left Behind. Pub. L. 107–110, 115 Stat. 1425 Title I [Title I, section 1119(g)(2)], enacted January 8, 2002.

Quinn, M., Hagen, L., Wright, L., & Bader, B. (April 18, 2001). *How teachers and paraeducators can work together to create positive learning environments: Teachers' and paraeducators' roles in maintaining safe and orderly schools.* Pre-Conference Presentation, Council for Exceptional Children Conference.

Study of Personnel Needs in Special Education (SPeNSE). (2003). Available at www.spense.org.

Chapter 2

Factors That Impact Behavior
Good and Bad

What You Will Learn

> **Learning Objectives:**
>
> In this chapter you will learn to identify the factors that impact behavior both positively and negatively. There are internal and external factors (both for the student and for teaching staff) that affect the learning environment. Relationship building with students and staff will be important, so you will be able to describe steps you should take to build trust and respect. You will be able to identify observable and measurable behaviors and take data on them. You will be able to describe the antecedents of behaviors and the consequences. You will identify how data can help you learn from your mistakes.

First, we look at students' basic needs and discuss the things students do to get attention as well as their motives. Next, we look at factors that are vital in building relationships with students to gain their trust, increase their motivation, and convince them to work with you: listening, building trust and respect, and showing that you are honorable. These concepts are also applied to student and teacher relationships and even to other paraprofessionals you may be working with.

We also look at what is often referred to as the ABCs of behavior—the Antecedents and Consequences relating to Behavior—including adult behaviors as an antecedent. And in the last section of the chapter, we take a look at observation and data taking as an essential skill if we want to monitor and intervene with student behavior.

Basic Needs

In 1943 an American psychologist named Abraham Maslow proposed a theory regarding human motivation. This theory has come to be called Maslow's Hierarchy of Needs. Maslow stated that humans are motivated by their unfulfilled needs, starting with the most basic needs. When these basic needs are not met, people will struggle with the motivation to meet higher level needs. The basic needs will dominate their thoughts and behavior. Maslow's hierarchy is illustrated as a pyramid, with the most basic needs at the bottom and higher needs at the apex.

Physiological Needs

Maslow stated that the most basic human needs are the **physiological needs**, or needs of the body. These needs are represented as the base of the pyramid. People need food, water, air, and shelter to survive. If a person doesn't have these essentials, he or she will focus on little, if anything, else. This level also includes shelter from the elements. Obviously if these needs are not met, a person would likely not survive for very long. But more importantly for the classroom, a student who has gone without food for a long period of time—or who has come to school without eating breakfast, or not knowing where he will sleep that night—will have difficulty focusing on learning. School personnel do not keep teaching math and language arts when they know their community is being threatened by a tornado. Safety and shelter immediately become the highest priority in the school. Likewise, for individual students the basic instinct for survival can mean that they filter out everything else.

Maslow's Hierarchy of Needs

Need for Safety

The second level in Maslow's Hierarchy of Needs consists of a human's **need for safety and security**. People need to feel safe from a variety of dangers in life. Most importantly, people need to feel physically safe. People who are worried that they may be injured focus almost entirely on the need to be safe. Students who are afraid of a bully concentrate their time and energy on ways to be safe from the bully rather than focusing on reading, math, or other course content. Students who experience violence at home expend a lot of their mental energy on keeping themselves safe from that violence. During class time they are more likely to be planning how to avoid the bully during recess (or how to pacify or avoid a violent family member when they return home) than concentrating on the curriculum. Ridicule or embarrassment from teachers or others is also a threat to safety. School lockdowns are an attempt to keep students and staff safe—because there is an eminent threat to safety. Likewise individual students who feel threatened will take the necessary steps to protect themselves as a priority.

Need for Love and Belonging

The third level involves the human **need for love and belonging**. According to Maslow, once people have met their lower level needs, they begin to look to other people for attention, love, and a sense of belonging. It is at this third level—when basic needs are met—that you will find students trying hard to gain the attention of others and make friends. Students who are isolated from their peers or detached from those around them often feel sad, lonely, and depressed. It is difficult to worry about higher levels of needs—especially giving attention to studying or homework—when they feel so alone. Students need to feel loved by family and friends; they need to feel that they belong in the school community, and attention from teachers and other adults can help to fulfill this need.

Need for Esteem

The fourth level of human needs, as described by Maslow, is the **need to feel self-esteem**. People need not only to get attention and simply have people around them but also to feel that those people respect them. Student self-esteem has been a common topic of discussion amongst educators in recent years as we've recognized the need for students to gain confidence in themselves. They need to feel competent and valued. In Chapter 1 you read about praise and other positive reinforcement that allows you as a paraprofessional to recognize students for the things they do well. Maslow considered the need for respect from others as the lower end of esteem, while the need for self-respect was a higher need within this level. When you point out to students their achievements and talents, ideally they come to recognize their own abilities, which leads to higher self-esteem. This concept applies to all students, even those who may be delayed in their physical or mental development.

Self-Actualization

Finally, the highest level of needs—according to Maslow—is the need to become our best selves, which he called **self-actualization**. Maslow believed that we are driven toward a goal of reaching our full potential. In this level of needs, a person may focus on morality, religious devotion, or a need to serve others. Some students may focus on art, music, or other forms of creativity. Other students may focus on scientific discovery, athletics, or a difficult skill. They are more willing to reach out and try new things, such as learning new hobbies. Individuals will focus on the area that is important to make them their best selves, and this applies to both students and adults. As a paraprofessional, think about the things that you do to develop yourself into a better person. It may be classes you take, books you read, concerts you go to, or church attendance. Increasing the skills that make you better at your job of helping students is part of self-actualization.

In schools, students who are hungry, tired, or feel they are in danger (whether real or imagined) will find it difficult to focus on learning. Students who have no friends or worry about the health and safety of a loved one may also struggle to focus on schoolwork or other activities. Though they may still come to school, church, sporting events, or whatever higher level activities they are involved in, they likely will not be motivated until their basic needs are met and they can therefore focus on that higher level.

Here's an opportunity to apply what we've been discussing. Think about a common student behavior—a bid to get attention. Now describe where it fits in Maslow's Hierarchy of Needs.

Getting Attention

Which level of Maslow's Hierarchy of Needs does *attention getting* match?

The following paragraphs should help you to decide:

Jim Knight, a professor at the University of Kansas, trains instructional coaches who go into classrooms to coach teachers for instructional enhancement. In his 2007 book, *Instructional Coaching: A Partnership Approach to Improving Instruction*, Knight refers to John Gottman's 2001 book, *The Relationship Cure,* in which Gottman suggests that emotional bids are at the heart of personal relationships. They call attention-seeking behavior making "a bid"—a bid for an emotional response. This may be a look, a touch, an expression, or an outward action.

This bid is to get attention, love, and assurance that one is needed, wanted, and important. Teachers and paraprofessionals can watch for these actions and be aware that each bid is a call for an emotional response. Some students are subtle in their bid. Susie raises her hand frequently the first day of class and repeats her name before answering or asking a question. Her bid is to get you to know her name. She wants you to learn her name and know who she is. Other students' bids may involve less appropriate behavior: calling out, hitting, or asking repeated questions (when the answers to the questions don't seem to be as important as someone looking at and listening to the questioner).

The challenge is for paraprofessionals and teachers to watch for and identify a bid for attention, to discuss it together and identify the need or motivation that is prompting the bid, and then to design the best response to it.

If you said that attention getting is the "need for love and belonging," you were correct. Attention getting is an effort to get a response from you. And remember

Chapter 1, where you learned about positive and negative reinforcement? If your response to the attention seeking is negative—"Abu, how many times do I have to tell you to raise your hand?"—Abu may find this attention better than no attention at all. On the other hand, if you recognize Abu when he raises his hand without being reminded to do so, you are giving him positive reinforcement. "Abu, thank you for remembering to raise your hand!" This type of recognition will address his need for belonging but will also lead to esteem building as he engages in appropriate behaviors.

Helping Meet Student Needs

Paraprofessionals, teachers, and other school personnel can do much to assist students to move from the basic levels of need to the higher levels. In the next section, we talk about the things paraprofessionals can do to build relationships with students and help them to achieve their highest level of self-actualization. First, healthy and meaningful interactions with students require that you build trust and respect. This trust is built one student at a time and one interaction at a time. It will be more difficult and take longer with the student who has learned from his or her short experience of life not to trust adults. But underlying the concept of trust and respect is the importance of your character, competence, and motives—essentially your personal and professional integrity. We briefly discuss each of these, and you will have an opportunity to consider how these apply to you and your work setting.

Trust and Respect

Trust is something that is a familiar concept, yet building trust is not always easy, and it is something that is often difficult to describe. The description for building trust often includes being trustworthy. Steven M. R. Covey (son of the well-known author and inspirational speaker Steven R. Covey) wrote a book titled *The Speed of Trust* in which he identifies five "waves" for how trust operates in our lives, with a "key principle" for each one:

1. Self-trust (key principle: credibility).
2. Relationship trust (key principle: consistent behavior).
3. Organizational trust (inside the organization; key principle: alignment).
4. Market trust (outside the organization; key principle: reputation).
5. Societal trust (key principle: contribution).

Covey's emphasis is on the importance of trust within business organizations, but you can see that the first two waves of trust he identifies relate to individuals and individual interactions in almost any setting.

Interactions with students are better when there is trust and respect. The more a student trusts in you, the better your relationship will be with that student. And as someone who often helps students who are struggling and perhaps embarrassed by their shortcomings, your students especially need to feel they can trust you. You need to have credibility.

Trusting Character

How does one build trust with students? Two factors that support trust building are character and competence. Character means you behave consistently and with integrity. Competence means you know what you are doing.

As a person with integrity, you can be trusted because you will never betray a confidence. You will keep your word of honor. Karl G. Maeser, a German educator who immigrated to the United States in the 1850s, spoke of trust and honor when he said,

> I have been asked what I mean by "word of honor." I will tell you. Place me behind prison walls—walls of stone ever so high, ever so thick, reaching ever so far into the ground—there is a possibility that in some way or another I might be able to escape; but stand me on the floor and draw a chalk line around me and have me give my word of honor never to cross it. Can I get out of that circle? No, never! I'd die first.

When you behave in a trustworthy way, you are demonstrating that you can keep your word. You don't keep it only part of the time and the other part say, "Well I said I would . . . but it isn't that important now." Students need to know that you always keep your word. You may be one of the few people they know who do that, and some of them may be astonished by it if they have been let down often enough. But it will certainly earn you their respect.

Trust Competence

Sometimes a student may trust you, but the student may also know you do not have the authority to act on a problem. As a paraprofessional, you many not feel that you have all the skills that are needed to deal with some of the behaviors you see in the classroom. (This would be competence—and may take hours of additional training.) However, if the student believes that you have strong character, that you care about her success and that you will keep your word, then she is much more likely to trust you and more apt to comply with your requests. This will be true even if she realizes that you do not have complete authority over a situation, as long as you are true to your word. And as this occurs over and over again, the student's behavior will eventually improve because she knows your character and how you as a role model have had a positive impact on her. This is what is meant by *Trust Competence.*

Several university students were asked to think back to their high school days to identify someone on the teaching staff they trusted and then identify what that person had done to gain their trust. Here is a sampling of what they said:

> "When I'm a teacher I want to do what my teachers did. To gain the trust/ respect from my students, I will (1) ask questions and take interest in their personal life (weekend plans, after school jobs), (2) have them write prompts/ journal entries about things that are important to them, (3) ask questions about school, what they like (subjects), of all the subjects they are studying, which is their favorite."

"I have found it to be effective when teachers and paraprofessionals show genuine interest in things important to the student. I have also noticed that as a student I was more willing to open up when I knew they were on my side. They explicitly told me that they were rooting for me."

"They listened and remembered things they'd asked about me. They showed real interest. They gave me sincere and personal compliments/praise. It was special when they complimented the good in me that they noticed. They seemed to be sincere overall."

"It is important for teaching staff to interact with students when they enter and leave the classroom, and acknowledge them outside of the classroom setting. Go to activities they are involved in (sports, plays, church activities). Write praise notes or give sincere praise to the students."

"When my teachers shared who they were and worked with me to gain my trust, I learned that teachers had feelings and emotions too, just like me and all the other students. They had happiness and fear and expectations. They let me know how they truly felt. I hope that I can be the same type of teacher in the future, kind of showing a little vulnerability, so that my students can have a better chance of trusting me."

"My leaders discussed my interests with me. They would tell a funny joke/ story about mistakes that they'd made. We would talk about each other's family background. On occasion we'd play a game together. They expressed confidence and trust."

"My favorite paraprofessional understood me and my difficulties. This was done through observations and by meeting with me and the teacher. She gave positive compliments on my behavior and academics. Somehow she managed to take an interest in my out of school activities."

"I think this is a "line upon line" principle. When you take notice of a student, they begin to recognize you care. The caring, as viewed by the student, will become solidified as you enquire about and remember elements of their life. After the student realizes the depth of your commitment, they trust teachers with stories and insights. Students can then tell the adults that you appreciate their trust in you."

Several university students were asked to identify an adult they trusted in high school and how that person had gained their trust. They said:
- They took an interest in me and in my personal life.
- They let me know they were rooting for me.
- They gave me sincere and personal compliments/praise.
- They shared who they were, so I learned that teachers had feelings and emotions too, just like me and all the other students.

(Continued)

- They managed to convey—through being observant and meeting with me and the teacher—that they understood me and my difficulties.
- They were consistent and deeply committed to their students.

Exemplifying Maslow's Hierarchy of Needs, these university students identified the factors that built their relationships with adults in their high schools. Note that listening and remembering what the students deemed important were considered signs of caring about the students and led to gaining their trust and respect. This, in turn, motivated them. Listening, building trust and respect, and showing that you are honorable are concepts that also apply to the paraprofessional/teacher relationship. Consider how you perform as you look at the items in the Personal Assessment of Trust Builders form. Evaluate your performance with specific examples relating to the classroom and working with students, and then again when working with teachers and administrators.

Motive

We have referred to integrity several times already in this chapter, particularly one aspect of integrity—the integrity of intent or motive. When students know your reason for being in the classroom is to help them learn and they know that their learning truly motivates you—it inspires their trust that you are genuine in your purpose.

So what is your **motive**? We sometimes call the motive the "function" of the behavior. Is your intent to help? It is through your actions that students know you care about them. You listen to them. You ask questions about the things that are important in their lives—their families; sports, drama, or other extracurricular activities; music; peer relationships; cars—whether you think those things are important to you personally or not. They become important to you because they are important to your students.

One of the authors of this book has in her possession a loving note that was written to her husband in beautiful feminine handwriting. The couple had been married for some 30 years and had a serious emergency in their lives. The note was found in his shirt pocket as they prepared for the evening. It reads:

Dear Owen,

I want to say goodbye, but didn't want to wake you because you were sleeping so soundly. It has been great being with you! I hope I will be able to see you again.

Jan

What were the intentions? What was the motive of this woman toward a married man?

Explanation: Owen's family had a history of heart disease, so it should have been no surprise when he had a serious heart attack and subsequent bypass surgery. The intensive care nurses were capable, competent, and caring. Owen's doctors and nurses were surprised by the speed of their patient's recovery. So when Jan, the head nurse, was leaving to take her planned time off, she was surprised to learn that

Personal Assessment of Trust Builders

My performance: I ...	Always	Sometimes	Never	I could improve this by ...
Show genuine interest in the students and their personal lives.				
Ask questions about the students and their lives both in and out of school (e.g., their hobbies, weekend plans, after-school jobs, favorite school subject or teacher or sports team, the World Cup or the Super Bowl, the school dance, etc.).				
Interact with students when they enter and leave the classroom.				
Acknowledge students outside of the classroom setting (e.g., eat lunch with them, walk to class with them).				
Show a little vulnerability (e.g., admit when I make a mistake, talk about what I'm going to do to correct it).				
Give sincere compliments (e.g., write notes of sincere praise, take the time to notice the good things students achieve).				
Incorporate students' interests and preferences into the work I do with them.				
Understand the students and their difficulties (e.g., when they show frustration or anger it does not surprise me and I am able to receive it in a positive way).				

Owen would be released before she returned from her holiday. Kind and caring, she wrote the sweet note. Her motive was to celebrate her patient's recovery and to acknowledge her pleasure in playing a part in that recovery.

When a positive, caring motive is known, negative assumptions are put aside. Trusting relationships continue to build.

Personal Assessment of Trust Builders

Read the statements listed on the nearby form and make an assessment of your performance in these areas. You may feel that you already do these things, but there is usually room for improvement. So take the time to consider how you might go even further to support students by extending what you do.

There are a large number of areas to consider, so as you look at your self-assessment identify just one or two areas to work on. Set a goal and a time by which you will meet that goal. Then make sure you take the time—perhaps after a week or two—to review whether you have met that goal. But don't forget to recognize the areas where you feel you do a great job. Take some time to celebrate. Treat yourself to a chocolate bar, a new book, or a trip to the movies. Or just bask for a moment in the feeling of satisfaction that you are doing your job well. These can be your positive reinforcements for a job well done!

Making Mistakes

Oops! You made a mistake. Admit it, laugh at it, correct it, consider why you made it, and thank the person who discovered it. If you are unsure of what went wrong, talk with your supervisor and together identify the mistake and the correction procedure. Remember two heads are better than one, meaning two people using their minds together may be able to solve a problem that one cannot. Each may have a different perspective to share, and together you can identify what went wrong, what to do about it, and how to prevent it from reoccurring in the future. The book of Ecclesiastes in the King James Version of the Holy Bible puts it this way: "Two are better than one; because they have a good reward for their labor. For if they fall, the one will lift up his fellow; but woe to him that is alone when he falleth for he hath not another to help him up" (Ecclesiastes 4:9).

Use the Proactive Thinking to Prevent Problems form to help think through problem solving and prevention. Try to think of different types of things that you feel went wrong in the past weeks or months and consider a variety of different ways of remedying the situation and preventing it from happening again.

Always Learning

If you are one of those paraprofessionals who travel from classroom to classroom, you are especially lucky. As you provide assistance to teachers and students, you have an opportunity to see a variety of different ways of doing things and thus learn new strategies and ideas. Observant eyes can identify something new and useful every day, sometimes every hour. These learning opportunities are presented with each teacher-student interaction. What the student does—and how the teacher reacts to that behavior—is a learning moment. You may like to write these good

Proactive Thinking to Prevent Problems

What Went Wrong (briefly describe the situation)	Possible Remedies (think of as many ways as possible to put things right)	Prevention Measures (plan for things you can put in place to try and stop it from happening again)

Choose one area to work on over the next two weeks. Then return to your prevention ideas and assess how effective they were. If they were not successful, work with your teacher to identify a new plan. If they were successful, celebrate together!

Always Learning—Documenting the Positive Experiences

What Went Right	How I Will Use This	Other Strategies to Try

ideas down in a "New Ideas" notebook so you will remember and can call upon these ideas and strategies as you encounter new behavior challenges. We've also provided an Always Learning form that you may like to use for recording the positive learning experiences you've had as you've worked in different classrooms.

There may be times that you may disagree with the action the teacher takes—but the real opportunity comes when the paraprofessional may say, "Although that action was not what I consider to be the best, here are some options that I think may work better in this situation." Careful evaluation and analysis of actions that could be taken can help a paraprofessional add more options to his or her toolbox of strategies for improving behavior.

Helping Teachers Too

Up to this point in the text we've discussed the needs of students and looked at the things you can do to help them meet their needs. It would be marvelous if every student moved smoothly and swiftly up Maslow's Hierarchy of Needs to the top level of self-actualization—although in reality this is a lifelong quest for all of us. It would be great if paraprofessionals and teachers could spend the greatest portion of their time supporting learning instead of looking at correcting behavior. The foundation can be built by applying the things you've learned in this chapter and Chapter 1. But now let's broaden the concepts to include the teachers with whom you work. Think of ways you can help and support teachers as you read the following sections.

Building Trust and Respect

The primary goal of the classroom is for paraprofessionals and teachers to work together for the benefit of student learning. The classroom is not anything like a competitive sport where the each player is trying to best the other. It must be a model of teamwork at its best. And the research tells us that the best teams are built not only on competence but also on an emotional connection. Teachers and paraprofessionals who work as an effective team often share observations about their teamwork with examples like, "She seems to read my mind. When something needs to be done and I'm busy, she just goes ahead and does it." Or, "He cares about the students and wants them to be successful. He is the best paraprofessional I've ever had." Or, "I don't have a teaching degree, but she treats me with respect and values my suggestions. Although we bring different expertise to the classroom, as people, we are equals." These are references to relationships and emotional connections as much as competence.

Here are two things that will help to build and maintain the effectiveness of your work with your teacher because they contribute to building relationships: humor and listening.

Humor

Humor is the ability to perceive, enjoy, or express that which is amusing, comical, incongruous, or absurd. It can be overused, but appropriate classroom humor is constructive and inclusive. It shows you are warm and "human" and that you are willing to laugh. Have you heard the saying, "Laugh, and the world laughs with you; Weep, and you weep alone" (Ella Wheeler Wilcox)? Enjoy the classroom, students, and teachers and the many adventures they bring. Some of the ways you might use humor in the classroom are:

- Pop culture references.
- Laughing at oneself.
- Laughing with students (but never at them).

> A day without laughter is a day wasted. —Charlie Chaplin
> If you're too busy to laugh, you are too busy. —Proverb
> If we couldn't laugh, we would all go insane. —Robert Frost
> I don't trust anyone who doesn't laugh. —Maya Angelou

Listening

Although listening can seem like a passive "activity," we know there are powerful ways to be active listeners. In his book *The 7 Habits of Highly Effective People* (1989), Stephen Covey discusses the concept of empathic listening. He says, "seek first to understand, then be understood." This wise advice helps paraprofessionals and others carefully listen to the message the teacher is sending. Focus. Ask yourself, "What is he trying to tell me?" Check for understanding by asking for more information or for clarification. Did you understand the message? This shows that you're focused, want to respond in appropriate ways, and want to be involved.

How Are You Doing?

Take some time to evaluate how you are doing. Have you been building trust and respect through your character and competence? Do you show respect to students, teachers, and others? Are you actively listening? Read the checklist below and self-evaluate.

Checklist for Building Trust

- Do I "Say what I will do and do what I say I will?"
- Am I consistent in making and keeping commitments to others and myself?
- Am I open to learning new ideas that may cause me to rethink issues or to redefine my values?
- Do I justify telling "little lies" to misrepresent people or situations, or do I put a "spin" on the truth to get the results I want?
- Can I acknowledge when someone is right and I am wrong?
- Do I help students to see and know that I have their best interests in mind?
- Am I consciously aware of my motives? Do I refine them to make sure that I am doing the right things for the students and teachers?

The checklist provides you with prompts for examining and documenting your own attitudes and practices in relation to student behavior, as well as those of the other adults in your work setting. We ask you to identify any contradictions or mismatches as well as the commonalities of approach, and to consider any action you might take to enhance and contribute to positive behavior in the classroom. Some of these items will require persistent and lengthy attention, while others may have simpler, faster solutions. But you can enhance your attitudes and practices in some small way today—and again tomorrow.

ABCs of Behavior

So far in this chapter we have considered a variety of influences on student behavior, including the relationships of trust that we can build with our students. But before we move on to the next section and consider how we document and evaluate student behavior, we need to discuss the behavior that we see, what happened **before** the behavior, and then, of course, what happened **after** the behavior occurred. This will allow us to look at the proactive measures we can take to establish and maintain a more positive behavioral ethos in our classrooms. This strategy is sometimes referred to as the ABCs of behavior, where:

A is the antecedent,
B is the behavior,
C is the consequence.

As an adult in the classroom, you can be aware of the things you can do to prevent the behaviors you wish not to see, and you can shape the behaviors you want to increase.

Antecedent Events

The critical point in the analysis of behavior is to consider what happened BEFORE the behavior occurred. We call this the antecedent event. It is especially important to pay attention to these events when you are looking at the behavior of students because these antecedents trigger the behavior.

Antecedent

An-te-ced'-ent (noun, adj.) Going before; preceding.
a.   A preceding occurrence, cause, or event.
b.   An antecedent is any physical object or occurrence in the environment.
c.   The important events and occurrences in one's early life.

Let's look at some of the antecedents that may be the "trigger" for a behavior. An example: you are driving your automobile and you come to a stop sign (antecedent), so you step on the brakes and stop (the behavior). If you do not perform the behavior, your consequence may be a car accident or a ticket by a police officer who sees you violating the law!

Credit: Christopher Wells Barlow

Another antecedent may be a student bullying another student by saying mean things. This may trigger a behavior of crying in young children or physical retaliation such as punching, hitting, or other fighting in older students. The behavior is the response to the antecedent (bullying).

In the case study of the boy who shouts out without raising his hand, you can shape the behavior by reminding students **before** you ask a question. Simply saying, "As we perform this math problem together, I'm going to ask some questions. Remember to raise your hand and wait to be called upon before you answer." This gives the students notice of your expectation and reminds them to raise hands (antecedent) and you will call on them (behavior). The next section will discuss consequences in more detail.

The Consequence

The consequence is what happens after the behavior. Chapter 1 looked at positive and negative reinforcement as consequences of behavior. The chapter summary below gives you an opportunity to apply the information you've covered in the text so far. A form is provided on page 60 to help you apply the information to your situation.

Focusing on Specific Behavior

Frustrated teachers (or paraprofessionals) may sometimes be heard to say things like: "That boy—he never sits still!" Or, "He's always out of his seat!" Or, "He shouts out all the time!" In our exasperation over what feels like continuous disruptive behavior we can easily fall into a pattern of making these sorts of generalizations. And yet, are they really true? If we're clearly setting expectations and teaching them to our students, it is important to be accurate in monitoring their behaviors so that we have a solid baseline for discussing those behaviors and a clear method of assessing improvements. We acknowledge that students shouldn't be out of their seats or shouting out at all. Even low levels of these behaviors can be very frustrating for the adult and for other students in the class. However, something more precise is needed if we wish to take a systematic approach to managing and changing student behaviors. So, in this section of the chapter, we'll be looking at some of the principles associated with monitoring and recording student behavior as a basis for our discussions with students about that behavior and as a first step in changing it if necessary.

Look at this list of "behaviors"—things we may think of as verbs and therefore things that people "do." Which of these would you say is observable and measurable?

walking	talking	reading
writing	paying attention	thinking
listening	collaborating	researching

These are all behaviors we might associate with classrooms, and we'd consider most of them desirable in our students. But which of them can you actually see happening? Can you see someone thinking? Or listening? Well, no. What you see are the outward signs, which *seem to suggest* that the person might be thinking or listening.

The thinker may look thoughtful, but she could be thinking about anything, not necessarily about the task at hand. The listener may be looking in the right direction, facing the speaker, with his eyes open and an interested look on his face, but

Source: iStock #702842

his mind may be miles away and his attention on quite a different focus than the classroom activity in which he should be engaged. Even behavior such as reading is difficult to observe unless the student is reading out loud. Silent reading might be suggested by a book in hand, eyes turned toward the page, perhaps even lips moving for a young reader, but we have no way of knowing whether the student is actually reading merely by observation.

You can state (and record) whether a student has a book open in front of him, whether his gaze appears to be directed toward the book, and whether he is talking to peers or not—as long as you recognize that these are just possible indicators of reading (and appropriate behaviors for the classroom). But these are not proof that the student is reading. If we wish to establish a clear picture of how a student is behaving (what he or she is actually *doing*), we must focus on behaviors that we can see or hear unequivocally and that we can therefore record/count.

Observable and Measurable Behavior

An observable behavior states what the student is doing. It is a visible action, an external feature, not something that is going on inside the student's head. In order to be measurable, a behavior must first be observable. In addition, the behavior must be defined clearly enough for an observer to be able to determine whether the behavior is occurring, to count the occurrences of the behavior, and/or to note when the behavior began and ended (duration of the behavior).

Here are some examples of behaviors that are observable and measureable:

- Student drops pencil.
- Student uses a graphing calculator to identify the vertex, axis of symmetry, and intercepts of a quadratic equation.
- Student writes complete sentences from sentence fragments.
- Student raises hand before giving an answer.
- Student correctly names the US presidents in the twenty-first century.
- Student describes the relationship between mass and volume as it relates to density.

Notice that some of these are observable and measurable in terms of their product (*writes complete sentences*) whereas others are observable as a process (*raises hand before giving an answer*).

Examples of behaviors that are not measurable include: thinking, analyzing, contemplating, and judging because these take place inside the brain. We can know the behavior only when it is said, written/recorded, or acted upon.

Recording Observations

There are a wide variety of ways in which we can monitor and record student behaviors. We suggest three here that can easily be used in a regular classroom setting—open observation, time sampling, and event sampling. It is worth noting that they all require some time, and they all are more easily accomplished if this is your only task—i.e., you're not trying to work with a group of students and monitor/record at the same time. You can discuss the possibilities for monitoring/

recording behaviors with your supervising teacher. Even a short observation session (10–20 minutes) can yield useful information. If this is done on a regular basis, it builds a clear picture of the student's behavior over time.

Things to Address When Observing

- The behavior must be carefully and explicitly taught to the students if you expect them to do it.
- Select a behavior that is observable and measurable.
- The behavior must be well defined (off task, acting out, or being discourteous are all too vague).
- Determine the time interval for observation.
- Focus on and record only the behavior to be observed.
- Take accurate data.

The methods of observation and recording that we discuss here are:

- Open observation with field notes.
- Time sampling.
- Time sampling at intervals.
- Event sampling.

As you read about each of these, analyze which would work best for you if you were to record specific student behaviors. Then take the opportunity to try at least one of them out. With your teacher, decide the behavior that you wish to observe. Be very specific. Be sure that your definition of the behavior is so narrow and specific that others would understand what you are observing and be able to observe exactly what you saw and recorded. Decide which type of behavioral recording is best suited to monitor the behavior. And lastly, decide when you will observe the behavior. Do you want to observe the behavior in a number of situations or just once? Do you want to observe in the morning and again in the afternoon? Data collected at different times and in different situations will give a fuller picture of what is happening.

Open Observation with Field Notes

Open observation, simply put, means watching the student and taking notes on what you see. It is also called by a variety of different names, such as *running records* and *scripting* (although scripting is more detailed in that you write down everything that is said). This type of data collection is a continuous record of what is going on over a period of time. It provides a wealth of detailed information, but it is quite time consuming and takes a good deal of concentration as an observer. It also produces a lot of loose information, which may be difficult to organize or present as a clear picture of the student's behavior. In the box you can see an example of notes taken during an open observation at uneven time intervals.

10:01–10:04	Mariah is looking about the room. Others have their books out and are reading. She looks at each student, then turns and looks at the clock. Shouts out, "Miss P. It's 10 o'clock!"
10:05–10:09	Mariah pulls book from desk and slowly turns the pages to the page listed on the whiteboard. She appears to be reading.
10:10–10:12	Mariah is looking about the room again. She pulls a piece of string from her pocket and wraps it around her fingers, then unwinds it, and is wrapping it again. Mutters something under her breath I couldn't understand.

This type of continuous data collection can also be recorded using a timeline—marking a line across a piece of paper and noting what the student is doing by making notes at the relevant points in the line.

It helps if you mark the line with time intervals (you can see an example in the box). Then you can keep track of the student's behavior in relation to:

1. how long the student spends in total doing particular things (being on task, wandering around the classroom), and
2. whether the student's behaviors change according to the time (whether he gets distracted after about 5 minutes, for example). Again, this can be time consuming, but it can also be very revealing to watch a student constantly, even for 20 minutes, so that you get a clear idea of what he does and for how long. Time sampling is more about sustained behaviors (on-task, off-task) than specific instances of short behaviors (hand raising, calling out, etc.).

Time Sampling

Time Sampling—Observing On Task (OT) Behavior of Three Students

10:00	John Nathan Angela	On task (OT) OT OT
10:03	John Nathan Angela	OT OT Talking to neighbor
10:06	John Nathan Angela	Tells Angela to be quiet OT Begins working again
10:09	Etc.	

Time sampling—as the name suggests—consists of noting and recording student behavior during a given period or interval of time rather than continuously recording what is happening. It does not give a complete record of everything the student is doing during the whole of the observation period, but it does produce a sample of the behavior.

When you use time sampling, you must first choose your time interval (for example, 30 seconds). Then you observe the student only briefly at the beginning of the time interval and record what you see. You then look away from the student until the beginning of the next 30-second interval. Recording is usually done using a grid with the time intervals marked out and either a checklist of target behaviors or space to note which behaviors you see. We've included a sample recording sheet in the box, but this one uses two-minute intervals.

Example of Time Intervals

Look at the clock every two minutes and record what the student is doing.

10:00	10:02	10:04	10:06	10:08	10:10
Out of seat	Appears to be reading text	Looking around room	Reading text	Sharpening pencil	Doodling on blank paper

---

It is useful if recording and observing happen at the same time and if every time unit stipulates the time of the observation, such as 10:00 until 10:20 each day. These time intervals can be chosen randomly or systematically. If you and the teacher choose to use systematic time sampling, the information you obtain will apply only to the time period in which the observation took place. For example, at 10:10 every day (during math) the student raises his hand and says he needs to go to the restroom. This technique is applied to studies on incidence of frequent behaviors, such as hand flapping or shouting out, so it may not be appropriate to the setting in which you work.

In contrast to sampling only one specific time each day is a time sampling method that involves the acquisition of representative samples gained when you observe the student at different time intervals. Doing observations at different (and random) times throughout the school day may give a better picture of the behavior you are observing. You may be able to see if it occurs more frequently across all times of observation.

A big disadvantage of time sampling is that it is not useful if the behavior occurs infrequently or unpredictably because you will often miss the event in the short time period of observation.

Event Sampling

Event sampling is more useful if the behavior happens infrequently or unpredictably. An example may be temper tantrums or angry outbursts. In this style of sampling, the observer lets the event determine when the observations will take place. For example, if the question involves observing behavior during a specific class period or area of the school, one would use event sampling instead of time sampling.

Work with your teacher as you prepare to observe. Students should know that you are completing an assignment and that you will not be available to address other needs while you are carrying out observations. You can train them in advance that when you have the clipboard, for example, you will not be able to work with them on other things. Tell them that you will be taking data infrequently through the day/week and ask for their cooperation. As you do this on a regular basis they will become accustomed to it and learn to carry on without your support and without being distracted by it.

Sit in a location in the classroom where you can see and hear the behaviors of interest, but place yourself out of the way of student traffic patterns (e.g., away from the sink or water fountain, away from the exit). Stay focused on the behavior you are to record. Above all it is important to take accurate data because this will guide the teacher's decision making on instruction and behavioral adjustments.

Protocol for Observing

- Sit somewhere out of the way of classroom traffic.
- Sit where you can see and hear the behaviors of interest.
- Focus on the assignment and always take accurate data.

There are some additional considerations when you are monitoring student behavior in this way. You may need to monitor and record a student's behavior while you are working with a small group or leading a learning activity. This is sometimes unavoidable, and in fact recording while working has both advantages and disadvantages (see the nearby box for a list of advantages and disadvantages).

Participant Observation

Observing behavior and recording data while participating in an activity with the students is referred to as a "participant observation" because you are participating in the activity (as opposed to only observing and being slightly removed from the activity, which is sometimes referred to as "non-participant observation"). This is difficult to do when you are also teaching, motivating students, and guiding all the other orchestration that is necessary in a classroom. A solution may be to have students monitor and record their own behaviors. In this case it is best to focus on recording a positive behavior that eliminates the possibility of the student engaging in the undesired behavior.

An example of this would be to have a student record how many times he raises his hand to answer a question, rather than to have him record how many times he shouts out in class. You can see that it would be much more motivating for the student to record instances of a desirable behavior for which he or she can be rewarded on displaying the results than recording instances of negative behavior for which he or she can be punished on presenting the results. In the latter case the student has no motivation to be accurate, but in the former case he or she has every incentive. Students often like to graph their own results if they are to record particular behaviors over a period of time. And this can be motivating—especially as they're competing against themselves and against a goal they've had some say in—rather than competing against other students and working toward goals they may not feel apply to them or see as achievable.

If the behavior of concern applies to more than one setting within the school (for example, in the classroom and in the playground), it is useful to conduct some of your observations in both settings. If the issue is that the student is using inappropriate language, for example, or perhaps refusing to do what an adult asks, this is quite likely to occur in more than one location. And, it may not occur with the same frequency. So if the student showed more of an appropriate behavior in one class period than another (or at lunch break rather than in the classroom) you could look at the different influences in the two settings. Then you could try to match or duplicate those influences from the setting where the behavior is displayed more often. You could of course also ask the student why he or she behaves more appropriately in the one setting than in the other.

It's also often useful to observe another student for a comparison. (And under the IDEA, the identification of some disability areas requires observation of students *and* a comparison with their peers.) So if you feel that a particular student is shouting out without raising his hand too often, observe another student who shouts out without raising his hand. You may find that your target student is no worse than other students in the class, but for some reason you've noticed the behavior in him more than in other students. If it turns out to be a more generalized problem, you and the teacher can tackle that with the whole class rather than just targeting the one student.

Advantages and Disadvantages of Participant vs. Non-Participant Observation

Participant Observation	Non-Participant Observation
It may be difficult to record and lead the learning activity at the same time (suggesting that the recording method must be as simple as possible).	Recording is simple as you have no other responsibilities.
You have access to all of the detail of what students say and do, as you are sitting amongst them.	You may miss some of the detail of what students say and do as you are sitting at a distance.

(Continued)

You can keep students on task.	If they are working independently and you're observing/recording, you will be unable to help them stay on task.
You must be careful not to influence their behavior too much, otherwise you will not get a true picture of how they normally behave.	When you are observing and recording you will be unable to provide guidance and support for them, but you will get a better picture of how they behave without supervision or when supervised by a particular adult.

Earlier we discussed the issue of overstating a problem, such as "He always shouts out." Using the data you collected, you may find that the really irritating behavior of a particular student doesn't occur nearly as often as you had thought—which is one possible positive outcome of this exercise. But the more important outcome is that you now have concrete evidence of how often a student engages in inappropriate behavior and the basis for presenting that to the student and discussing with him or her how this can change. You or the teacher can use the numbers from your observation to help the student set a target for change.

A student who observes his own behavior—the student who tallies the number of times he raises his hand to answer a question, for example—can learn to take his own data. This enhances his awareness and can improve his behavior. As you continue to monitor and record, you will hopefully see a reduction in negative behavior and an increase in the associated positive behavior. This is partly due to an increased awareness on the part of the student, which in itself can lead to behavior change, and you can celebrate that change for the better with the student.

There is an old saying, "You don't fatten a pig by weighing it." Frequent or regular monitoring and recording alone are not likely to bring about desired behavior change. In the same way that poor piggy needs feeding if he's to tip those scales and get the prize at the fair, so your students need to be provided with the information or strategies they need to make change. These are some of the questions to consider in upcoming chapters as we discuss the proactive ways to work with students on their behavior improvement.

Typical behavior	What's the antecedent?	What are the usual consequences?	Do they work?	What could I do about this?

Summary

In this chapter you learned to identify the factors that impact behavior both positively and negatively. There are internal and external factors (both for the student and for the teaching staff) that affect the learning environment. Relationship building with students and staff will be important, so you will be able to describe steps you will take to build trust and respect. You will be able to identify observable and measurable behaviors and to take data on them. You can identify and describe the antecedents of behaviors and the consequences. You will identify how data can help you learn from your mistakes.

We've mentioned having the student raise a hand before answering a question posed by the teacher or paraprofessional. Let's look at a few of the other behaviors that typically occur in the classroom. Write these down as they occur to you using a large A for Antecedents, B for behavior, and C for consequences. Write whether or not the consequences worked. What will you do next time?

Learning Outcomes

Chapter 2 helped you gain the following learning outcomes:

- You can name the factors that affect student behavior—both positive and negative.
- You can identify internal and external factors, including aspects of the learning environment (work groupings, physical arrangements, routines), and motivational issues.
- You can pinpoint specific behaviors by identifying and recording.
- You can show how to take observation data using different forms of recording.
- You know about the ABCs of behavior, including adult behavior as an antecedent, observing behaviors, and taking data.

Looking Ahead

In the next chapter we will look at ways to help students succeed. You will learn to set procedures including rules and routines by setting clear expectations and using effective teaching methods, including teaching social skills. We also will focus on the need for a whole-school approach and the necessity of collaborative behavior.

Bibliography

Burton, A. P. (1953). *Karl G. Maeser: Mormon educator.* Salt Lake City: Deseret Book Co., p. v.

Covey, S. (1989). *The 7 habits of highly effective people: Powerful lessons in personal change.* New York: Simon & Schuster.

Covey, S.M.R. (2006). *The speed of trust.* New York: Simon & Schuster Adult Publishing Group.

Gottman, J. M. (2001). *The relationship cure: A five-step guide for building better connections with family, friends, and lovers.* New York: Crown.

Knight, J. (2007). *Instructional coaching: A partnership approach to improving instruction.* Thousand Oaks, CA: Corwin Press.

Koehn, M. (June 16, 2013). Transforming school culture. [Web log comment]. Retrieved from http://smartblogs.com/education/2014/06/16/transforming-school-culture-through-mutual-respect/?utm_source=brief.

Maslow, A. H. (1943). A theory of human motivation. *Psychological Review, 50*(4), 370–396. Retrieved from http://psychclassics.yorku.ca/Maslow/motivation.htm.

Chapter 3

Plan A

Setting Students Up for Success

What You Will Learn

Learning Objectives:

Upon completion of this chapter, you will know the importance of setting clear expectations and communicating those to students. You will be able to identify what is acceptable behavior and what is not, according to particular circumstances. You will be able to provide a rationale for setting rules and routines. By studying the chapter and applying your knowledge, you will be able to explain the importance of using effective instruction and to give examples of effective strategies. These are examples of the powerful behavior management strategies that support student learning. Many of them may already be in place in your work setting, such as helping students know behavioral expectations, not just recite/memorize them. You will be able to recognize these as you apply the knowledge you gain through this chapter.

As the title of this chapter suggests, here we focus on some of the proactive ways in which classrooms and other work settings can be set up to maximize positive behavior.

Plan A: Setting Students Up to Succeed

We refer to this chapter as Plan A because the first and primary purpose of any classroom behavior regime or strategy is to establish and maintain positive, appropriate behavior. Recognizing that not all students will oblige us by behaving appropriately, we address strategies for dealing with inappropriate behavior in Chapter 5. But notice that Chapter 5 is referred to as Plan B. This is because our first concern should be how we can promote and encourage appropriate behavior in our students (Plan A); Plan B is what we do for students who can't manage or who choose not to behave appropriately under Plan A. Optimal interventions address much more than the aggressive behavior of specific students; rather, interventions seek to create a school environment that will allow for the academic and social success of all students.

> The first and primary purpose of any classroom behavior regime or strategy is to establish and maintain positive, appropriate behavior.

Calling this current chapter Plan A should also give a clear message that we need to actually have a plan to establish and promote positive behavior. We can't just hope it will happen. We need to be proactive and look ahead. We need to consider possibilities and be prepared for them. And so we make a plan. And then we set that plan out for our students so that they have a clear understanding of what's expected of them—and hopefully include them in some of the planning process, such as devising classroom rules and discussing rewards, so that it also becomes their plan.

As you read you'll note that the procedures used to make a classroom run smoothly, with all its organization and harmony, will also apply to a family home, a community organization, and other establishments. As you study the list, think of ways these apply to one of your personal settings, such as your home. Some of the things we do to set precedents for success include:

- Establishing classroom rules.
- Setting clear routines.
- Setting clear expectations.
- Using effective teaching methods to teach appropriate behaviors and expectations—along with other content.

You may think that these are a teacher's responsibilities, and you are right. But there are two considerations here.

1. The best teachers will ensure these measures are in place, but some teachers will not appreciate the necessity of setting up clear routines or expectations. Some will have a full repertoire of effective teaching strategies; some will not. Paraprofessionals can therefore find themselves assigned to classrooms that lack some of these essential elements.
2. Paraprofessionals are often required to work with groups of students, including those with difficult behavior. In these group-work situations, the responsibility for establishing rules, routines, and expectations is yours as a paraprofessional; you also need to use effective teaching strategies.

So this chapter is of direct importance to you and your work because you learn the skills to get you off to a good start. These skills also get the students off to a good start and help to maintain appropriate behavior. In the last part of the chapter, we also consider why it's important to teach our students social skills, one of which is the skill of collaboration.

Setting Clear Expectations for Student (and Adult) Behavior

Do students know what we want from them? A word that is constantly used in education is *expectations*. Teachers have high expectations for all students. School boards, administrators, state and federal education agencies, and legislators have high expectations for teachers and their students. Coaches and other community members have all sorts of expectations for students. Parents have high expectations for their children. And what about the students? They too have expectations of what will happen when they sit in a classroom and "live" in a school. Expectations are everywhere. If school personnel and parents hold the same expectations, then this consistency helps to prevent confusion. But it is very difficult, if not impossible, for students to meet our expectations if they have not been told and taught precisely what those expectations are.

The rationale behind a clear and consistent approach may be obvious, but it is sometimes overlooked. Students need clear expectations because:

- They give students a sense of security.
- They provide a standard for student behavior—something to set as their aim.
- Students can feel a sense of achievement when they do what's expected.
- Students can receive approval (reinforcement) for their behavior.

Clinical and social psychology experts agree that children need to know what is expected of them. Dr. Robert Rosenthal, a Harvard professor, systematically studied expectations and their influence on "self-fulfilling prophecies."

In 1964 Rosenthal conducted an unusual experiment at an elementary school near San Francisco. He wanted to know what would happen if teachers were told that certain kids in their class were destined to succeed. So, he gave all the students a test. He then chose several students from every class and told their teachers the test had predicted that these students would dramatically improve their Intelligence Quotients (IQ). (In reality, these students were chosen randomly, with no real reason to believe they would be smarter.)

Dr. Rosenthal then continued to study the students and found that over two years the teachers' expectations actually did help the students improve. He said, "When the teachers had been led to expect greater gains in IQ, then increasingly, those kids gained more IQ [points]."

As you review the need to set high expectations for students, think about expectations for you as an adult.

Clear Expectations of Adults

- Do you feel more secure when you know what's expected (by your employer, by your spouse or significant other)?
- Do you like having a standard that you can strive for and feel good about achieving?
- Do you feel good about yourself at the end of the day or on completion of a task?
- Can you identify your achievements based on the job expectations?

Sometimes paraprofessionals do not have written job descriptions and, therefore, no explicit expectations for the job. You will surely feel much more secure if you know what is expected. Because you are an adult, you most likely will self-advocate by asking the person who hired you or your supervisor to define those expectations.

The University of Alabama Parenting Assistance Line (UA-PAL) gives advice to parents about the need for consistency in expectations, and we have already made some reference to consistency in the Introduction. But the principles also hold good for teachers and other educators in school settings, so we feel that it is important to expand on those ideas here. You can find the UA-PAL website details in the Bibliography, along with a great deal of useful advice for parents that applies equally well to others who work with children and young people. In the box below you will find the reasons that UA-PAL gives for providing consistency. Although the advice is aimed at parents, as you read, note how it applies to paraprofessionals too.

Why Is Consistency Important?

- Consistency gives children a sense of security. They learn they can rely on their parents and trust that their needs will be met. This helps in the bonding process.
- Children with consistent parents experience less anxiety.
- Developing a daily routine with regular rising times, bedtimes, after-school schedules, and meal times will cultivate a more peaceful home life.
- Consistency helps children develop a sense of responsibility because they know what their parents expect from them.
- Children who have consistent rules with predictable consequences are less likely to "push the limits" and constantly test their parents by misbehaving. They learn quickly that "no" really does mean "no."
- Investing early in consistent parenting pays off huge dividends later. There will be considerably fewer temper tantrums and less arguing and bargaining as the children grow.
- Without consistency, children must "guess" daily what actions are appropriate. They wonder if everything that takes place happens because they did something to make it happen.
- Inconsistent parenting causes confusion, poor self-esteem, and oftentimes very negative values.

Now let's apply those principles of consistency of expectations (noted in the nearby box) directly to the classroom.

Principles of Consistency

- Consistency gives students a sense of security. They learn they can rely on teachers and paraprofessionals and trust that their needs will be met. This helps in developing strong relationships.

- Students experience less anxiety when teachers and paraprofessionals expect the same things by being consistent.
- A daily routine with regular times and schedules will cultivate a more peaceful classroom life.
- Consistency helps students develop a sense of responsibility because they know what their teachers and paraprofessionals expect from them and can therefore take responsibility for their own actions.
- Students who have consistent rules with predictable consequences are less likely to "push the limits" and constantly test their teachers and paraprofessionals by misbehaving. They learn quickly that "no" means "no."
- Investing early in consistent practices pays off huge dividends later. There will be considerably less acting out, arguing, and bargaining as the students go through school.
- Without consistency, each day students must "guess" what actions are appropriate and what limits are placed on their behaviors. They wonder if everything that takes place happens because they did something to make it happen.
- Inconsistent classroom practices cause confusion, poor self-esteem, and oftentimes very negative values.

Paraprofessionals and other teaching staff are not children, but we still have some of the same needs. So when we talk of *children* we're not just talking about grade school children. We're also referring to the youth and young adults you may work with in high school. Young people need expectations taught and reinforced because they experience a great deal of uncertainty as they move through their teenage years. They do not need to have an additional sense of uncertainty added unnecessarily by a lack of consistency from the adults who work with them in school.

Of course it may seem that children and young people spend most of their time pushing boundaries and challenging expectations that have been set for their behavior. But that is part of the learning process—they need to check where the boundaries really lie and what the expectations really are. Pushing boundaries could even be considered a necessary condition for learning. It's a natural curiosity and creativity abounds.

The Smart Classroom Management website (details in the Bibliography) also provides reasons why we must be consistent in our classroom management procedures. You will find those in the box on page 68. They recommend that we memorize the list and "internalize its importance" so that we can "relax in its reassurance." We think that's a nice idea. See what you think.

Because you are in the classroom with a teacher, or you may take a small group to another location, we have slightly modified the ideas from Smart Management. The concepts of consistency are still vital, but the impact of two adults in the classroom must receive some consideration.

Reasons for Consistent Management of Behavior

It's Unfair Not to Be Consistent

Both paraprofessional and teacher must be consistent in what they do. To enforce your agreed-upon consequences sometimes and not others is grossly unfair to students. And regardless of your reasoning, regardless of the sensitive nature of the circumstances, or the unique personality of the misbehaving student, the rest of the class doesn't know any better, and thus will be sure to enter it in their unfairness file.

It Causes Resentment

If you don't follow the classroom management plan as it's written, the students will naturally conclude that you're playing favorites—and fiercely resent you because of it. This can be particularly galling when those few who are given more latitude than others are the same ones who continually disrupt the class and ruin the fun of learning. And, if you, the paraprofessional, fail to follow the management plan when you are with a smaller group—the teacher may also resent you and your work.

You Lose Student Respect

Whenever you say you're going to do something and don't do it, you lose a layer of respect from students. The central message they get from you is that you can't be counted on. To the students, you're just another wishy-washy adult who makes promise after promise but doesn't come through. Perhaps it goes without saying that you will also lose the teacher's respect.

Your Authority Will Be Tested

When the students with the most challenging behavior learn that you are not so committed to enforcing consequences, they know that the classroom management plan is written in pencil instead of ink. Now if the teacher enforces the rules and applies consequences, but you the paraprofessional do not—then it is you who will be tested.

Heaven forbid if you are required to supervise these students on the school playing fields or another location away from the people who they know will stick to enforcing the rules. They'll test you and challenge you every chance they get. They'll continually skirt the edges of your rules, probing for weakness. They'll push the boundaries.

Student Behavior Will Worsen

Wherever there is weak accountability or semi accountability, behavior, respect, and kindness take a nosedive. Of course, the inverse is also true: where there is accountability, polite behavior, respect, and kindness are sure to follow. A classroom where teacher and paraprofessionals are polite and respectful to each other and who consistently support each other in the behavioral expectations of students will be a positive constructive environment.

Learning Will Suffer

You simply cannot protect the rights of students to learn and enjoy school if you don't follow through with the classroom management plan. Students have a right to come to school and learn without interference and disruption. And unless the teacher and paraprofessionals rely on a plan for holding misbehaving students accountable, learning will suffer.

You Will Be Forever Frustrated

Without 100% reliance on the classroom management plan to curb misbehavior, you will naturally fall into potentially harmful methods like yelling, scolding, sarcasm, arguing, and the like. You will also find yourself hoping the students will behave, pleading with them to behave, and trying to convince them to behave through such silly actions as bribery. This is a remarkably frustrating and ineffective combination that will cause you to question your choice of career.

Adapted from Smart Classroom Management, www.smartclassroomman agement.com.

Consider this case study, where you can review the problems related to failure to apply rules with consistency and fairness.

The Case

In an elementary school (not to be named here), there was an uprising between teachers and paraprofessionals. Teachers were angry with paraprofessionals and paraprofessionals were angry with teachers. Student learning was suffering. The school principal called one of the authors of this text to mediate. Through information obtained at meetings with each of the groups, we learned that the school had a whole-school discipline system that consisted of giving tickets to the students who were misbehaving. When a student received a ticket, a consequence was to follow.

Only paraprofessionals were given schoolyard supervision responsibilities. The teachers' duties were to prepare lessons while the students and paraprofessionals were outside.

While outside, some students misbehaved and received tickets from the paraprofessionals, but when everyone returned to the classroom the teachers either threw away the tickets or told the students, "The ticket doesn't matter." No negative consequences were applied. No discussions were conducted about how students should behave properly.

Over the weeks, poor behavior increased and the effectiveness of receiving a ticket as an incentive to improve behavior diminished or stopped. Students began back-talking and showing disrespect—especially to paraprofessionals.

Take a Moment to Consider the Issues in This Case

Look at the textbox named Reasons for Consistent Management of Behavior. Which of the checked statements apply here?

Based on your reading of the chapters to this point, what should be done to improve this school's atmosphere?

Analyzing the Situation

First, if you thought the school should move to a positive behavior support system, you are absolutely right! Giving recognition for good behavior is a much better way to increase positive actions than focusing on negative behaviors.

Also, however, a careful plan for the few students who occasionally misbehave should be identified, written out clearly, and taught to ALL school personnel and ALL students. Everyone should know what the consequences will be, and those consequences must be consistently applied. This applies to the consequences for both positive and negative behaviors.

Classroom Rules and Routines

Consequences and rules go hand in hand because it is difficult, if not impossible, to have one without the other. We looked at consequences first, because in many instances paraprofessionals go into a classroom where the rules are already set. Although you are not ultimately in charge of the classroom, there will be times when you must establish rules for behavior. It may be when you are supervising in the schoolyard or the hallways, or when you are working with a small group.

Experts recommend:

- That we have only four or five rules—any more than that and the students won't remember them.
- That they be expressed in positive terms rather than as a series of *Don'ts*.
- That whenever possible they should be discussed/decided with the students, because being part of the decision making is more likely to promote ownership and willingness to adhere to the rules.
- That rules should be posted somewhere prominent and reviewed on a regular basis.

Rules: Experts recommend that they should be:
- Kept to a maximum of four or five.
- Expressed in positive terms.
- Discussed with students.
- Placed on view for the whole classroom.

 Consider the Following

What rules do you have in your classroom or your own work setting? Take a minute to note them here:

Do the rules meet the recommendations listed above?

For those that don't, try rewriting them here:

The American educator Harry Wong discusses the need for clear rules and routines in classrooms. In fact, he is so convinced that rules and routines need to be thoroughly understood that he has recommended that teachers spend the first weeks of the semester teaching those rules—teaching them, modeling them, having the students discuss and role-play them, playing the *What if . . . ?* Game (see the nearby box). For the first two to three weeks of the semester, teaching the rules and nothing else! He justifies this advice by reminding us that children who thoroughly understand the rules are usually willing to follow them, removing the distraction of students misbehaving due to a lack of understanding of how they're supposed to behave or what a rule really means. After those initial weeks teaching only rules and routines, Harry Wong says teachers can get on with the job they're paid to do—teaching the curriculum—and they can get on with it with little or no disruption.

 The *What if . . . ?* Game

This game allows for exploration—in this case, exploration of how the rules apply in different situations.

Let's take for example a rule such as, *We use quiet voices in this classroom.* The teacher may start a discussion by asking, *What if . . . you've raised your hand for help with your work, and no one has come to help you? Do you still have to use a quiet voice? Or is it okay to shout out to get the teacher's attention?* Students can then discuss what they think, and—in a situation such as this where shouting out would not be acceptable and the *quiet voices* rule would still apply—they could be encouraged to suggest alternative ways of getting the teacher's assistance. Then the students should be encouraged to think of other *What if . . . ?* situations for further discussion of this rule until all possible exceptions have been explored.

Although this is a game, it explores many possibilities, so be sure to resolve each *What if . . . ?* as it is discussed. Don't leave students in any doubt as to the different situations in which the rule applies versus those in which the rule can be disregarded.

Harry Wong also makes an important distinction about routines. They begin, he says, as procedures—teachers telling students how they would like things done. They only become routines once students have learned them and incorporated them into their classroom behavior. And this requires rehearsal, as with the rules.

The number one problem in the classroom is not discipline; it is the lack of procedures and routines—a classroom management plan.

—Harry Wong

Take a moment to think of some of the various procedures that have been established by the teacher(s) you work with. List some of them here. We've started the list for you.

Classroom procedures include:

* What to do on entering the classroom.
* How homework is collected/logged.
*
*
*
*

You may also find it useful to consider which of these procedures are problematic for students. Why do you think they may be problematic—is it because they haven't been thoroughly learned/taught and therefore aren't yet routines for the students? What are some ways in which this could be improved?

When Things Go Wrong

Sadly, there are classrooms that go wild. We are referring not to a class where one or two students misbehave, but rather a situation where none of the students really behave properly. In these out-of-control classrooms, the problem, as Harry Wong suggests, is most often because the rules and consequences haven't been set—nor have they been thoroughly taught to the students. Teachers and paraprofessionals may be at odds with each other and nothing seems to be going right. Above all, learning is not taking place—or at least the type of learning parents have in mind when they send their children to school. Where does anyone begin to get things under control?

Heather Rader, a contributor to the online magazine *Choice Literacy*, provides an interesting analogy along with insight into the classroom features that she feels make the greatest contribution to effective classroom management. Take a look at the nearby box and see if you agree with her suggestions.

I overheard my oldest two kids moaning as they surveyed the huge pile of clean laundry. I'd been out of town for several days and everything was a little backed up.

"C'mon," I encouraged. "Just grab the big stuff first." I directed them to grab the tablecloths, sheets and towels, fold them and put them away. Within five minutes, with all the "big stuff" put away they were happily tackling the still sizable but now workable heap.

With any task, knowing the "big stuff" to move first is essential. It's those items that provide momentum for the rest of the work to come.

In a classroom where behavior management is an issue, I look for and ask about evidence of three pieces. Are there written behavioral expectations to refer to? Is there a quiet signal that works? Is there time for children to talk and move? If not, those are the sheets, tablecloths, and towels that we can move first. Although none of those pieces are quick fixes, it is amazing once they are out of the way what emerges as possible work.

—Heather Rader

As we reflect on an out-of-control classroom, there are a few "big things" that need attention. First, **the rules and routines** must be established. Most teachers prefer to involve students in establishing the rules. So an adult may go to the classroom, slow things down, and talk to the students about the cost of chaos on their learning goals. They may discuss which rules and routines will help make the classroom better for student learning, and why. Expert teachers agree that when students help make the rules, they have more ownership in them and are more likely to follow them. These teachers have also learned that the use of a clear set of accompanying consequences will help create a happy, healthy classroom setting. Their students feel more comfortable and safe. Both the teacher and the students experience fewer surprises during the period. There are established routines for nearly every daily task.

Another "big thing" is to be **proactive in instructional planning**. Bad behavior breeds like cockroaches in a classroom where little or no instruction takes place. Effective teachers plan ahead thoroughly for teaching. The great teacher is not racing about the classroom trying to find materials or hurriedly writing instructions on the whiteboard. He or she has already prepared the instructional materials and knows how and when they will be used.

A "big thing" that was discussed in detail in Chapter 1 is **positive recognition and reinforcement**. The great teacher (or paraprofessional) uses positive, specific praise statements frequently. This can include setting the stage by standing at the door of the classroom to welcome students as they arrive. In this way, each student hears her name used as she is welcomed into the classroom. This also clues the teacher in to each student's mood. He knows who seems happy or angry. He has a better idea whether or not the angry student is likely to vent that anger and he begins to build a plan to prevent that "melt-down," if possible, before it happens.

Little Things to Do That Support Positive Behavior

1.	Let the student know that he is important by knowing his name and using it to call on him.
2.	Use specific words when you tell the student what he did that was right.
3.	
4.	
5.	
6.	
7.	
8.	
9.	
10.	
11.	
12.	
13.	
14.	

He also knows who is going to need a bit of encouragement and who is going to need extra attention and "Tender Loving Care" (TLC).

Now that we've considered some of the "big things," as Heather Rader calls them in her laundry analogy, identify some of the "little things" that you can do proactively to support positive behavior in the classroom. Some of these may have been mentioned in earlier chapters, too, but it is a good idea to generate a list that you can refer to later when you need additional ideas. A few examples have been entered to help you begin your list. You may wish to post the list somewhere in your work setting as a reminder to use these little things and so that you can add to it as you think of more examples—or see them practiced by fellow educators.

What Constitutes Acceptable/ Unacceptable Behavior

To this point, as part of Plan A we have looked at establishing expectations and rules. But as part of this discussion of setting expectations, rules, and routines, we could pause here to consider what we think constitutes acceptable behavior. This is important because our expectations relate directly to what we think is acceptable versus unacceptable behavior—what we expect students *will* do and what we expect them *not* to do. An action that is appropriate in one setting may be VERY inappropriate in another setting. Likewise, some actions may be "age-appropriate" for a baby but would be considered out of control and inappropriate for a teenager.

An interesting exercise is to watch other people with their children. This may be other family members, people we see at the market or the beach or on the bus, or people at church or other social groups we belong to.

Consider the following Scenarios

The Crying Baby

You're at the public park and sitting not far from you is a young mother whose few-month-old baby is crying. The baby is in a stroller and the mother is sitting on the bench nearby talking to another adult. And she's ignoring the baby's crying. Mom doesn't seem to notice the crying, but it's bothering you. Why might that be true? What it is about a crying baby that people don't like? And the mother is ignoring the baby's cries. Does that seem right to you?

Think and write about what bothers you about this situation and whether you find it acceptable or unacceptable.

The answer to this scenario will vary from one person to another—and that's okay. The important point here is to identify for yourself which behavior you feel is appropriate, and why. The baby may be hungry and crying is an appropriate response for that because at the early stages of life a new baby can't say, "Hey mom, I'm hungry!" However, if the mother ignores the baby for an extended period of time, you may say that her behavior is inappropriate. She should take action to feed the baby rather than allowing the baby's distress to increase.

The Thirsty Adolescent

A student in the classroom often raises his hand and requests to leave his seat to get a drink of water. Class has just begun and you know that he just came in from the hallway where you saw him at the water fountain, and yet he is asking to leave the classroom again. It hasn't bothered the other students yet, but during instruction yesterday you counted his requests. He left four times to get a drink and twice to go to the restroom. What is puzzling is that the work does not appear to be too hard for him and he passes the assessments.

Think and write about what bothers you about this situation and whether you find it acceptable or unacceptable

---

Again, the answer to this scenario will vary from one person to another. The teacher may say it is not acceptable, but you, the paraprofessional, may say this behavior gives a warning of another problem. Is he trying to test the rules? Or is he trying to see if the teacher and paraprofessionals have the same expectations for him? It may be that the student has diabetes, which makes him thirsty. It is a bigger problem if the diabetes is undiagnosed and these signs are merely passed off as bad behavior. The important point here is to identify for yourself if you feel a behavior is inappropriate, and to identify why. Then decide what you will do about it.

In each of the cases, you will note that the behavior is acceptable or unacceptable according to **the reason** for it and **the context**. Usually something else needs to be discovered to give you all the information you need to make a decision about the appropriateness of the behavior. To learn more about the behavior, we usually need to take notes or complete other forms of observational data. We may need to talk to the student. In an earlier chapter you learned to take data. Meeting with the student with data in hand is a great way to remove emotions from the situation—and avoid saying, "You never . . ." or, "You always . . ." Data provides the details, and the more we know, the better decisions we can make. When presented with data, students often make better choices.

In your work setting there will be a whole range of behaviors that vary in the degree to which they are acceptable or unacceptable. Are children allowed to run around and scream in school? Well yes, they are. Providing they are in the schoolyard. It's normal behavior for young children. We encourage the running around (perhaps less of the screaming) because it allows children to get exercise, let off steam, reduce the fidgets they might otherwise have when we need them to sit still, and pay attention to their learning tasks. We might be surprised to see our teenage students running around in the same way that the younger children do, but we probably wouldn't consider that it needed a sanction or to be prohibited.

Help Students Know Behavioral Expectations, Not Just Recite/Memorize Them

As we discuss the circumstances in which behavior is appropriate or inappropriate, we come to realize that rules may be memorized and strictly followed—without students really understanding them. Have you ever encountered a situation in which a student misbehaves, but when you point out that misbehavior and ask about the rule the student can tell you the rule exactly—despite having just broken it? This is a common phenomenon. Many children who misbehave can recite the class rules. Why is this? In some cases they have not generalized the rule to other settings. But in all cases they have not yet internalized the rule or adopted it as part of their own behavior. As you read the following case study, think about the rules and how they are applied in different situations then complete the form on the next page.

Example/Case Study

My little 5-year-old friend is full of jumping beans—he's just a boy through and through. He likes to leap about, pretending to be Spiderman, so he's always jumping and climbing. He just can't walk down the sidewalk—he has to leap from one side to the other. He can't walk down steps—he has to jump down two (or three, or four!) at a time. He also likes to throw things. And he's allowed to throw the cushions in the sitting room. It makes for a good game. It's harmless and the worst that happens is that a book is knocked off the side table. But when we go out, he picks up stones and throws those. This is an intelligent 5-year-old. He knows that stones hurt and can do damage. But his natural instinct is to pick things up and throw them.

His mother brings him to my house to visit. She stops him from jumping and throwing because—although he may be allowed to do them at home—she thinks it's not an appropriate thing for him to do at someone else's house. At the age of five, will this change of expectations confuse him? Is he able to understand when rules apply and when do they not?

Case Study Form

What would you do in this situation? Here are a few questions to stimulate your thinking:

- Is he more likely to learn the rules established at home, or will he think the rules apply only at the houses where he is a visitor?
- Will he decide that the rule he learned while visiting is the absolute rule and then stop jumping at home?
- What are some ways to help him learn that some things that are okay at home are not okay elsewhere?

When all paraprofessionals and teachers (and even principals) agree on the same expectations and consequences of student behavior, the rules have been established and taught, and the students have learned to generalize the rules, then we must focus again on the importance of using effective instructional materials.

The Importance of Using Effective Instructional Methods

In reality, instruction is the foundation of everything that happens in classrooms. We instruct student on appropriate behavior, but our primary purpose is to instruct them on content such as mathematics and language arts and in more general thinking and problem-solving skills. As we mentioned in the Introduction, effective instructional methods are one of the most powerful tools we have for managing behavior. Why is this? Let's think of an example that could apply to you as an adult. As you read this example, see if you can identify the essential characteristics of effective instruction and how these serve as behavior management tools.

Suppose you go to a meeting. You expect it to be interesting and useful. The speaker has been advertised as an expert, and it's a subject you're interested in learning more about. You've also been invited to go by colleagues you respect, and they've recommended the meeting as something that will suit you and help you in your work. You arrive on time, take a seat, and anticipate the meeting with optimism and a sense of expectancy. You're willing to learn and happy to be taught.

Unfortunately the speaker turns out to be dull. The content of the meeting turns out to be quite different from what you'd been led to expect—it really has no relevance for you personally, and you find that you can't really understand much of what the speaker is talking about. You try to pay better attention, to see if you can come to grips with what the speaker is saying, but you give it up after a while and your mind wanders. You don't feel that you can leave, but you're faced with the prospect of sitting for another hour or so, enduring, when the material is irrelevant and uninteresting, not to mention difficult to understand. And you could be doing something else that is more important and more motivating!

So what do you do? You probably find some other way of passing the time. Perhaps you think about what you need to do when the meeting is over and you can finally get away—you've got some errands to run, so you spend some time thinking that through. That reminds you that you need to go to the store, so you try making a mental list of the things you should buy. You wonder if you can get away with writing a list—you've got a notebook in your wallet—so you take it out and start to write. People will just think you're writing notes about the speaker's topic, so that's okay. And then you remember there was someone you should have called before you got into the meeting. You can't do that now, but you could send a quick text. So out comes the cell phone—you've already set it to silent, so no one will hear you. And while you've got the phone in your hand perhaps you can check on the Internet for the price of an item you're thinking of buying. Then you check the store hours to make sure they'll still be open when you finally get away. So in fact the meeting turns out to be a very productive time for you—you've relieved the boredom and done something useful. And you feel a lot less guilty because you haven't been wasting your time.

Source: iStock #24139911

Can you see the parallels with your students? Faced with **dull, irrelevant material** from the speaker/teacher, students will think of something better to do. The same is true if the **material is too difficult** for them to grasp—or if the **material is too simple**. They'll allow their thoughts to wander—perhaps, like you, to think about what they're going to do once they can get away from this dull stuff. So they become distracted and lose track of lesson content. Or perhaps—and this is something you probably wouldn't do as an adult—they entertain themselves by distracting other students. None of that is helpful as far as their learning goes—even if they don't get out a piece of paper and start writing a list, even if they're not allowed to use their cell phone in the classroom. The speaker/teacher has lost their attention and they're no longer engaging with the material being taught. We know from the research that *engagement* (paying attention to instructional material and activities) is an essential ingredient for learning.

> Students will often misbehave when teaching material is:
> - Dull.
> - Irrelevant.
> - Too difficult or too simple.
> - The pace moves too slowly.

Low-Level Disruptions

Your disengaged students are likely to act out and devise activities that they think are more entertaining. But as you see from our adult example, there are various types of behavior that can be considered low-level disruptions. Earlier in the chapter was an example of clean laundry that needed to be put away, but family members were overwhelmed with the huge pile. They focused on the big things, which reduced the pile to something that was small enough to deal with.

In the classroom there are often low-level disruptions that happen over and over and over! These are not significant in themselves, but what makes them the most irritating is the frequency of the action. These low-level disruptions include talking (when students should be listening), disturbing fellow students, making silly noises, and so on.

> Low-level disruptions may be more annoying than the major incidents—if they are not addressed.

Tracey Lawrence, an elementary school teacher in the United Kingdom with a focus on behavior and attendance, in a blog published through http://theguardian. com, notes that it's low-level disruptions that can have a higher impact on the learning atmosphere of a classroom than more extreme behavior. She offers teachers 10 ways to deal with such low-level disruption. We've modified these ideas slightly to assure that they include paraprofessionals. You'll find her suggestions in the nearby box.

1. Adjust the Volume

With loud classes, avoid raising your voice. It only increases the noise. Lowering your voice can be much more effective. If the volume of your voice is always high, it loses its effect. Note that if you are loud with small groups, you'll disturb other groups.

2. Move Around

Your presence is extremely powerful. Don't stay stagnant in one place or at the front of the class. Move around. Stand or sit beside students to help them avoid becoming distracted. Talk to them about their task. Give them deadlines. For example say: "I'd love to see two more ideas by the time I come back, as your ideas are really interesting." Then walk and visit another student/pair but make sure you come back.

3. Shut out Negativity

Don't allow negativity to enter the classroom. If a student isn't ready to come in, stop them and provide a brief distraction. Allow the student to calm down so that they can enter in a calmer frame of mind.

4. Be Prepared

Prepare your resources before you begin. It allows you to challenge the student's energy as much as you can. Rustling papers and setting out resources while students wait only encourages low-level disruption.

5. Manage the Space

Along with the teacher you are the decisive element in the classroom to control the space. Stand at the door as they enter. Talk. Work to change moods. Say "hello" regardless of whether you have their eye contact or not. Always say goodbye at the end of class or the end of the school day.

6. Keep Calm

Have a calm outlook. If you can't leave the room but are getting annoyed, flick through your [teaching notes or papers] or walk away from the situation to calm yourself down before returning.

7. Don't Deviate from the Work at Hand

There is no need for an excessive response to low-level disruption. Don't interrupt teaching to deal with it.

8. Be Positive

Deal with low-level disruptions by using positive language. "We sit in our chairs so that our handwriting is beautiful." It doesn't give the student the opportunity to opt out and also sets the expectation.

9. Share Your Expectations

Don't assume students understand what your version of acceptable is. Tapping, shouting, and throwing could be acceptable at home. You've identified expectations in the text above, but you need to make it clear that they're not acceptable in class.

10. Have a Routine

Students can be uneasy when they do not know what is going to happen in the day. They like to know what is coming up in their day so if things are going to change give them warning . . . and explain what to expect.

Tracey Lawrence points out that these ideas are not guaranteed to always work, but they have been tried and tested in classrooms.

So let's sum this up in a positive light and state clearly what's needed. In order to be an effective behavior management tool, instruction must:

- Be presented in an engaging manner.
- Include content that has relevance for the student.
- Be pitched at a level that the student can understand.
- Be delivered at a pace that meets the student's needs.
- Be reinforced through activities.

We're not saying that it's easy to accomplish this for all students, and indeed your presence in the classroom is a witness to this. Most paraprofessionals are employed to support students who struggle to access the curriculum. Many students have behavior issues as a result of that struggle.

Teaching Social Skills and Collaborative Behavior

Although the United States Constitution does not mention education, it does delegate associated responsibilities to the states, and therefore, each state's constitution has a provision for the education of our children. When states first declared school and school attendance, the compulsory education systems were obviously quite different from the present. The classroom was a place where children sat at desks, in rows, and only moved from their seats for very specific reasons—when given permission to go to the bathroom, to run an errand for the teacher, to go outside for recess or sports lessons, or at the end of the school day. This was true even for the youngest students, and content was taught largely through lecture methods, with one adult standing at the front of the classroom delivering the curriculum and students doing a great deal of copying from the chalkboard, working in silence and alone. Social interaction was confined to recess, lunch breaks, and movement around the school and was not considered to be part of instruction.

Compare that with the modern classroom—particularly in elementary schools, where students now often work collaboratively, consulting with each other and seeking help from peers on their work. They move around the classroom between different activities, and groups of students may be working on half a dozen different types of activities within the same room, under the supervision of more than one adult. The amount of social interaction—even during instructional sessions—is significantly greater in modern classrooms than it was even 30 years ago.

The Purpose of Public Education

Being a good citizen, a good employee, or a great student requires social skills such as the ability to get along with others. The purpose of public education has been affected by major changes in American society. Over time, the following have all been goals of public education:

- To prepare children for citizenship.
- To cultivate a skilled workforce.
- To teach cultural literacy.
- To prepare students for college.
- To help students become critical thinkers.
- To help students compete in a global marketplace.

"School: The Story of American Public School," PBS, accessed at www.pbs.org/kcet/publicschool/get_involved/guide_p2.html.

Today, along with the learning interactions and exploration, there are field trips and a variety of other hands-on activities that take place away from the classroom. In addition to the basic social skills involved in interacting with others (such as learning manners with please, thank you, etc.), there are other social skills that students need. Skills such as:

- Listening to and accepting another person's ideas.
- How to take criticism of work or behavior.
- How to approach another person to initiate an interaction.
- Avoiding or deflecting conflict.
- Expressing an opposing idea without being argumentative.

You may say that these are difficult even for adults, but students who lack social skills will probably not know how to:

- Take or give a complement.
- Take and follow an instruction.
- Respond appropriately to a social interaction initiated by another student or an adult (review *bids for attention* in Chapter 2).
- Seek help when they need it.
- Work collaboratively with peers.
- Make joint decisions.

These are behaviors that can—and must—be taught, because without them it is very difficult for a student to operate well in the modern school setting. But they are also important because the student who lacks them is likely to behave inappropriately.

Fintan O'Regan, who works as a behavior and learning consultant in the United Kingdom, offers a formula for effective whole-school approaches to behavior: SF3R, which he describes as the "pillars of good teaching and parenting."

SF3R

S   Structure—which includes clearly defining the ethos of the school—the principles that determine the rules and expectations.

F   Flexibility—not just having Plan A and Plan B but a whole host of other options for dealing with the diversity of students and situations that make up the typical school setting.

R   Rapport—the trust and respect that develop between adults and children when there is a determined effort to be positive and actively acknowledge children's views and needs.

R   Relationships that connect all of those involved in the instructional setting—positive and productive partnerships that facilitate learning.

R   Role models who provide direction and purpose for others.

Plan of Action

As a result of your reading and reflection on the principles discussed in this chapter, it's now time to formulate/add to your plan of action.

Ask yourself:

1. What will I do that I've not done before in relation to building positive student behavior?
2. What are some additional things I can do now that I've studied the chapter?
3. What will I stop doing that I've been doing until now in relation to student behavior?

Summary

It is always productive to take time to evaluate your actions and to identify those things that you will do differently next time. As important as improving may be, it is also important to take time to celebrate those things you do well!

Learning Outcomes

After studying this chapter and reflecting on the contents, you can now demonstrate understanding of the following principles of setting precedents for success, including:

- Explain the importance of using effective instruction and give examples of effective strategies. You can provide a rationale for setting clear expectations.
- Communicate what is acceptable behavior and what is not.
- Identify the importance and use of rules and routines.
- Explain the importance of using effective instruction and give examples of effective strategies.
- Explain the importance of teaching social skills, including the necessity of collaborative behavior.
- State ways to help students know behavioral expectations, not just recite/memorize them.
- List examples of the powerful behavior management strategies that support student learning, many of which may already be in place in your work setting.
- Identify the usefulness of those strategies as you apply your knowledge.

Looking Ahead

Just like the trailer to a good movie, we're looking ahead to the next chapter where we discuss the many ways to reward students! Grab a bowl of popcorn and prepare to learn ways to compliment effective instruction AND appropriate behavior.

Bibliography

Ashbaker, B., & Morgan, J. (2013). *Paraprofessionals in the classroom: A survival guide.* Upper Saddle River, NJ: Allyn & Bacon.

Lawrence, T. (June 3, 2014). Focus on behavior and attendance. *The Guardian.* http://theguardian.com.

Linsin, M. (June 18, 2014). How to build effortless rapport. Smart Classroom Management. www.smartclassroommanagement.com.

Morgan, J. (2007). *The teaching assistant's guide to managing behaviour.* London: Continuum Books.

O'Regan, F. (2013). SF3R 4 Behaviour. *Special, 13*(3), 36–37.

Rader, H. The big stuff. *Choice Literacy.* https://www.choiceliteracy.com/articles-detail-view.php?id=1996.

Rosenthal, R., & Jacobson, L. (1968). *Pygmalion in the classroom.* New York: Holt, Rinehart & Winston.

Rosenthal, R., & Jacobson, L. (1992). *Pygmalion in the classroom.* (Expanded ed.). New York: Irvington.

University of Alabama Parenting Assistance Line (UA-PAL). Discipline & guidance: Consistency. Accessed at www.pal.ua.edu/discipline/consistency.php.

Chapter 4

Rewards

What You Will Learn

Learning Objectives:

In this chapter we will be considering in greater detail the principles of Least Restrictive Behavioral Interventions (LRBI), as outlined in Chapter 1, in relation to the rewards we make available to students.

Although we have already considered Plan A, we will look in greater detail at rewards. You will learn what reinforces different types of behavior, how frequently to praise or reinforce, and how to use rewards for appropriate academic behavior and for social skills.

You will learn the importance of choice in relation to student behavior, the choices that students and educators can make, and the importance of discussing this with the students so that they clearly understand their options.

Lastly, we also look at helping students to make choices as steps to help them learn self-determination.

Today the typical duties of paraprofessionals are much more sophisticated than in the past. Duties, which include instructional and noninstructional activities, may cover areas such as:

- carrying out part of a teacher-directed behavior management program,
- data collection,
- providing one-to-one tutoring (behavior and social skills, along with academics),
- organizing instructional and other materials,
- assisting with assessments,
- conducting parental involvement activities,
- documenting student progress,
- assisting with the organization of the classroom environment,
- acting as a translator,
- personal caregiving,
- monitoring playgrounds,

- monitoring bus duty,
- library duty,
- assisting access to building/facility, and
- support and enhancement of professional programs.

Paraprofessionals have even served as members of a crisis team for students with emotional disabilities. As you review this list, can you identify any of the activities that do not require positive praise and rewards and effective instruction in behavioral skills? Student accomplishments and behavior should have positive behavior supports whatever your area of responsibility.

Little Things Grow

In the USA students spend approximately 1,400 hours at school during a school year. That's a considerable portion of their lives, so the learning environment that is created is of the utmost importance to students. Sadly, some schools have serious incidents such as shootings, gang activities, and drug-related violence. This underscores the need for the development of an effective organizational structure to promote appropriate social behavior in school settings. While the serious behavior problems have caught national attention, it is the less intense behaviors that cause stress to teachers and that are blamed for teacher burnout. Examples of these less intense problems are talking out, defiance, and failure to follow the rules. Teachers and paraprofessionals sometimes become frustrated and resort to negative, punitive methods in dealing with these frequent but minor behavior problems.

Before we discuss some of the ways we can counteract and reduce instances of negative behavior, consider this blog from Montie Koehn, who stresses the underlying need in classrooms for mutual respect.

After nearly a decade as a classroom teacher in Oklahoma City Public Schools, I started feeling what all educators hope to avoid: burnout. It escalated to the point where I told my principal I would rather take a non-professional job at a local fast food restaurant or retail store than continue teaching.

But from that low came an opportunity that would forever change my life on both a personal and professional level.

Understanding my frustration and realizing intervention was required to keep me in the profession I had once enjoyed so deeply, the principal at my school directed me to complete a summer professional training program designed to reignite educators' passion for teaching. During that summer institute, I learned the power mutual respect has in transforming school culture.

A pivotal aspect of fostering mutual respect among teachers, students and staff is adhering to the following eight expectations, which I've witnessed fundamentally change the way schools function:

1. **We will value one another as unique and special individuals**.
   We're all unique, and our differences should be celebrated and embraced.

This is an especially important idea to instill in young students, as their self-esteem and self-perception are in formative stages.

2. **We will not laugh at or make fun of a person's mistakes nor use sarcasm or putdowns.** In addition to feeling physically safe at school, students have a right to share their ideas and opinions without fear of negativity. Emotional security is important to personal growth.

3. **We will use good manners, saying "please," "thank you," and "excuse me," and we will allow others to go first.** This might seem like an insignificant emphasis on politeness, but good manners are foundational to selflessness and empathy. Leading by example with polite behavior and respect for others will help instill those qualities among students.

4. **We will cheer each other to success.** This emphasis on community and an "all boats shall rise" mentality helps students support their peers and acknowledge the accomplishments of others. We all do better when we all do better.

5. **We will help one another whenever possible.** Encouraging students to look out for their peers fills communities with conscientious, helpful and generous citizens. Teamwork is a life skill that serves students well far beyond the classroom.

6. **We will recognize every effort and applaud it.** Everyone experiences failure—times when our best effort didn't produce the desired outcome. While failure is disappointing, the effort of trying to accomplish the goal is always worth recognizing.

7. **We will encourage each other to do our best.** To mitigate complacency and create a climate where excellence is rewarded, help students set high standards for themselves and others. Educators can model this behavior by maintaining high personal standards and supporting other teachers in their work.

8. **We will practice virtuous living.** Recognize that how students treat each other as people is foundational to a healthy life at school, at home and in the community. By emphasizing empathy, good character and other important life principles, educators create well-rounded and thoughtful students.

These eight expectations, which I first discovered more than 10 years ago, have provided the cornerstone for instruction throughout my career. I've seen these basic tenets change hearts, instill hope and create learning environments filled with mutual respect.

Not only did she avoid burnout, today Montie Koehn is a principal at Kennedy Elementary School in Norman, Oklahoma. She has been an educator for more than 20 years and was the National Distinguished Principal of the Year (2010–11) and Oklahoma Elementary Principal of the Year (2010–11).

You can find the website for her blog (Voice of the Educator) at the end of the chapter.

Take another look at those eight expectations suggested by Montie Koehn and reflect on each of them in terms of how you may already promote them and what you could do to establish them as part of your students' repertoire.

Montie Koehn's Fostering Mutual Respect: How Well Am I Doing?

1.   **We will value one another as unique and special individuals.**
How do I communicate this expectation to students?

What do I do to show that I value students as unique individuals?

2.   **We will not laugh at or make fun of a person's mistakes.**
How do I communicate this expectation to students?

What do I currently do if students make fun of each other's mistakes?

3.   **We will use good manners.**
How do I communicate this expectation to students?

What do I do when students show good manners? And when they don't?

4.   **We will cheer each other to success.**
How do I communicate this expectation to students?

What do I do to encourage students to encourage each other?

5. **We will help one another whenever possible.**
   How do I communicate this expectation to students?

   What do I do to encourage students to help each other?

6. **We will recognize every effort and applaud it.**
   How do I communicate this expectation to students?

   What opportunities do I offer for recognition and celebration of effort as well as success?

7. **We will encourage each other to do our best.**
   How do I communicate this expectation to students?

   What do I do to reinforce this behavior in students?

8. **We will practice virtuous living.**
   How do I communicate this expectation to students?

   What do I do to help students develop as well-rounded, thoughtful people?

Attend to the Positive

When our primary focus is on negative behavior and rule violations, we are attending to the inappropriate behaviors; this focus detracts from academic instruction time. Likewise, the focus on negative behaviors minimizes opportunities to teach positive, appropriate replacement behavior. Use of punishment and negative or punitive strategies may briefly mitigate behavior problems in the classroom, but these strategies are not a permanent solution.

Teach Behavior

We've emphasized the importance of teaching and learning several times already, so at this point you might ask yourself the question: What is learning? Take a moment to think about how you would define learning.

You may have considered such elements as *Learning is* . . .

- Increased knowledge or understanding.
- New skills.
- Building on previously acquired skills or knowledge.
- Increased confidence.

These (and many others) are all elements of learning. But an important concept that is often overlooked is that learning is also a behavioral issue. Students can *learn* to behavior properly. They can *learn* the class rules and how to comply with them. Thus learning can be defined as a *change in behavior.* Again, this definition can be applied to behavior in all types of settings.

1. Academic. We teach a lesson on using capital letters at the beginning of sentences. For the next piece of writing, if a student uses capital letters in appropriate places, we say he has learned to use capital letters because his writing behavior has changed in this way.
2. Social. As he walks home from school, a student is bullied by older students while taking a shortcut through the park. He soon learns to walk home a different way—along the streets where there are other people and the other students don't dare to bully him. He has changed his behavior by taking the more crowded and longer route home.
3. Emotional. A young child throws a tantrum in order to get what she wants. The parent chooses to give in to the tantrum (for a whole lot of reasons, but let's say they're in the candy aisle at the store where there's plenty to tempt a toddler). The toddler throws a tantrum the next time she and her mother go down the candy aisle at the store. If the mother gives in to the tantrum, the child will have learned a new and useful behavior to get what she wants. This is a negative example, but it serves as a reminder that learning, as behavior change, is not always in a positive direction.

Many of these changes in behavior do not happen instantly—some take many years to occur. Learning naturally takes more time for more complex or difficult skills. The attitude of the learner also affects the rate of learning or behavior change.

So as we consider learning as changed behavior, and the opportunities we have to change students' behavior by teaching them, let's remind ourselves of the characteristics of effective teaching.

- Effective teaching keeps students engaged. When lessons are delivered in new and interesting ways, including a mix of presentations, experiments, discussions, and other approaches for variety, students will have the best chance for behavior and learning success.
- Lessons must be presented on an appropriate level for students' learning—neither too difficult, nor too easy.
- Consider the physical seating arrangements and their effect on learning: the grouping of students for instructional activities, and the creative use of space to support group activities as well as quiet study. Physical arrangements must take into account the need to separate students who are easily distracted.

Lessons that truly engage students reduce misbehavior without the need for any other techniques. But the same principles apply when you are deliberately teaching behavior techniques as if you were teaching academic content and skills. Obviously, teachers have the main responsibility to plan lessons and keep them interesting, but as a paraprofessional, you should always monitor the types of support you use and note whether or not they keep students engaged in the content and positively motivated.

Let's look now at the disruptions that can occur and how to support positive interventions. We begin by looking at using only the least restrictive when dealing with problem behavior. In Chapter 1 we made brief reference to the concept of Least Restrictive Behavioral Interventions (LRBI), and we discuss it in more depth and breadth here.

Least Restrictive Behavioral Interventions (LRBI)

The LRBI approach originated as a plan developed by the Utah State Office of Education to assure that students with disabilities receive an appropriate education. The plan gives best practice suggestions for the protection of student rights to teachers, school personnel, Local Education Authorities (LEAs), and the state; encourages parents to be involved in the selection of behavior interventions; and incorporates a model of Positive Behavioral Interventions and Supports (PBIS) and Response to Intervention (RtI). Implicit in the LRBI is to give best practice suggestions to ensure that effective educational practices are in place throughout educational programming, even when more intensive intervention procedures are selected.

We have proposed its use in relation to positive or appropriate behavior for two reasons: First, because we feel that it has much **wider application** than special education settings. And second, because how we deal with appropriate behaviors should closely **parallel how we deal with negative behaviors**.

The Wider Application

Although developed in Utah for special education students, the basic principles of LRBI relate to all classrooms. You will find an overview of the three levels of intervention recommended for LRBI in the box on page 95, and we recommend that you familiarize yourself with the principles. But let's look at the wider context of the classroom. The primary function of classrooms and other education settings is learning, which assumes that teaching is taking place.

The purpose of a history lesson, for example, is to advance students' understanding of historical events that have shaped our world, as well as the underlying causes of those events and their consequences. Do you remember the saying: "History repeats itself"? That serves as a good reason to study it. We also want our students to learn to think like a historian—to question and explore, to learn to document and record, to interpret and apply. These are the types of knowledge and skills we might associate with a history lesson.

Missing from this list entirely is any reference to behavior. And we know that behavior and learning are inextricably linked. When inappropriate behavior enters the picture, the extent to which students learn and develop the relevant skills will be lessened. On one level, this is simply a question of the student having disengaged from the lesson material to engage in inappropriate behavior and the teacher being obliged to stop teaching in order to deal with the inappropriate behavior. They are both "off the job." And that is sometimes literally the case. Teaching stops for perhaps a minute, perhaps 10 minutes, while the teacher addresses the behavioral issue. So a one-hour history lesson potentially becomes a 50-minute history lesson. Multiply that by all the lessons a student attends during a school year, and whole days can be lost from teaching and learning because teachers have to take time to deal with behavioral issues. However, it's not only the disrupter who learns less, it's also the disrupted—and that includes not only the teacher, but also all the other students in the class who've stopped learning because the teacher has had to stop teaching in order to deal with the behavior.

× # =
You Do the Math!

If only 5 minutes are lost (because the teacher has to deal with a behavioral issues) from each lesson each day of school, that's:

    5 minutes × 180 days of school × 5 class periods = 4500 minutes, or 76 hours, or almost 13 days of school per year!

    Imagine how many hours and days are lost when more than this amount of time is stolen from each day.

What is also lost when the lesson is interrupted is momentum. Having dealt with the inappropriate behavior, the teacher has to pick up the threads of the discussion or presentation, recapture the attention of her students, refocus or remind them of what was discussed before the interruption, and then carry on.

There is also every possibility that while the teacher is dealing with one instance of inappropriate behavior, others may occur. Students whose studies are interrupted become more likely to find their own entertainment, which may take the form of inappropriate behavior. There is also a potential increase of inappropriate behavior or an escalation when other students join in.

The more quickly the inappropriate behavior can be dealt with, the better. Hence the notion of *least restrictive response*—a response that imposes the fewest possible restrictions on the student that his/her behavior warrants, but also the fewest restrictions on the teacher and teaching. Get on with the real purpose of the classroom by dealing very quickly and simply with the behavior and moving on or returning to the lesson agenda. Let's not waste more time with unnecessarily lengthy (and severe) behavioral interventions.

Three Levels of LRBI

The LRBI plan consists of three levels:

Level One

Low-level interventions should be in place in all classrooms. These serve to prevent problems and include such things as:
- Appropriate, motivating curriculum.
- Rules/Expectations.
- Group reinforcement.
- Behavior momentum.
- Redirection.
- Parent conferences.

Level Two

A higher level of intervention calls for the involvement of teaching staff and parents. It may include such interventions as:
- Behavior Contracting (writing a contract with a student and all parties sign it).
- Mentoring (requires parent permission).
- Correction of Behavior Error (minor).
- Exclusionary Time Out (such as missing recess).
- Food Delay (such as late lunch). This requires parent permission.

Level Three

This is a high level of behavior intervention and it requires parental involvement/permission. It is much more intensive and individualized. It is only for the "few" students who have not responded to lower level interventions. All staff are trained to implement these interventions and a behavior interventionist is involved. Schools obtain a signed consent from parents for any of these interventions:
- Forceful Physical Guidance.
- Manual Restraint.
- Seclusion or Time Out.

(Continued)

It is understood that effective educational programming, appropriate classroom management, and other universal proactive supports must be present in every classroom and that at least two interventions are used within each level before moving to the more restrictive interventions. It is also understood and mandated that the individual intensive interventions are monitored for student safety as well as for progress. Higher level interventions are discontinued as soon as progress is made. And as discussed in earlier chapters, high rates of opportunities for success and positive reinforcement should be in place.

Parallels Between Negative and Positive Behaviors

We often discuss inappropriate behavior—and often that's the first sort of behavior that comes to mind when we talk of behavioral interventions. But when our primary focus is on negative behavior and rule violations, and we are attending primarily to the inappropriate behaviors, this focus detracts from academic instruction time. Likewise, the focus on negative behaviors minimizes opportunities to teach positive, appropriate replacement behavior. Use of punishment and negative or punitive strategies may briefly mitigate behavior problems in the classroom, but these strategies are not a permanent solution. We need positive interventions focusing on positive behavior.

An intervention is any sort of response. To intervene is to get involved in some way, to interrupt what's going on, or to try to make a difference. This can relate to both inappropriate and appropriate behavior. Here we want to look at least restrictive intervention in relation to positive behavior. We're really looking at the interventions we otherwise might call rewards or reinforcement. We will consider interventions for negative behaviors in Chapter 5 when we discuss sanctions.

Definition of Intervention/Intervene

a.   To involve oneself in a situation so as to alter or hinder an action or development.

b.   To interfere, usually through force or threat of force, in the affairs of another.

c.   Treatment, attention, care provided to improve a situation.

Examples of Interventions from Other Professions

In medicine or the medical care area, the intervention for an illness or injury may be a splint, medicine, or medical attention to a wound. Here are a few others:

*   Sore muscles may require a massage—kneading and rubbing parts of the body to increase circulation and promote relaxation.

- Addictive substance abuse may need detoxification—a treatment for addiction to drugs or alcohol intended to remove physiological effects of the addictive substances.
- An individual who is deafblind is one who has a combined loss of vision and hearing where neither the person's vision nor hearing can be used as a primary source of accessing information. An Intervener is a trained individual who provides mediation or intervention between the person who is deafblind and his or her environment, enabling him or her to communicate effectively with and receive nondistorted information from the surrounding world. An Intervener acts as the eyes and ears of the person with deafblindness.
- And, of course, sometimes the best "intervention" is no intervention—to let things take their natural course.

The intervention is selected by the medical professional in charge of the patient on the basis of the patient's individual needs.

Example of Interventions in Classroom Behavior

Like the medical doctor, the educator has a range of options for intervening with student behavior:

- Sometimes it is best to deliberately **ignore the behavior**—unless it is dangerous.
- Inappropriate behavior can often be dealt with effectively and efficiently through the use of **nonverbal interventions**:
  - Without saying anything, try using eye contact, pointing, gestures.
  - Move into close proximity to the offending student.
  - Gently touch the student on the arm or shoulder and point to the book or other work.
- Direct your corrective comments to **the behavior** rather than the student. The student is responsible for the behavior, but it is much more helpful to show the student that it is the behavior that needs changing.
- Never react with anger, even when dealing with larger rule or behavior infractions—display the **tolerance and patience** that you would have your students show to each other.
- **Help students develop skills to de-escalate their anger or other emotional outbursts.** Students can be taught to control their anger. But it is not something that they automatically learn on their own. Give them ideas of what they can do:
  - Count to 10 before saying/doing anything (an old-fashioned remedy but still good).
  - Go to an empty classroom until calm.
  - Put your hands in your pockets (or lap) instead of swinging or slugging.
  - Some people like to "talk it out" while others need quiet time alone or they find it helpful to write.
  - Help the student to understand her needs and to use that as a behavior solution.

- Express **confidence** that the student can change and learn good, positive behavior.
- Use other students to **model correct behavior**. This does not have to be staged—if you watch for appropriate behavior occurring near the misbehaving student, praise or reward it in some way and the misbehaving student may take the subtle hint.
- As soon as the offending student changes his or her behavior, give the **same praise or reward** that was previously given to the other student who was modeling appropriate behavior.
- Use **bibliotherapy**. Tell stories and read books or poems about students who were in situations similar to the student's life/disability/behavior. This can be a useful and nonthreatening way to teach a behavior concept.
- **Choices** play an important role in all of our lives. Help students to understand that they are free to make choices, but some choices may lead them on a pathway that is away from their goals.
- **Celebrate**. Paraprofessionals are well situated to help students see their improvements. Identify ways to celebrate those improvements. Behavioral improvements are as important to celebrate as reaching academic goals.
- **Identify places in the classroom or school where students can go to calm down**. *One of the authors taught a group of emotionally disturbed students. The students were assigned to her classroom more than half of the school day (self-contained). Many of the students had serious problems they were dealing with (a boy's father was in prison for murder, another's mother was dying from cancer, a girl's father went to prison for embezzlement) in addition to having difficulties with schoolwork. There were days when a student could not concentrate and just needed time to get his or her emotions under control. The place to calm down in the classroom was a big, sturdy rocking chair. Yes, a rocking chair! These students did not need punishment because they were not ready or able to engage in educational activities. They needed time, patience, and a chance to de-escalate. No one spent more than 20 minutes in the rocking chair—by their own choice—but what a big, positive difference it made in getting them ready to work.*
- **Don't stop providing reinforcement and praise when a student seems to reject you**. Sometimes it is a trust issue, and the student isn't quite sure if he can trust you yet. He may intentionally break a rule to see what you will do and to learn whether or not you will be consistent in following the rules and providing the prescribed consequences. But this doesn't stop you from finding other reasons to praise the student. A trap that many teachers fall into is that they stop praising and rewarding a student who has misbehavior. This is a slippery slope because once you begin to focus on misbehavior—then that is often all you notice.
- **Reward students for showing responsibility**. Shift the emphasis of the classroom management system from the teacher to the students.

Whatever the situation, educators should try to not overreact to misbehavior and should use the least restrictive intervention necessary for effect management of that behavior.

There are many low-intensity interventions you can use to curb inappropriate behaviors:

- Planned ignoring—giving no attention to the student who is misbehaving.
- Signal interference—eye contact, pointing, or other discreet gestures to show that you noticed the inappropriate behavior.
- Proximity control—moving closer to the student.
- Praising the appropriate behavior of other students—this is usually effective if the other students are seated nearby.

Another Example of LRBI

Here's a fine example of a least restrictive intervention from a setting outside the classroom, but it nicely illustrates quite how simple interventions can be.

George is three years old and he's a handful. He's probably on the Autistic Spectrum but that hasn't been properly assessed yet. So some of the subtleties of social interaction don't quite work with George. Call his name and he may not respond, so you can't distract him from inappropriate behavior in that way. But he does manage some interactions. One of the things he's really good at is roaring like a lion.

Credit: Christopher Wells Barlow

And we've all done it, haven't we? We teach young children to make the sounds of different animals and reward them for it by laughing, applauding, or otherwise giving them attention—even having them perform for grandma or other visitors. But if you ask George to roar like a lion, that's what he does—over and over and over again. You can get very tired of having a young lion roaring in your face—and George takes his role-play very seriously.

But one day I noticed—when George's mother and dad had had enough of the roaring and had asked him to stop, without success—a very clever ruse. Dad simply asked George: What sound does a mouse make, George? And—like magic—the roar of the lion became the squeak of a mouse. No dramatics. No bribery. No big deal. And no negative effects. Suddenly George was the quietest and meekest boy imaginable as he imitated a mouse.

Credit: Christopher Wells Barlow

Now how's that for a fine example of the least restrictive intervention? And why is that such a very clever intervention? For two reasons:

1. There were no histrionics, no yelling, and no threats. Dad just spoke to George in a calm voice. So we can interpret *least restrictive* as partly meaning that our response or intervention doesn't actually add to the disruption that the inappropriate behavior has caused.
2. When Dad's request that George *stop* roaring didn't have any effect, he changed his request: he asked George to *do* something that prevented the roaring. You can't squeak like a mouse and roar like a lion at the same time. They are **mutually exclusive**.

This second point is a very useful one in relation to modifying student behavior. When we ask a student to stop doing something or use the word "Don't," it introduces a negative aspect into the situation. But if we ask them to do something that excludes the behavior we want to stop, then we're asking them to **DO something rather than STOP doing** something.

This is particularly useful with young children—we distract babies when they're banging a toy against the floor or table, for example, by offering them something else (usually something softer or less noisy if they continue to bang it against the floor).

But it can work just as well with older students. And we can get so we do it automatically. Our students are hanging around talking at the beginning of a lesson, so we ask them to take their seats and open their books. That interrupts the hanging around, which helps to reduce the talking and gives them something more purposeful to do. But we don't have to even mention the hanging out or the chatting—or refer to the things that they were not doing in negative terms.

Rewarding Both Academic and Social Behavior

We must consider the fact that rewards can come from sources other than our own input. Students give each other reinforcement or sanctions. So consider the case of showing public approval of a student's appropriate behavior. Although your approval would normally be reinforcing, the student might get a negative reaction from peers (called teacher's pet, or ridiculed). The peer feedback or reaction is likely to be more powerful—especially among teens—and can cancel out the positive effect of the approval you offered. It just might not be considered "cool" to be approved of by an adult—especially for teenagers, who generally don't like to stand out from the crowd.

A study conducted in Australia with about 750 elementary students found that nearly all the students said they wanted to be praised equally for academic achievement and good behavior. However, most said they wanted to be praised on an individual basis for the *effort* they put into their work rather than their ability. Telling a student he is smart, clever, or good was not preferred. They preferred recognition for effort, achievement, and good behavior.

This is a good reminder that:

1. We need to consider the social context when we intend to reward students.
2. We need to praise both product and process (results and effort).

Here's what some teachers and paraprofessionals said their students find rewarding:

"We have had students with severe behavior problems at our school, kids who simply act out because they are so mad at the world. By offering rewards, we are trying to show them that by attending school and getting an education, they get something out of being in school. There are the immediate rewards, such as prizes and treats, and we're hoping to get them to the long-term rewards, such as a job, college, and a future."

"My school uses rewards to help students put aside their worry about home problems. We want them to find a reason to be at school. We want them to find reasons to apply themselves."

"As we progress through the year, my teacher and I gradually increase the amount of work needed to earn the external rewards. We gradually phase them out altogether as the students begin to show responsibility for their own behavior and work ethic. This also helps them to see the association between completing work, behaving, and getting good grades."

"I work with students who are identified as emotionally handicapped under IDEA. Our students earn points for meeting their individual behavior goals. Then, with their points they can trade them in for computer time or other free time, soft drinks, candy, chips, pencils, etc. This also helps them learn math as they figure how many points they've earned (plus) and how many more they will need (minus) to purchase the desired item."

External/Internal Rewards and Extrinsic/Intrinsic Motivation

The ultimate aim of providing a system of tangible rewards for students is to move them on to feeling rewarded by intangibles. The internal rewards are what adults respond to—along with the ability to delay that gratification for longer periods of time. These are important because of the realities of life—when your students are in their forties and employed, no one is going to try to get them to do their work promptly or behave ethically in their profession by promising them extra recess.

Tangible External Rewards

Points	Stickers	Choice	Free Time
Extra Recess	Pizza Party	Field Trip	Notes

Intangible Rewards

Approval	Satisfaction	Sense of Achievement

The knowledge that you have tried hard and met a challenge

Studies have found that when students believe the main focus of learning is to obtain external rewards (pass an exam, get good grades), they often perform worse, may think of themselves as less competent, and report greater anxiety. Some studies have found that the use of external rewards actually decreases motivation for a task for which the student initially was motivated. However, when they believe that exams are simply a way for them to monitor their own learning, students do much better. Students seem to enjoy taking responsibility for themselves—they find it motivating.

Credit: Christopher Wells Barlow

Researchers at Brigham Young University have found that one of the most powerful tangible reward systems uses notes to the students. Paul Caldarella found that writing thank-you notes can teach students behavioral skills and improve relationships. He found that instituting praise notes—or written compliments—in the classroom, at recess, or in the teacher's lounge reduces behavioral problems. He even found that tardiness decreased. And on the adult level, coworkers found their relationships improved. While praising someone verbally is great in the moment, it might be forgotten over time. The advantage of written notes is that they can be specific, timely, and can be read over and over again by the student.

> The ultimate aim of tangible rewards is to help students develop appreciation for and be motivated by/experience the feelings of satisfaction that come from doing well and controlling one's own behavior and reactions.

What Constitutes a Reward?

How are you doing with rewards? What do your students think? Take half a day and monitor the rewards that you give out. Make sure you use a simple system for recording as you monitor so that it doesn't interfere with your work. Then take some time—perhaps another day—to quickly survey the students about what they consider to be rewards—with the permission of your supervising teacher, of course. Do it only as an informal chat so it doesn't get too detailed and formal. You might just have them complete this sentence, "a reward for me is. . . ." When you have both pieces of information—your own monitoring data and your students' opinions—take stock of whether what you're typically offering matches what your students actually say they find rewarding.

> A reward is designed to increase the likelihood of a behavior happening again/more often.

Some Rewards May Be More Like Punishment

When is a reward not a reward? Let's go back to the definition of a reward as something that a person finds motivating and satisfying. Remember that we are using positive behavioral supports and the Least Restrictive Behavioral Interventions, so if you were to list the rewards you offer and order them from least intense and least time-consuming to most intense and most time-consuming, the ones you should be using most often as part of your daily routine and repertoire would be those at the top of the list. Those at the bottom would be used very infrequently and reserved for serious behavioral incidents (and probably only in consultation with a teacher).

We can examine some of the common consequences meted out in classrooms and consider whether they constitute punishment or reward. The exercise in the box below will help you to do this.

 Reward or Punishment?

Examine some of the common consequences meted out in classrooms and consider whether they constitute punishment or reward.

Consider . . . The student who is attention seeking.

A student who is attention seeking wants what? Well attention, of course. And whose attention does the student generally want? That of an adult rather than another student. We can give that student as much attention as he or she wants, but we must be sure to give it as a reward for appropriate behavior rather than as the reward for inappropriate behavior. Otherwise, we will be rewarding or reinforcing inappropriate behavior, especially if the student can get more of our attention that way. We must reverse the trend and give more attention for positive behavior.

Consider . . . Social activities and games.

An example that applies to adults came to our attention recently. A group of mature adults had gathered together socially, and one of the group suggested they all play charades. There were some groans from those who didn't like playing games, but the person who'd suggested it was one of those people who seem undaunted and determinedly cheerful, so the game went ahead. A volunteer was found to start the game, and there were a good number of suggestions for the charade until . . . suddenly the person who'd organized the game declared that whoever guessed correctly would have a turn at presenting the next charade. This resulted in a noticeable change in behavior, particularly the volume of conversation. Suddenly people were whispering answers to each other and very few were willing to actually call out suggestions. What had happened here? Why the change?

When participation in the game was a choice, almost everyone in the group was willing to participate. However, once there was the declaration that the person with the "correct" guess (the winner) became the next presenter, the whispering and the reduced conversation suggests that instead of that being perceived as a reward, it really constituted a threat. Not physical, of course, but just the possibility of an unwanted consequence—having to present a charade—as a consequence of giving a correct interpretation was enough to deter people from participating fully in the game.

Think of how this may apply to some of the activities you may ask your students to participate in and whether some of the intended rewards actually de-motivate students.

Frequency of Praise/Rewards

A welcoming smile each day may be enough for some students. But, with the many pressures of grades, peer acceptance, and other day-to-day challenges, most students will need and want more. In an important study on teacher praise, James Brophy found that only 6% of interactions in the classroom involved praise. He noted that even in classrooms where teachers used praise once every five minutes, the average student would only be praised once every two hours—that's only three times a day or 15 times a week. Ask yourself whether that is enough to keep students motivated.

We must also balance praise or rewards with correction or criticism. Balancing the positive with correction procedures, Caldarella recommends four praise statements for every one correction.

Intermittent/Unpredictable Frequency

Paraprofessionals and the teacher may have determined a specific behavior to reward, such as a quiet and quick transition from math to literacy groups. Now you can "catch" the students being good. But the research suggests you will want to vary the timing of this or other rewards hourly and daily, but not at the same time each day. If the praise is completely predictable (and that includes the same phrases every time) it becomes too rote and routine to be effective. Be assured that students will continue to respond positively to praise even if it is not provided *every time* they engage in the requested behavior. So although frequent praise is most desirable, constant and unvarying praise for the same behavior is not desirable or necessary.

Professors at Vanderbilt University recommend using about six praise statements every 15 minutes to ensure that more students receive more praise.

In the box below, you will find some reminders of how we can help students develop their social skills so that they can add those to their repertoire of behaviors we can reinforce by offering rewards and praise.

Checklist of Teaching Tasks to Verify

- Teach the behaviors that will maximize the student's social success and minimize failures.
- Use assignments that will help students use the social skills in "real" life.
- Make sure students have mastered the skills they are to generalize.
- Make training as realistic as possible.
- Enlist the help of peers, parents, and school personnel with prompting and reinforcing the social skills.
- Prompt and reinforce appropriate behavior.

(Continued)

- Teach self-management skills.
- Provide retraining and reminders of social skills.
- Carefully document the effectiveness of training to ensure that social skills instruction is improving social skills.
- Make certain that the target social behavior is specific enough to demonstrate (being a good sport, helping your neighbor).

Importance of Choice

Perhaps one of the most important concepts in relation to student behavior—and one that we feel deserves more attention than it typically gets—is the notion of *choice*. Students who haven't been offered options routinely will often have difficulty with choices. Learning how to manage choices and the consequences that go along with each choice is something that needs to be taught/learned. It is important that teachers and paraprofessionals provide enough guidance for students on how choice operates in the classroom and how students can determine outcomes for themselves.

Making Choices

"He made me do it!" students will often say. Although we acknowledge that students can be coerced into behaving in particular ways—especially when bullying or intimidation are involved—the reality is that students almost always have a choice in the way they behave. This is a revelation for many students, who feel that their negative responses are natural, spontaneous, and "can't be helped." The realization that students can choose for themselves is a real mark of growing understanding and maturity.

Even very young children can be taught this principle. When young preschoolers have done something inappropriate—refusing to share toys, throwing food on the floor, hitting, or kicking—we take them aside and talk them through what they have done and what they could do next time to make the situation better. We essentially have them stop and think about their choices and help them realize that they could have chosen to react differently in that situation. We do this in the hope that the next time they are in the same situation, they will make a better choice. But we must acknowledge that even some of our oldest students may not have grasped and taken on this concept. They may persist in the immature belief that they have no control over what happens. This is a learned behavior, and we can help them to unlearn it. Recognizing one's own autonomy and choosing to use it wisely is a life-skill that we want all of our students to develop.

Choices and Self-Determination

Psychologists Richard Ryan and Edward Deci examined the theory of self-determination as it relates to education settings. The definition of self-determination? A person's ability to control his or her own destiny. And a critical part of the concept of self-determination involves the combination of attitudes and abilities that will lead students to take control by setting goals for themselves and taking the initiative to reach those goals. Basically, it is defining for oneself the direction or path of your choices. Ryan and Deci also found that when students are intrinsically motivated (as we referred to in an earlier section of this chapter), their quality of learning is better. This, of course, does not surprise you. You know that if you get to do something you find interesting or enjoyable, then you are much more engaged in the activity. The same concept applies to students.

The field of special education has embraced the concept of self-determination in recent years. For much too long, decisions were made for people with disabilities with little or no involvement from the individual. The decisions were motivated by good intentions—everyone wanted students with disabilities to do well—but they overlooked the desires and hopes and dreams of the individual with disabilities. As our society has become more sensitive to the needs and rights of those with disabilities, we have moved to the concept of self-determination as a crucial element in the life plan. Success has been shown in three areas relating to self-determination: autonomy, competence, and relatedness.

1. Students have greater **autonomy** when:
   - they feel supported to explore,
   - they can take initiative,
   - they can develop and implement solutions for their problems.
2. Moreover, students experience greater learning **competence** when:
   - they are challenged,
   - they are given proper feedback.
3. Students experience **relatedness** when
   - they perceive others listening and responding to them.

When these three needs are met, students are more likely to be intrinsically motivated and actively engaged in their learning.

However, a continuing challenge in education is the growing requirement for students (and therefore teachers) to meet the demands of the Common Core curriculum. This may limit some of the curriculum choices for all students. But, one of the ways educators engage students in learning is by getting the students more involved in setting their own educational goals—within the context of that curriculum. When this happens—because they have choices—they are more likely to reach those goals. This can have long-term effects beyond the classroom. Researcher Michael Wehmeyer found that students with disabilities who are more self-determined are more likely to gain employment and to live independently in the community after high school than are students who are less self-determined.

Using choices in their lives helps students to identify their own needs and develop strategies to meet those needs. As self-determination is taught, secondary schools are finding it is a better way to motivate students to meet their needs and to become more responsible for their lives. Leaders in the schools are emphasizing the use of self-determination curricula with students with disabilities to meet federal mandates to actively involve students with disabilities in the Individualized Education Planning (IEP) process.

"He made me do it!"

Although we acknowledge that students can be coerced into behaving in particular ways—especially when bullying or intimidation are involved—the reality is that students almost always have a choice in the way they behave.

For many of your students, this may be a very novel concept.

Examples of Teaching Choice

So how do we go about teaching students that they have a choice and that their behavior isn't inevitable and doesn't have to be a reaction to other people? Like any other idea or piece of information that we feel a student needs to explore or acquire, the idea of choice can—and should—be taught systematically. And students need to learn that the choice of a particular behavior naturally leads to a particular consequence—positive or negative.

In Chapter 2 we talked about the ABCs of behavior: Antecedent (before), Behavior, and Consequence (what happens after the behavior). If students are to choose their own behavior, then we can't actually intervene at the level of the behavior. Let's put that another way: we can't change student behavior. Why? Because only students can change their behavior. So what's left to us? We intervene either at the level of the antecedents—the triggers for behavior—or at the level of consequences (positive or negative).

Do not give rewards in response to promises . . . such as, "I will be better in the future." Rewards are for actual improved behavior.

Looking at consequences is often the most useful angle from which to approach the question of why students choose to behave in particular ways. We can engage them in a discussion of the types of consequences they prefer, then talk about how they can go about getting those consequences. Obviously, students cannot choose some consequences. An all-expenses-paid trip to Disneyland or being excused from school for the rest of the day (or the week if they've been very good!) are choices that are not going to be available to your students. And overly generous rewards don't have to be made available to students if they complete their homework or any other ordinary tasks in school. However, from a menu of available consequences, students should have what we might consider a constrained or limited choice of outcomes. And when they make choices, they are bound to choose something that they will enjoy.

We might discuss with students:

- If you had a choice of going out to recess or staying in the classroom to do extra work, which would you choose? Some students would choose to stay in rather than go out to recess, for a whole lot of reasons.
- How they think they go about choosing the preferred thing (by choosing the behavior that will generate the desired consequence).

- If there is a page of mathematics to do, how many of the math problems they're going to tackle before you check if they've got them right. Tell them you're not going to stand over them and watch them work. You're going to circulate and help anyone who needs your help. That offers them a choice and some sense of having control over their own school experience.
- What their preferences might be for possible rewards or positive consequences for appropriate behavior, given a range of possibilities that you identify. Then students can be given a choice of rewards for desirable behavior. For example, they can choose to have time on the computer or time to read (and, of course, a choice of which book).

How Much Choice Do You Have?

This might also be a good point at which to consider how the principle of choice applies to your own behavior as an adult in the classroom. We also can choose consequences or outcomes by being selective about our own behavior and exercising deliberate choice. Once you have decided which consequence you'd really most like, then you have to consider what behavior on your part is most likely to lead to that consequence.

Think for a moment. Do you want:

- Students who like you?
- Students who respect you?
- A friendly relationship with your students?
- To set high standards of behavior and help your students to achieve those standards?

Perhaps the answer to all of these questions is YES! Or perhaps some of these are more important than others. Whatever your answers, decide what the consequences (ABCs) of behavior will be for each of these. There may be more than one consequence for each of these goals.

For Example

The desired consequence: you want students to respect you.

The necessary behavior to obtain that consequence (list things here, such as being fair, showing students respect, being consistent, standing up for them, etc.):

-
-
-

Once you have decided which consequence you'd really most like, consider what behavior on your part is most likely to lead to that consequence. Write those actions here:

Remember that administering consequences should always be coordinated with the teacher. This supports consistency in the classroom and ensures that everyone is thinking along the same lines. And the consequences should never be something to hurt or punish the student. Remember that we want to help students develop their independence through good choices. It is sometimes helpful to take time to privately discuss with the student how a different choice might have turned out better for him. And it is always a good idea to be a role model for your students by making good choices—although you may also find it useful to sometimes discuss with them how difficult it might be for you to make good choices (being patient, consistent, using a least restrictive intervention, etc.) when they are behaving inappropriately.

Summary

In this chapter and the previous one, you've read about motives, positive/negative reinforcement, and least restrictive behavior interventions. But it is the most basic of planning and teaching strategies that make the classroom function.

- Effective instruction that is designed to meet the students' learning needs.
- Teaching appropriate behaviors through a positive approach.
- Clearly defining expectations.
- Rewarding and recognizing students for their appropriate behavior.

Learning Outcomes

Remember that the less intensive behaviors—if not recognized and dealt with—often develop into the most serious behavior problems. After studying this chapter, you should now have mastered the following learning outcomes to enable you to intervene in the most effective way:

- You can use the principles of Least Restrictive Behavioral Interventions (LRBI) in relation to student rewards.
- You can explain the importance of choice in relation to student behavior.
- You can identify and explain the choices that students and educators can make.
- You can discuss the importance of discussing choice with the students so that they clearly understand their options.
- You can list the different types of behavior reinforcers.
- You can identify how frequently to praise or reinforce.
- You can use rewards for appropriate academic and social behavior.
- You can state why it is important to help students make choices.
- You can identify ways in which choice leads to self-determination.

Plan of Action

As a result of your reading and reflection on the principles discussed in this chapter, it's now time to formulate/add to your plan of action.

Ask yourself

1. What will I do that I've not done before in relation to student behavior?
2. What will I stop doing that I've been doing until now in relation to student behavior?

Looking Ahead

In the next chapter, readers are given an opportunity to consider where school failure begins and to track back from exclusions to a point where a more effective path might be taken with difficult students.

Bibliography

Ashbaker, B. Y., & Morgan, J. (2011). *Assisting with early literacy: A manual for paraprofessionals.* Upper Saddle River, NJ: Pearson Education, Inc.

Ashbaker, B. Y., & Morgan, J. (2001). *A teacher's guide to working with paraeducators and other classroom aides.* Alexandria, VA: Association for Supervision and Curriculum Development.

Brophy, J. (1981). Teacher praise: A functional analysis. *Review of Educational Research, 51,* 5–32.

BYU Magazine. (Summer 2014). Noting the praiseworthy: Paul Caldarella. p. 16.

Field, S., & Hoffman, A. (1994). Development of a model for self-determination. *Career Development for Exceptional Individuals, 17*(2), 159–169.

Koegel, L. K., Koegel, R. L., Boettcher, M., & Brookman-Frazee, L. (2005). Extending behavior support in home and community settings. In L. Bambara & L. Kern, *Individualized supports for students with problem behaviors: Designing positive behavior plans* (pp. 350–390). New York: Guilford Press.

Lewis, T. J., Jones, S.E.L., Horner, R. H., & Sugai, G. (2010). School-wide positive behavior support and students with emotional/behavioral disorders: Implications for prevention, identification and intervention. *Exceptionality, 18,* 82–93. doi: 10.1080/0936283 1003673168.

Maggin, D. M., Wehby, J. H., Moore-Partin, T. C., Robertson, R., & Oliver, R. M. (2009). Supervising paraeducators in classrooms for children with emotional and behavioral disorders. *Beyond Behavior, 18*(3), 2–9.

Morgan, J. (2007). *The teaching assistant's guide to managing behaviour.* London, UK: Continuum Books.

National Association of Special Education Teachers. (n.d.). Self-determination. Accessed at www.naset.org.

National Gateway to Self Determination. (October 2012). Research to Practice in Self-Determination Series. The National Training Initiative on Self-Determination and the Association of University Centers on Disabilities. Accessed at www.ngsd.org/.

OSEP Center of Positive Behavioral Interventions and Supports. Available at www.myboe.org/portal/default/Group/Viewer/GroupView?action=2&gid=928.

Pickett, A. L., Likins, M., & Wallace, T. (2003). *The employment and preparation of paraeducators: The state-of-the-art 2003 (7th).* Retrieved from National Resource Center for Paraprofessionals website: www.nrcpara.org/resources/employment-and-preparation-paraeducators-state-art-2003.

Quinn, M. M., & Mathur, S. R. (Eds.). (2004). *Handbook of research in emotional and behavioral disorders* (pp. 327–351). New York: Guilford Press. Retrieved from https://illiad.lib.byu.edu.

Ryan, R. M., & Deci, E. L. (2000). Self-determination theory and the facilitation of intrinsic motivation, social development, and well-being. *American Psychologist, 55*(1), 68–78.

Sugai, G., & Horner, R. H. (2008). What we know and need to know about preventing problem behavior in schools. *Exceptionality: A Special Education Journal, 16*(2), 67–77. doi: 10.1080/09362830801981138.

Sutherland, K. S., Wehby, J. H., & Copeland, S. R. (2000). Effect of varying rates of behavior-specific praise on the on-task behavior of students with EBD. *Journal of Emotional and Behavioral Disorders, 8*(1), 2–8. doi: 10.1177/106342660000800101.

Voice of the Educator: Koehn, M. (June 16, 2014). Transforming school culture through mutual respect. Accessed at http://smartblogs.com/education/2014/06/16transforming_school_culture_through_mutual_respect/.

Wehmeyer, M. L., & Schwartz, M. (1997). Self-determination and positive adult outcomes: A follow-up study of youth with mental retardation or learning disabilities. *Exceptional Children, 63,* 245–255.

Chapter 5

Plan B

Sanctions

What You Will Learn

Learning Objectives:

In this chapter you will learn about the essential characteristics of sanctions (timely, appropriate in scope and focus, simple, and meaningful to the recipient student). This ties directly to the importance of linking classroom-level sanctions to the wider school context of behavior management. And you will know the concept of student choice—as it relates to inappropriate behaviors and the associated sanctions. Most importantly, you will learn some of the potential negative outcomes of persistent and unresolved inappropriate behavior, including the costs to society at large and the students as individuals.

You will be able to summarize the importance of positive behavior intervention supports to prevent behavior that requires the restrictive sanctions studied in this chapter.

In Chapter 3 we discussed Plan A—what we do to encourage and maintain appropriate behavior in our students. This is the primary purpose of management plans and strategies. They must encourage our students and make it worthwhile for them to behave appropriately; they must provide an environment and the necessary incentives for students to behave in ways that will facilitate learning. That means minimal inappropriate behaviors and the associated disruptions they bring.

> The primary purpose of behavior management plans and strategies is to provide an environment and the necessary incentives for students to behave in ways that facilitate learning.

Now we need to discuss Plan B—the contingency plans for those occasions when students do not respond to Plan A. But first, let's be honest about this—the majority of students in the majority of classrooms in our schools behave appropriately most of the time. And when a few of the students misbehave, most of them are amenable to correction and willing to adjust their behavior in response to minor adjustments we make on a daily basis as this minor misbehavior occurs. Even the best student can occasionally speak out of turn, express reluctance to engage in an assigned task, or act with unkindness toward a peer. This is human nature—as adults, we even do it ourselves.

The 1989 Elton Report in the United Kingdom stated:

> A sample of just over 250 secondary [school] teachers in the West Midlands [UK] was asked about the types of misbehavior they found most troublesome in their classrooms. The behavior that was rated most troublesome by a wide margin was 'talking out of turn.' Then came 'hindering other children' and 'calculated idleness.' Physical aggression came last in rank order. The main conclusion drawn by the researchers from their survey was that teachers are, in general, much more concerned about persistent minor misbehavior than the occasional dramatic confrontation.

This is still largely true today. Most teachers will never be threatened with a knife or gun at any time in their careers. But all teachers—and paraprofessionals—will have to deal with students who are disruptive or noncompliant.

Remember that too much emphasis often is placed on compliance rather than genuine communication.

Only about 15% to 25% of students in US schools have some type of identified behavior or learning problems, and of those a much smaller percentage—less than 6%—are considered eligible for special education because of behavior problems. So the majority of our Plan B actions will be of the minor kind, rather than major incidents of severe aggression or noncompliance. Students who display those types of behaviors are also likely to have a behavior plan or behavioral goals on their IEP, so if you work with these students you will need to familiarize yourself with their IEP goals and the behavioral strategies that may be specified.

Much research has been carried out over the years on how we should respond to inappropriate behavior. Ideas have changed significantly since the times of the switch, the cane, and the use of corporal punishment. The vocabulary we use has likewise changed. Where the common terms were *discipline* and *punishment,* we now more commonly talk of *positive behavior supports, interventions,* and *sanctions.* The specific action taken by teachers and paraprofessionals will depend on the severity and frequency of the individual student's action. This should be carefully studied, and paraprofessionals are in a good position to take data on the things they see in relation to behavior. This helps teachers and paraprofessionals collaborate on understanding the frequency with which rules are broken, the severity of the behavior, and the actions that should be taken.

We offer a brief reminder here about identification of target behaviors. In order to be specific and to help all faculty members remain consistent in their conversations about student behavior, it is important to identify the problem behavior but to describe it in neutral terms—avoid words like *always* and *never*, and refer to the problem behavior rather than to a problem student. Explain the behavior and actions taken to correct it, including the results. Try to generate alternative explanations that are positive for the behavior. Act on one or more of the new, positive explanations. When the behavior improves, don't compare it with the old behavior (e.g., "That is a lot better than when you were doing . . .") but focus instead on the newly improved behavior itself.

No matter the level of the behavior you are addressing—from only a minor infraction to a total meltdown—there are some basic principles that apply across the board. And all this with the caveat that the basic principles discussed in earlier chapters of effective evidence-based instruction, reasonable rules, motivation, etc. must all be in place in a positive environment. But let's begin by taking a closer look at sanctions.

What Is a Sanction?

In the same way that a reward is anything that motivates and satisfies a student, a sanction is anything the student finds unsatisfactory—a deterrent or de-motivator that will discourage the student from engaging in or persisting in inappropriate behavior. It is therefore something designed to decrease, discourage, or eliminate a behavior that is deemed inappropriate.

What Is a Sanction?

A sanction is something designed to decrease, discourage, or eliminate a behavior.

Let's think about those. In most work settings there is some system of sanctions for adult employees—the ultimate being dismissal but, before that, even disapproval in different forms. There may be limits placed on your privileges, for example, or you may not be entrusted with certain types of responsibilities or activities. In some work settings, an employee whose behavior is cause for concern may be placed on probation, with careful monitoring of the behavior for a period of time. Reasons may be tardiness, leaving early, inappropriate use of cell phones or work computers, or dishonesty.

Even in a family setting or among friends, there are potential negative consequences and sanctions that people can impose on you as an adult if they disapprove of something you have done (or not done). If you borrow something from your neighbor or a family member and don't return it or return it damaged, you are unlikely to be able to borrow from them again. Your reputation has diminished in some way and trust may have been lost. Use the worksheet on the next page to look more closely at the sanctions that might be present in your life.

Sanctions: Adults Experience Them Too

As an adult, there are sanctions imposed for certain types of inappropriate behavior that you may engage in. What are some of the sanctions imposed on you by someone else? Make some brief notes about the situation and what the sanction will be if you do not comply. We have started the list with paying taxes—a phenomenon we're all familiar with and that carries potential sanctions.

1. What are the sanctions for a failure to pay taxes?

2. What other types of sanctions do you feel control your behavior as an adult?

3. Are there any in your work setting?

4. What about in a family setting or among friends—are there potential sanctions in those settings?

Essential Characteristics of Sanctions

One of the things that the research has taught us is that when we feel that sanctions are appropriate, they should have certain characteristics in order to be effective. They should be timely, appropriate in scope and focus, meaningful to the recipient student, and simple.

In order to be effective, sanctions should be:
    T   **A**   **M**   **S**
    <u>T</u>imely.
          <u>A</u>ppropriate in scope and focus.
               <u>M</u>eaningful to the recipient student.
                  <u>S</u>imple.

Timely

My mother always taught me that if you catch a dog chewing on your shoes, you correct him straight away to let him know he's doing something unacceptable. If you wait and do it later, he won't understand why you're punishing him. The principle holds true for the human young as well. A sanction delivered too long after the inappropriate behavior will not be an effective deterrent. Although it may be understood logically by the student to be the result of inappropriate behavior that occurred earlier in the day, to have maximum effect the behavior and the sanction need to be as close together time-wise as possible. This is particularly true for the youngest students but also applies to older students; too much delay with a sanction weakens its effect.

Appropriate in Scope and Focus

This is simply a question of a minor "offense" deserving only a minor sanction. Overly harsh sanctions make for justifiably resentful students. When a student protests, "But all I did was . . . !" he may well be justified in complaining if the sanction is overly severe. But harsh sanctions also lead us quickly down the path toward school-based sanctions and thence to exclusion—which is a path no one should willingly or lightly contemplate. We have already discussed the concept of Least Restrictive Behavioral Interventions (LRBI) in connection with rewarding appropriate behaviors. This also applies to any sanction—it should be the least restrictive or least severe response to the behavior in question. Sanctions do not actually have to be particularly punitive in order to be effective. As we know, an expression of disappointment from an adult whose opinion matters to the student is often enough to make the student realize she has done wrong, wish she hadn't, and discourage her from repeating the behavior.

When the classroom rule is to raise your hand, the teacher or paraprofessional who wants to stop a student from shouting out answers before he is called on would remind all the students of the rule at the beginning of the activity. Then, when the student forgets and shouts out an answer, she may ignore the student (and the answer) and first call on someone else who is raising a hand, saying, "You are raising your hand, please tell us the answer."

This is a subtle reminder that the rule is to raise your hand and if you don't, you may be ignored. However, this is an instance where it would be useful for the paraprofessional to take data on the behavior by counting how often the student shouts out and what happens when the shouting out is ignored. If the behavior increases, it can be surmised that ignoring the student is not working to change his behavior and something else needs to happen instead.

Notice too that the sanction here is the absence of attention. The teacher is not introducing something into the situation to act as a punishment, such as detention or even the loss of recess. Withholding something the student wants is also a common form of sanction and this minor infraction of shouting out only merits a minor sanction (ignoring the behavior), unless it proves to be persistent.

Amelia Smith, who was raised in Utah in the early twentieth century, reflected on her father's method of disciplining his children: "If any of us needed to be corrected for some misbehavior he simply put his hands on our shoulders and looking into our eyes with a hurt look in his own, said, 'I wish my kiddies would be good.' No spanking or other punishment could ever have been more effective." The relationship between Amelia and her father must have been so good that his disappointment was enough to discourage her from misbehaving again. So this tells us something else about appropriate sanctions. They can be very mild but still be extremely effective when there is an important relationship involved.

Applying Amelia's example to the student who shouts out, if the behavior persists, a kind but firm statement of disappointment may reduce the shouting and increase hand raising. This usually is best when the student is called aside and not exposed to embarrassment in front of the whole class.

Meaningful

What you absolutely do not want to hear a student say in response to a sanction is, "I don't care!" If they really don't care about the sanction imposed, then it's no sanction at all. It will not serve the intended purpose of discouraging or reducing a particular inappropriate behavior. So for the student who doesn't like going out to recess, removal of recess will not represent a sanction. For the child who likes to work alone, having them work away from other students will not be a sanction at all and may do nothing to decrease the behavior that prompted the sanction.

As an adult, if I violate a law by driving over the speed limit and get stopped by a police officer, I know what the punishment will be—a speeding ticket and its unavoidable fine (and perhaps a sanction on my car insurance premium). When laws are established, the penalty is set to make the punishment *meaningful*. And it usually works. Paying the fine is a financial sanction that we don't want to deal with again, so it helps to keep us within the speed limit. And, of course, multiple tickets can result not only in multiple fines (increasing the financial loss) but also in loss of your driver's license, which for most people is a very effective deterrent. Have you ever received a ticket for speeding? Perhaps you haven't and so just the possibility of getting a ticket may keep you driving within the speed limit. We could say that the threat of a sanction—just the possibility—is enough to keep you within the law. You don't actually have to suffer or receive that sanction.

Refer to the earlier principles of sanctions: timely and within an appropriate scope. The speeding ticket scenario above also demonstrates both of these principles. The officer puts on the police car lights at the time he sees you speeding. So you know immediately that something is wrong—and a quick glance at the speedometer confirms your infraction. There is no delay. The officer does not stop you the next day for a speeding violation that took place the day before.

Having the sanction be **appropriate in scope** is especially important. The speed rules have been established and posted. You know what they are because you studied the rules before passing your driver's test for the license. You also know the penalty. So you never have to worry that the officer will walk up to your car, pull his revolver, and shoot your foot because you were pushing on the gas pedal too hard! The sanction is appropriate for the rule that you broke. Likewise, a student would not be expelled from school because he forgot to raise his hand before excitedly knowing and shouting out an answer.

Simple

It really is not necessary to design complex sanctions or punishments. They are much more difficult to administer (or remember) and more likely to lead to dispute as the details have to be explained and discussed. Overly complicated sanctions also simply waste time that could be better spent on teaching and learning. So a set of simple sanctions that can be easily understood and administered is by far the best option. This idea of simple sanctions also brings us back to the idea of *least restrictive* interventions, discussed in Chapter 4.

A sanction is designed to decrease the likelihood of a behavior occurring or recurring.

Linking Classroom Sanctions to a Whole-School Approach

In the past many schools found that they were dealing with an increasing number of behavior problems such as fighting, bullying, and a general lack of discipline. It was not a reflection of teachers, staff, or principals who did not care, but rather it was the failure to adopt a school-wide, consistent model for Positive Behavioral

Interventions and Supports (PBIS). Although this particular terminology has only begun to be used recently, the principle still holds true: a whole-school, positive approach to behavior is essential for providing students with an environment where appropriate behavior is encouraged and supported. Today many schools have adopted PBIS as an effective way to prevent problems and to cope with those that arise in a fluent, consistent way.

Establishing a whole-school PBIS may be out of the scope of paraprofessionals. However, it is important to understand and to support the implementation at the site where you work.

The Technical Assistance Center on Positive Behavioral Interventions and Supports was established by the US Department of Education's Office of Special Education Programs (OSEP). Its purpose was to define, develop, implement, and evaluate a multitiered approach to technical assistance that would improve the capacity of states, districts, and schools to establish, scale-up, and sustain the PBIS framework. Emphasis is given to the impact of implementing PBIS on the social, emotional, and academic outcomes for students with disabilities. This is not merely a system for behavior management but is designed to benefit every aspect of a student's school experience.

You can refer to the webpage www.pbis.org/school/swpbis-for-beginners (also listed in the Bibliography) for in-depth information. This section of the PBIS website is specifically dedicated to those individuals who are interested in learning more about school-wide positive behavioral support. PBIS, when applied at the school-wide level, is sometimes referred to as: SWPBIS or SW-PBIS. For the remainder of this chapter, SWPBIS will be used when referring to School-Wide Positive Behavioral Interventions and Supports.

The underlying principle is teaching behavioral expectations in the same manner as any core curriculum subject. Typically, a team of approximately 10 representative members of the school will attend a two- or three-day training session provided by skilled trainers. This team will be comprised of administrators, classified staff, and regular and special education teachers. The school will focus on three to five behavioral expectations (rather like a set of school rules) that are positively stated and easy to remember. In other words, rather than telling students what not to do, the school will focus on the preferred behaviors. Here are some examples from other schools:

- Respect Yourself, Respect Others, and Respect Property
- Be Safe, Be Responsible, Be Respectful
- Respect Relationships and Respect Responsibilities

After the SWPBIS team members determine the behavioral expectations that suit the needs of their school, they will present them to the whole staff to ensure that at least 80% of the staff buys into the chosen expectations. This serves to ensure consistency from class to class and adult to adult—an essential for successful implementation of SWPBIS. The team will then create a matrix of what the behavioral expectations look like, sound like, and feel like in all the nonclassroom areas. This matrix will have approximately three positively stated examples for each area. Here is an example line from one school:

Respect Property

Bus	Keep feet and hands where they belong.	Throw unwanted items in wastebasket.	Keep food and drinks in backpack.
Cafeteria	Place tray on kitchen window shelf after scraping leftovers into wastebasket.	Wipe table with sponge provided.	Clean food spills off floor.
Restroom	Flush toilet after use.	Use two squirts of soap to wash hands.	Throw paper towels in wastebasket.
Playground	Report any graffiti or broken equipment to adult on duty.	Return playground equipment to proper area at end of recess.	Use equipment as it was designed.

This would be filled out for each nonclassroom area and each behavioral expectation.

Another primary activity for the SWPBIS team is determining how the behavioral expectations and routines will be taught in and around the school. There are many lesson plans available for teaching respect, responsibility, and so on, and the PBIS website has many examples available. Many schools choose to use several days at the beginning of each year to take the students around the school to different stations where the skills are taught for specific settings.

For example, a bus may be brought to the school and the children will practice lining up, entering the bus, sitting on the bus, and exiting the bus using hula hoops to denote proper body space distance in lining up to enter the bus.

This may seem like a very persnickety level of detail, and even an unnecessary waste of school time when students could be engaged in learning academic content. But the truth is, many students need this level of specificity—the actual physical example of what's required of them and practice drills to embed understanding. You'll remember that in Chapter 3 we referred to Harry Wong's advice that teachers use the first weeks of school to firmly establish behavioral expectations, discussing rules with students and using the *What if . . . ?* Game to explore possible exceptions to the rules. These SWPBIS recommendations apply the same principles to the whole school rather than just individual teachers.

The next task for the SWPBIS team is fine-tuning the office discipline referral process. The team will decide "What behaviors are an instant trip to the office and what behaviors are taken care of in the classroom." It is very important that every staff member knows the procedures and is consistent. If it is not permissible to use a cell phone in band class, for example, then it should not be permissible in art class.

In Chapter 3 you read and thought about the importance of being consistent in expecting students to know and follow rules. This consistency must be the same for all teachers and all paraprofessionals. So let's take a brief look at the various ways in which consistency should be demonstrated.

Consistency in Different Ways

Consistency between students. Any student who participates in a rule violation should get the same sanction as any other student for the same inappropriate behavior. The only acceptable difference might be if the student has persisted in this inappropriate behavior and the other is engaging in it for the first time. As noted in our previous example of ignoring the child who shouts out, the "repeat offender" should get a different sanction than the "first time offender." Cautionary note: This is usually, and most appropriately, determined by the teacher or the person who is in charge of the classroom.

Consistency across staff. It should not matter which member of staff deals with the inappropriate behavior. The student should expect the same reaction or consequence. Students shouldn't be able to play one adult against another or expect greater leniency from one particular member of staff rather than another. Individual teachers will certainly have different tolerance levels depending on the behavior, and students know this, but essentially the levels should be the same across all staff—and that includes paraprofessionals.

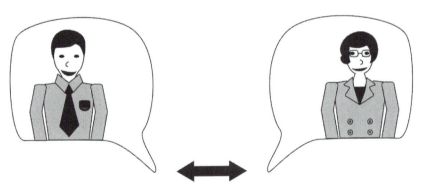

Credit: Christopher Wells Barlow

School staff supports decisions. As noted above, it shouldn't matter who sets the sanctions—if, for example, a student loses a privilege or recess it should not be restored by another member of staff. Even the principal should back up the member of staff and only intervene by discussing the matter privately with the member of staff if he/she disapproves of the sanction. Do you recall the case study in Chapter 3 where the teacher failed to support the sanctions issued by paraprofessionals? A School-Wide Behavior and Intervention Plan (SWBIP) can prevent this from happening. If you have no SWBIP, paraprofessionals and teachers can get together and make the decision to remain consistent in implementing sanctions within their own classrooms.

As you review the information up to this point in this chapter, summarize the information in the form on the next page to record your understanding of sanctions and the PBIS in relation to your paraprofessional role.

Sanctions and PBIS

- What is a sanction? What words come to mind when you read the word "sanction"? What are some synonyms for this word? Take a moment to consider these questions, and record some of your thoughts here.

- Write your thoughts on the importance of having a stratified range of sanctions where those imposed in the classroom setting dovetail with those imposed in the wider school setting. Remember TAMS as you develop your answers.

- Write your beliefs of the importance of consistency between classroom and school settings. Bearing in mind that the appropriateness of behaviors differs according to setting, why is consistency still essential?

- Discuss how you see your role within a SWBIP system.

- Discuss the importance of school staff support for the decisions made about sanctions. If, for example, a student loses a privilege or recess, should it be restored by another staff member?

Write a brief response to the following scenario.

One of the students you support for part of her middle school timetable runs past you in the school hallway during second period. You can see she's upset and call out to her to ask what's wrong. She tells you—between sobs—that the physical education teacher has just told her he's sending a note home because she was acting out in his class. "My mom will kill me when she gets that note." You know something of the girl's background and that her mother may well punish the girl harshly—you suspect physically—when she gets the note. You also know this isn't the first time she's acted out in the class—she's already had a warning and several minor sanctions for her behavior. What do you do?

Response to Case Study

Of course the sanctions that you, the teacher, or the principal employs to discourage students from repeating inappropriate behaviors must have links to the overall school policy or procedures for behavior management, whether the school has adopted a SWPBIS approach or not. Each school should have a behavior policy that applies to all staff and students. This policy should clearly stipulate which behaviors are acceptable and which are unacceptable and should outline a set of sanctions considered suitable for different inappropriate behaviors. Thus the sanctions used in the classroom should be derived from—or may be dictated by—the school behavior policy. And, of course, if there is abuse in the home, it must be reported to the authorities. On the next page you will find a form that will walk you through the process of reviewing the sanctions available to you as you encounter inappropriate behavior. It also directs you to consider similarities and differences between various teachers and between whole-class, teacher supervised settings and the group work that you may have responsibility for.

Choice Revisited

When we discussed rewards in Chapter 4, we also discussed the importance of teaching students that they have choices in the way they behave and, therefore, choices in the consequences they enjoy. This is true whether their behavior is appropriate or inappropriate. There may be a set sanction for a particular inappropriate behavior, so they may not have a *choice of sanction*. But what they do have is a choice over whether a sanction is imposed at all—because they can choose to engage in behavior that has no associated sanctions—*they can choose to behave appropriately*. The famous soviet writer Aleksandr Solzhenitsyn is quoted as saying, "it is time . . . to defend not so much human rights as human obligations." Teaching students their responsibilities is often considered a priority for schools, and this begins with learning to make appropriate choices.

One of the choices that students are making when they choose how they behave is a choice of the type of classroom environment in which they spend their days. The classroom where appropriate behavior dominates is a classroom where the focus is on purposeful teaching and learning, with minimal distractions, and the frequent giving of rewards. A positive atmosphere prevails. This is also likely to be a classroom of motivated students who are finding satisfaction in their achievements. And it certainly will be a classroom where the teacher (and other adults) enjoy their interactions with the students and also find a great deal of satisfaction in seeing the progress that the students make.

Student choice is not about the type of sanction imposed. That will already have been decided and recorded in the school behavior policy.
The choice available to students is to choose whether to behave appropriately.

Sanctions Around the School

- Identify the range of sanctions that are available in your work setting or other classrooms you have recently visited.

- Identify differences—if any—between different teachers you work with or have observed.

- How do sanctions differ—if at all—when you are working with groups of children rather than when the students are working under the direction of a teacher?

Remember, if you want to adjust sanctions for when students are working with you in a small group, you should check with your teacher to ask whether he or she finds this acceptable.

In classrooms where students choose to expend their energies on playing up and acting out, avoiding work, and generally making a nuisance of themselves, the atmosphere will be quite different.

- Momentum is likely to be lacking in teaching and learning activities as the teacher's attention is called away by inattentive or disruptive students.
- Well-behaved students have to endure the repeated spectacle of their peers being sanctioned, along with the associated resentment and possible escalation of inappropriate behavior.

Adult Choices

This is also a good point to remind ourselves of our choices as adults. We can choose to focus on identifying and sanctioning inappropriate behavior. Or we can choose to focus our attention and energies on identifying and rewarding appropriate behavior. Yes, those who behave inappropriately are supposed to receive a sanction. But one of the sanctions you have at your disposal is to ignore minor inappropriate behavior, as already mentioned. If the student who's behaving inappropriately wants your attention but doesn't get it through his or her inappropriate behavior, that in itself can act as a deterrent. That same student—if he or she sees and hears you praising or otherwise rewarding appropriate behavior—may then be motivated to behave appropriately in order to get your attention. That attention reward is what was desired in the first place—so find opportunities to turn your attention to the student *in response to appropriate behavior* rather than in response to inappropriate behaviors. Do it before the inappropriate behavior begins. Students who are getting plenty of attention have no need to misbehave in order to get attention. Take data from time to time to check that your strategy is working.

> If the student who is behaving inappropriately wants your attention and doesn't receive it, the "lack of attention" in itself can act as a deterrent.

Jerry Olsen and Paul Cooper, in their book *Dealing with Disruptive Students in the Classroom,* make the point that:

> The disruptive influence of the teacher's response to misbehavior should be less than the student's disruption. Some teachers create more disruption by disciplining students than misbehaving students cause in the first place.

Effective teachers and paraprofessionals ignore minor disruptions unless they are repeated, then they deal with the student privately.

Good Choices—And Some Not So Good

Take a moment to consider an example from your work setting. Think of a time when you made a good choice that resulted in a positive outcome for students. Write that here.

Now think of an example of an action that had a less than positive outcome and consider what you could have done differently to make a more positive outcome for students. This should be a situation where you had a choice of the action you took.

The Cost of School Exclusions and School Failure

The costs of failure to resolve bad behavior choices are potentially huge both for the students as individuals and, eventually, for society at large.

As we have already discussed in an earlier chapter, when the teacher has to take the time to deal with behavior, time for learning is lost. For students who persist in appropriate behavior to the extent that they are excluded from school, there's a significant financial cost to the taxpayer because an alternative provision is needed and other service providers become involved. Specialist provision for students whose behavior is especially challenging will always be far more costly than provision in a regular school environment. But the first direct cost to the student is loss of learning time. This accumulates until the student is likely to lack the skills necessary for future jobs as both academic and behavioral skills are vital to employment. Costs accumulate in terms of the individual being ineligible for college courses, out of work (or in low-paid employment), potentially unable to support self or family, or perhaps becoming involved in criminal activity. This may seem like a particularly bleak picture, but statistics show that students who are excluded from school largely do not do well later in life. As with employment, both academic and social skills are useful in life.

Where inappropriate behavior and exclusion are linked to emotional and learning disabilities, research shows that students are not as successful as their peers without disabilities in transitioning out of high school to employment or college, but they are entering the criminal justice system. Multiple studies have shown that

Plan of Action

As a result of your reading and reflection on the principles discussed in this chapter, it's now time to formulate/add to your plan of action. Reflect first and then write about any of the principles that struck you most forcibly as you've read this chapter.

Ask yourself: What will I do that I've not done before in relation to student behavior? Record some of your thoughts here.

Ask yourself: What will I stop doing that I've been doing until now in relation to student behavior? List **two things** that you are determined to give up in order to change for the better.

as many as 34% of individuals in the criminal justice system have a disability. While this is not extreme in terms of the total population, it is critical to individuals and their families if even one person is jailed for bad (and illegal) actions.

Other studies on people with emotional or behavior disorders found that those who were able to obtain a job were far less likely to stay in that job and fell behind in both wages and hours. Sadly, the jobs that they typically got did not allow them to earn enough to live independently. In addition to financial cost, the emotional cost of failure can be disastrous for a student, especially as he sees his peers succeed. He may find himself increasingly isolated as his behavior deviates increasingly from that of his peers. The economy may suffer the loss of a potential wage earner, but the individual suffers from lost dreams and hopes.

Dealing with Aggressive Behavior in Schools

Sadly, there are times when the best of school and classroom plans fail to prevent behavior problems. The cases are rare, but some students have emotional or psychological issues that are extremely difficult for them to control. We will discuss aggressive behavior only briefly in this chapter because in aggressive behavior situations, school professionals have the responsibility for ensuring that the appropriate supports are in place. This is well beyond your role and responsibilities.

Aggression is defined as a persistent pattern of behavior that causes or threatens physical or psychological harm. It can disrupt society generally, or schools specifically, by alienating peers, teachers, and even primary caregivers. According to the 2007 report of the US Department of Education National Center for Education Statistics, 7% of teachers indicated they had been threatened by a student during the 2003–04 school year, and 3% indicated an actual physical attack by a student.

What happens next, after a student has threatened violence to a teacher or to another student? Often students with these sorts of difficulties are quite quickly moved out of the school to a more restrictive setting. But it is important to keep in mind the discussion about exclusion of students. Exclusion from the general curriculum that their peers are following often causes them to lack the skills they need for employment or higher education, which we have already alluded to. The Council for Exceptional Children (CEC), the largest special education organization, conducts research on the standards needed by teachers who serve children and youth with exceptionalities. These CEC standards serve as a guide for teacher preparation programs in special education. The CEC's professional policies concerning children with behavior problems state:

> The exemption, exclusion, or expulsion of any child from receiving a free, appropriate, public education creates a greater problem for society and therefore should not be permitted. At the same time violent and destructive behavior is unacceptable in our schools. Acknowledging that such behavior occurs, CEC believes that schools have the responsibility to quickly and unilaterally move students who exhibit dangerously violent or destructive behavior to an alternative educational setting in which ongoing safety/behavioral and educational goals are addressed by appropriately trained or qualified personnel. This setting must meet the school's dual responsibilities of providing an appropriate, public education **and** a safe learning/working environment in an age, and culturally, appropriate manner.

A Word About Bullying

Bullying is a form of violence. Bullying is aggressive and repeated behavior based on an imbalance of power among people. It ranges from slapping, kicking, and other physical abuse to verbal assaults. And there is now a new frontier for bullying: cyberbullying, in which individuals (including kids) use e-mail and social media to humiliate, ridicule, or defame others.

Millions of students—about three in ten—are affected as a bully, a victim, or both, according to a 2012 study of students in sixth to tenth grade. The research was funded by the National Institute of Child Health and Human Development. Although definitions of bullying vary, most agree that bullying includes:

- Attack or intimidation with the intention to cause fear, distress, or harm that is either physical (hitting, punching), verbal (name calling, teasing), or psychological/relational (rumors, social exclusion).
- A real or perceived imbalance of power between the bully and the victim.
- Repeated attacks or intimidation between the same children over time.

Bullying can occur in person or through technology (electronic aggression, or cyberbullying). Electronic aggression is bullying that occurs through e-mail, a chat room, instant messaging, a website, text messaging, or videos or pictures posted on websites.

School-based bullying prevention programs are being implemented, with the ultimate goal being to stop bullying before it starts. A review of school-based bullying prevention programs yielded the following promising preventive elements:

- Improve supervision of students.
- Establish school rules and behavior management techniques in the classroom and throughout the school to detect and address bullying.
- Provide consequences for bullying.
- Have a whole-school antibullying policy.
- Enforce that policy consistently.
- Promote cooperation among different professionals and between school staff and parents.

Students need to understand that bullying will not be tolerated and that decisive action will be taken to deal with it. Students also need to have confidence that they will be believed and properly supported if they report bullying. You may wish to check for your school's policy on bullying to ensure that you are following prescribed procedures to help prevent bullying as well as support its victims.

Zero Tolerance*

"Zero tolerance" initially was defined as consistently enforced suspension and expulsion policies in response to weapons, drugs, and violent acts in the school setting. It meant that if a student brought a weapon to school—he was automatically expelled. Over time, however, zero tolerance has come to refer to school or district-wide policies that mandate predetermined, typically harsh consequences or punishments (such as suspension and expulsion) for a *wide degree* of rule violation. Most frequently, zero tolerance policies address drugs, weapons, violence, smoking, and school disruption in efforts to protect all students' safety and maintain a school environment that is conducive to learning. Some teachers and administrators favor zero tolerance policies because they remove difficult students from school. Administrators perceive zero tolerance policies as fast-acting interventions that send a clear, consistent message that certain behaviors are not acceptable in school.

Prevalence of Zero Tolerance Policies and Practices

According to data from the US Department of Education and the Center for Safe and Responsive Schools, at least 75% of schools report having zero tolerance policies for such serious offenses as:

- Firearms (94% of the schools reporting)
- Weapons other than firearms (91%)
- Alcohol (87%)
- Drugs (88%)
- Violence (79%)
- Tobacco (79%)

Among disciplinary actions mandated by zero tolerance policies, suspension is most frequently used for an extensive range of common offenses from attendance problems to disrespect and noncompliance. However, broad zero tolerance policies require that both *minor and major* disciplinary events be treated equally.

A 1997 US Department of Education study found that zero tolerance offenses that frequently resulted in suspension or expulsion included:
- Possession or use of a firearm (80%).
- Possession or use of a weapon other than a firearm (78%).
- Possession or distribution of alcohol, drugs, or tobacco (80%).
- Physical fighting (81%).

Problems Associated with Broad Zero Tolerance Policies

Research indicates that, *as implemented*, zero tolerance policies are ineffective in the long run and are related to a number of negative consequences, including increased school dropout rates and discriminatory application of school discipline practices. Proven discipline strategies that provide more effective alternatives to broad zero tolerance policies should be implemented to ensure that *all* students have access to an appropriate education in a safe environment.

Zero tolerance policies are complex and costly. Suspension and expulsion may set individuals who already display antisocial behavior on an accelerated course to delinquency by putting them in a situation in which there is a lack of parental supervision and a greater opportunity to socialize with other deviant peers. It takes them away from the academic learning environment where they can gain skills for future employment. Further, expulsion results in the denial of educational services, presenting specific legal as well as ethical dilemmas for students with disabilities.

Finally, there is no solid evidence that removing students from school makes a positive contribution to school safety or to society at large. A 2008 review of research by the American Psychological Association into the effects of zero tolerance policies recommended caution in applying zero tolerance and suggested a variety of alternative measures, including Restorative Practice (which you will learn about in Chapter 7) and School-Wide Positive Behavioral Interventions and Supports.

Other problems associated with zero tolerance policies include:

- Racial disproportionality: studies have shown that black students receive harsher, more punitive measures (e.g., suspension, expulsion, corporal punishment) than their non-minority peers.
- A greater negative impact on educational outcomes for students with disabilities.
- Inconsistent applications of zero tolerance policies, which often are not reserved exclusively for serious behaviors but are applied indiscriminately to much lower levels of rule infraction.
- An increasing rate of suspensions and expulsions throughout the country, even though school violence generally has been stable or declining.
- Increasing the length of expulsion to two-year, three-year, or even permanent expulsion.
- A high rate of repeat suspensions, suggesting that suspension is ineffective in changing behavior for these challenging students.
- Elevated dropout rates related to the repeated use of suspension and expulsion— the most likely consequence of suspension is additional suspension.

Consider what you learned in the earlier chapters about positive behavior supports, reinforcement, and effective instruction. Take some time to consider where school failure begins and to track back from exclusions to a point where a more effective path might be taken with difficult students. There may be a specific student who comes to mind in this regard, or you may just want to speculate and track an imaginary student. Write your thoughts here:

While there are no right or wrong answers to this activity, it is important to note that positive support tends to bring about positive action. For example, a recent study found that mothers who smile and laugh a lot have babies who smile more.

Zero Tolerance and Students with Special Needs

Zero tolerance policies may negatively impact students with disabilities to a greater degree than students without special needs. Although IDEA 04 '97 requires continuing educational services for any student with a disability who is suspended for more than *10 consecutive days* or *10 cumulative days* in one academic year, policies that require suspension or expulsion for certain behaviors put many students with disabilities *outside* of the education setting, apart from educators who could help address their needs. Furthermore, discipline practices that restrict access to appropriate education often make the problems even worse because they increase the probability that these students will not complete high school. School personnel charged with disciplining students with disabilities must be familiar with relevant components of IDEA because other alternatives have been mandated by federal and state laws. This in an effort to assure that students with disabilities have ongoing access to an appropriate education. In some rural locations this poses an additional challenge. For example, a student expelled from one high school may have to travel three hours over rough, unpaved roads to attend another high school.

Broad application of the zero tolerance policies has resulted in a range of negative outcomes with few if any benefits to students or the school community. Serious dangerous behaviors require consistent and firm consequences to protect the safety of students and staff; however, for many offenses addressed by zero tolerance policies, more effective alternative strategies are available. Systemic school-wide violence prevention programs, social skills curricula, and positive behavioral supports lead to improved learning for all students and safer school communities. And as noted above, working with students early, teaching appropriate behaviors, and reinforcing positive behaviors is a better way to improve behavior than excluding students.

All of this takes us back to positive behavior supports. Identifying the positive can prevent problems before they get to the sanction stage. The importance of this is emphasized by a study that examined factors that influenced a student's willingness to seek help for a threat of violence. Middle school students were asked how likely they would be to seek help in response to being bullied or threatened. It may be no surprise that the students who hold aggressive attitudes and perceive the school climate to be tolerant of bullying were less likely to report a willingness to seek help.

Summary

In this chapter we discussed the importance of sanctions, their essential characteristics, and their use in helping students understand choices and consequences. On completion of the chapter, you now can:

- Describe sanctions and give examples from your work or from the text.
- Describe the essential characteristics of sanctions: timely, appropriate in scope and focus, meaningful to the student, and simple (TAMS).
- Accurately describe the importance of linking individual and classroom behavior management to the school-wide expectations of behaviors.
- Understand and explain that every choice has a consequence. Good choices have good consequences.
- Know and explain the cost of inappropriate negative behaviors to students, families, and society at large.
- Have a greater awareness of how to deal with aggressive behaviors. Explain the concept of zero tolerance, as well as the potential shortcomings of such an approach.

Plan of Action

As you summarize the information from this chapter, you will need to analyze what types of sanctions you can support and even implement. Looking back at the Introduction, you completed an audit of your responsibilities in relation to student behavior. You identified and recorded the limits to your role. Now that you have specific details on sanctions, revisit the form and write your responses with greater detail. We have provided a blank form for your use at the end of the chapter.

Looking Ahead

Movie trailers originally were advertisements or commercials for a feature film that was coming soon to the cinema. They are called "trailers" because they were attached at the end of a current movie. However, industry leaders found that people had left the theatre by the time the trailer was being shown—so they moved it to the beginning. Yet the name stuck. Today it is still called a trailer, even though it may be at the beginning of a movie or even a stand-alone advertisement. We are adapting the term trailer to the next chapter's features.

In the upcoming chapter, you will learn about some of the disabilities that occur most frequently in the population. You will also learn about how those disabilities impact behavior and what strategies are most effective for supporting these students.

Note

*"Zero tolerance and alternative strategies: A fact sheet for educators and policymakers." Copyright 2008 by the National Association of School Psychologists, Bethesda, MD. Reprinted with permission of the publisher. www.nasponline.org.

Audit: Behavioral Responsibilities

These are my responsibilities with regard to student behavior:

-
-
-
-
-

These are things I'm <u>not</u> supposed to take responsibility for with regard to student behavior:

-
-
-

If I have questions regarding my behavioral responsibilities, these are the people I can go to:

-
-
-

If I have concerns about other paraprofessionals and their approach to student behavior, I can talk to:

-
-
-

Bibliography

American Psychological Association. (2008). *Are zero tolerance policies effective in the schools?* Available at: www.apa.org/pubs/info/reports/zero-tolerance.pdf.

Bear, G., Quinn, M., & Burkholder, S. (2001). *Interim alternative educational settings for children with disabilities.* Bethesda, MD: National Association of School Psychologists.

Centers for Disease Control and Prevention. Violence prevention. Retrieved from www.cdc.gov/violenceprevention.

Cooper, M. L., Thomson, C. L., & Baer, D. M. (Summer 1970). The experimental modification of teacher behavior. *Journal of Applied Behavior Analysis, 3*(2), 153–157. Article first published online: 27 FEB 2013. doi: 10.1901/jaba.1970.3–153.

Council for Exceptional Children Policy Manual. (2010). Section 3, Part 1, *Basic commitments and responsibilities to exceptional children,* p. H-7. Available at: www.cec.sped.org/Policy-and-Advocacy/CEC-Professional-Policies.

The Elton Report. (1989). Discipline in schools. London: Her Majesty's Stationery Office. Available at: www.educationengland.org.uk/documents/elton/elton1989.html.

Farrington, D. P., & Ttofi, M. M. (2010). School-based programs to reduce bullying and victimization. Systematic review for The Campbell Collaboration Crime and Justice Group. Available from: www.ncjrs.gov/pdffiles1/nij/grants/229377.pdf.

Fisher, H. L., Moffitt, T. E., Houts, R. M., Belsky, D. W., Arseneault, L., & Caspi, A. (2012). Bullying victimisation and risk of self harm in early adolescence: Longitudinal cohort study. *British Medical Journal, 344,* e2683. PMID: 22539176.

Houghton, S., Wheldall, K., and Merrett, F. (1988). Classroom behaviour problems which secondary school teachers say they find most troublesome. *British Educational Research Association, 14*(3), 297–312. Article first published online: 2 JAN 2013. doi: 10.1080/0141192880140306.

Morgan, J. (2007). *The teaching assistant's guide to managing behaviour.* London: Continuum Books.

Nansel, T. R., Overpeck, M., Pilla, R. S., Ruan, J., Simons-Morten, B., & Scheidt, P. (2001). Bullying behaviors among US youth: Prevalence and association with psychosocial adjustment. *Journal of the American Medical Association, (285)*16, 2094–2100.

NASP ASPIIRE Project (IDEA Partnerships). Available at: www.ideapractices.org.

NASP National Mental Health and Education Center for Children and Families. (n.d.) Available at: www.naspcenter.org.

NASP Resources. (n.d.) Zero tolerance and alternative strategies: A fact sheet for educators and policymakers. Accessed at www.nasponline.org/resources/factsheets/zt_fs.aspx.

Olsen, J., & Cooper, P. (2001). *Dealing with disruptive students in the classroom.* New York: Routledge.

Positive Behavioral Intervention Systems (PBIS). (n.d.) Accessed at: www.pbis.org/school/swpbis-for-beginners.

Quinn, M. M., Rutherford, R. B., Leone, P. E., Osher, D. M., & Poirier, J. M. (2005). Youth with disabilities in juvenile correction: A national survey. *Council for Exceptional Children, (71),* 339–345.

Safe and Responsive Schools Project. (n.d.) Accessed at www.indiana.edu/~safeschl.

Sanford, C., Newman, L., Wagner, M., Cameto, R., Knokey, A. M., & Shaver, D. (2011). The post-high school outcomes of young adults with disabilities up to 6 years after high school: Key findings from the national longitudinal transition study-2 (NLTS2). *US Department of Education* (NCSER 2011–3004), 1–106.

Skiba, R. (2000). *Zero tolerance, zero evidence: An analysis of school disciplinary practice.* Policy Research Report #SRS2. Bloomington, IN: Indiana Education Policy Center. Available at: http://ceep.indiana.edu/ChildrenLeftBehind/pdf/ZeroTolerance.pdf.

Solzhenitsyn, A. (June 8, 1978). *A World Split Apart.* Commencement address delivered at Harvard University.

Teachings of Presidents of the Church: Joseph Fielding Smith. (2013). Salt Lake City, UT: The Church of Jesus Christ of Latter-Day Saints. Available at: https://www.lds.org/manual/teachings-of-presidents-of-the-church-joseph-fielding-smith/chapter-4-strengthening-and-preserving-the-family?lang=eng.

US Department of Education. (1997 and 2007). *Principal/School Disciplinarian Survey on School Violence*. Washington, DC: National Center for Education Statistics.

Williams, F., & Cornella, D. G. (2006). Student willingness to seek help for threats of violence in middle school. *Journal of School Violence, 5*(4), 35–49.

Zigmond, N. (2006). Twenty-four months after high school: Path taken by youth with severe emotional and behavior disorders. *Journal of Emotional and Behavioral Disorders, 14*(2), 99–107.

Chapter 6

Behavior and Special Needs

What You Will Learn

Learning Objectives:

In this chapter you will learn about some of the most frequently occurring special needs and their impact on behavior. You will have a chance to apply your knowledge from earlier chapters of the clear link between behavior and learning and the use of reinforcement and sanctions to increase appropriate behaviors.

You will gain a basic understanding of the following special education needs or disabilities:

- Specific Learning Disabilities
- Autism
- Emotional and Behavioral Disorders
- Attention-Deficit/Hyperactivity Disorder

You will be able to state your role in working with these students particularly to the extent that you can offer sanctions and rewards.

This chapter considers a variety of special educational needs and their associated behavioral issues. The chapter is not intended to provide an exhaustive explanation of different disabilities (you can find websites for more information on these topics in the Useful Websites and Organizations section at the back of the book), but it is designed to provide information on particular disabilities and to consider whether students with these disabilities will invariably behave inappropriately. In addition we will consider whether we—and they—can, in fact, learn to manage their behavior.

Behavior and Special Needs

A variety of different types of disabilities or special needs do have behavioral issues directly associated with them. The most obvious of these are emotional and behavioral disabilities (EBD) and Attention-Deficit/Hyperactivity Disorder (ADHD).

However, there are also other types of special needs that can lead to a student displaying behavioral difficulties, even though the disability does not actually have a behavioral element, as it were. These include Learning Disabilities (LD) and Autistic Spectrum Disorders (ASD). In these latter cases, students may, for example, get frustrated because they are unable to do things that they see others do easily; they may also experience considerable anxiety. Both anxiety and frustration can lead to acting out behavior.

In the following pages, you will find brief descriptions of these four types of special needs and gain a better understanding of:

- What it is that causes the behavioral difficulties for students and those who work with them (*The Behavioral Issues*).
- How these behavioral issues can be addressed effectively (*Potential Solutions*).

We will also provide suggestions for websites and other sources of information about these special needs so that you can learn more, particularly if you are assigned to work with such students.

Learning Disabilities

A learning disability is a neurological disorder that affects the person throughout life. It is not a developmental stage or an illness that the person "suffers" from temporarily, but is a lifelong condition for which the individual must learn to compensate. It affects processes involved in understanding or in using language (spoken or written) and may look like an imperfect ability to listen, think, read, speak, write, or spell; it may also affect the ability to make math calculations.

Characteristics of Specific Learning Disabilities (SLD)

Specific learning disabilities affect processes involved in understanding or in using language, spoken or written, and may look like an imperfect ability to listen, think, read, speak, write, spell, or do math calculations. It is sometimes referred to as dyslexia because of the difficulty with lexicons (words).

Students with specific learning disabilities usually have normal intelligence, but they may have difficulty specific to an academic area of learning such as reading and language arts or math. But they are also likely to have difficulty with reasoning, recalling, and/or organizing information, and organizational skills. According to a 2014 report from the National Center for Learning Disabilities, nearly half of all secondary students diagnosed with a specific learning disability (SLD) perform more than three grade levels below their actual grade in reading and math.

Any one person is not likely to have learning disabilities in all of the following areas but may be affected by more than one, especially as some are interconnected.

- **Dyslexia**—a language-based disability in which a person has trouble understanding written language. It may also be referred to as reading disability or reading disorder.
- **Dyscalculia**—a mathematical disability in which a person has a difficult time solving arithmetic problems and grasping math concepts. Given the language content of math, a student with dyslexia will also have difficulties with some aspects of math.
- **Dysgraphia**—a writing disability in which a person finds it hard to form letters or write within a defined space.
- **Auditory and Visual Processing Disorders**—sensory disabilities in which a person has difficulty understanding language despite normal hearing and vision.
- **Nonverbal Learning Disabilities**—a neurological disorder that originates in the right hemisphere of the brain, causing problems with visual-spatial, intuitive, organizational, evaluative, and holistic processing functions.

Credit: Christopher Wells Barlow

The most common learning disabilities show up in the classroom as difficulty with basic reading and literacy skills. At this point it would be helpful to note that:

- Learning disabilities should not be confused with lack of educational opportunities caused by factors such as frequent changes of school or poor attendance.
- Children who are learning English as a second language do not necessarily have a learning disability. There will be only a few who do, but under the terms of IDEA, they must be tested in their native language for the determination to be made.

If students fall into either of these categories—they have received lower than normal levels of schooling or English is not their first/home language—there are specific types of support they will need, and there are often funding streams for such support. Because the source of the difficulty is different, so is the solution.

Learning Disabilities—The Behavioral Issues

Dr. Richard Lavoie, an expert in Learning Disabilities (LD) from New England, has written extensively about the characteristics of students with LD. You can find details of his website in the Useful Websites section at the back of the book. He makes several important points:

- There are a large number of potential characteristics that could indicate that a student has LD.
- No student will display all of these characteristics.
- The presence of these characteristics—which are largely *cognitive*—lead to *emotional* states that prompt inappropriate behavior, much of it innocent and unintended rather than deliberately noncompliant and disruptive.
- There are some common elements of LD to be aware of to help minimize the effects of these elements and thus reduce the likelihood of inappropriate behaviors occurring.
- The concept of fairness means everyone getting what they need rather than everyone getting the same thing.

Dr. Lavoie's workshop presentation is called *How Difficult Can It Be? The FAT City Workshop* because of the Frustration, Anxiety, and Tension that having LD produces in a student.

- (F) Frustration:
    - At not understanding what is required.
    - At the apparent speed and pace of lessons (because the LD student generally cannot process information as quickly as non-LD students and struggles to keep up).
    - At not being able to find the appropriate words quickly enough to express his ideas and feelings (because dysnomia, or word-finding difficulties, is also commonly associated with LD).
- (A) Anxiety:
    - That the teacher will call on him/her to answer a question and he/she won't be able to produce the answer quickly enough.
- (T) Tension:
    - Because of the constant state of stress that all of the above can produce for an individual with LD.

Although we are discussing school-age students, LD is not something that a child overcomes with age. The child with LD becomes an adult with LD. Fifteen percent of the US population, or one in seven Americans, has some type of learning disability, according to the National Institutes of Health. Learning disabilities often run in families. The condition does not change, only the skills and capacity to cope.

When we think of situations that produce frustration, anxiety, or tension, what comes to mind may be visits to the hospital or dentist (anxiety), not being able to understand instructions or official letters sent through the mail that have obvious importance (frustration), and uncertainty or conflict at work or home (tension).

Frustration, Anxiety, and Tension—Common Reactions

Take a moment to consider situations in which you may feel frustration, anxiety, or tension and answer the questions that follow.

First, make a note of the types of situations that cause you to feel frustration, anxiety, or tension.

Now consider: How do these situations make you feel? What sort of emotions are generated? What is your typical reaction in these situations?

The types of emotions that may be associated with these situations may include anger, intolerance, impatience, and even despair. They may lead to an inability to think clearly or even find the right words to express feelings or needs—just when you really need to let someone know how you're feeling. We may even experience a desire to just run away from the situation. This will hopefully help you to relate to your students—those who experience school as a source of frustration or anxiety or tension. Perhaps you can better understand what their inappropriate behavior may be prompted by and masking. Bear in mind, however, that whereas your anxiety may fade once you leave the dentist's office, some of your students may live in an almost constant state of anxiety while they are in school.

Learning Disabilities—Potential Solutions

Here are some suggestions for supporting students with learning disabilities. Many of these strategies can also assist students who have no diagnosed disability. These are useful strategies to use in class.

- **Think time**. When you ask a question, allow students time to think of an answer. Before you ask the question, tell the group that you don't want them to raise their hands straight away, because you want them to take their time thinking of an answer. This not only allows the student with LD the extra thinking time he needs, but also avoids the common situation where only the fastest students ever get to answer questions—and most of the rest of the students don't bother even to think of an answer, let alone raise their hands, because they know they'll never be fast enough to be called on.
- Provide **visual examples**, whether this is layout of an assignment or a photograph of how an area of the classroom should look when it's been cleaned up. This assists students with LD who have difficulties with visualization to see a model that they can then imitate.

During a hotel stay, one of the authors noticed a clever feature on the housekeeper's cart in the hallway. It had photographs that showed four areas of the hotel room—bathroom, closet, nightstand, and bed—as they should look once the room had been serviced. The reason for this was the ethnic diversity of the housekeeping staff and their associated lack of English, but the technique was effective in communicating requirements because it was an exemplar of what the finished product (in this case a clean room) should look like. If you want students with LD to help with cleaning up in the classroom, you may want to post photos around the room to show what they're aiming for.

- Provide **copies of notes** as a handout. Students with LD are unlikely to be able to multitask (listening and note-taking simultaneously), so they end up doing neither. An outline is often best—it allows students to keep track of where you are and reduces the amount of text. If you can use simple graphics for some of the items, all the better. This strategy will allow all students to spend more class time thinking and participating rather than constantly taking notes.
- Give **instructions one at a time**. All too often we say things like, "Now I want you to put your books away, put pencils in the jar, put rulers in the tray,

then go and get your coats and come back and sit on the carpet." This "instruction" is actually five instructions. It may seem like a much slower process to give one instruction at a time, but in reality it can save you time—and prevent the inappropriate behavior that you would have to deal with.

Autistic Spectrum Disorders (Autism)

The word "Autism" comes from the Greek word "autos" (self) because of the inner/self-focus of those with Autism and their inability to relate to or understand the feelings of others. Autism, or Autism Spectrum Disorder (ASD), is a disorder of neural development. As the name suggests, children with ASD will fall somewhere on a spectrum or range of impairment.

Some students show only mild impairment and may seem to most people to just be very quirky children. These students often have average or above average intelligence and they can function well enough in a classroom, but they struggle with social interactions. Students on the opposite end of this spectrum can have significant intellectual disabilities, may not speak at all (known as being nonverbal), and may seem disconnected from those around them. When working in schools, it is common to find some children on each end of the spectrum as well as everywhere in between, although those with the most severe autistic tendencies are likely to need placement in a special school.

Autism Spectrum Disorders

"Autism" comes from the Greek word "autos" (self) because of the inner/self-focus of those with Autism and the inability to relate to or understand the feelings of others.

According to the Centers for Disease Control (CDC), an estimated 1 in 68 children has been diagnosed with ASD. It occurs among all racial, ethnic, and socioeconomic groups and in both sexes, but five times more often in boys than in girls. These children receive a wide variety of special education services, ranging from specialized classrooms with educators who specialize in working with ASD students to being taught in the normal classroom with little or no accommodation made by the general education teacher. While working in schools, you will likely work with students with ASD. It is important that you know what types of behaviors these students will likely show so that you can successfully intervene, teach, and assist these students in the most appropriate ways.

Children can be diagnosed with ASD as young as 18 months to 2 years. At 18 months, signals of the possible presence of ASD include children's unwillingness to be cuddled or hugged, not responding to their own name, and not making eye contact (think of the neuro-typical child who will enjoy playing peek-a-boo at this age). These children are often first diagnosed with a developmental delay, but once they start school they are often identified because of their lack of language development.

It is not uncommon for people to think that ASD was "caught" or caused by some event that occurred around the diagnosis or appearance of symptoms. A few parents worry that vaccinations around this same age may be the cause of ASD. However, research has shown that vaccinations have no correlation with the occurrence of ASD. The symptoms may be identifiable as early as 18 months or so, but that does not mean Autism begins at 18 months. Recent studies have shown differences at birth in children with ASD, including regions of the brain not developing correctly in certain areas. (Please see the Bibliography if you would like more information about Autism.)

Autism—The Behavioral Issues

Children with ASD will show a wide variety of impaired behaviors but in three common areas:

- Social difficulties.
- Communication disabilities.
- Flexibility of thinking or imagination.

Students with ASD are all different. There is a saying that, "If you have seen one child with ASD, you have only seen one child with ASD," as no two children with ASD will have the same behaviors or behave that way the same number of times or to the same degree as another. It is important to remember that some of these behaviors may be seen in most children to some degree on occasion, but in order to be diagnosed with ASD students would need to present several of these behaviors—to a significant degree—consistently since the time they were very young.

Avoid the urge to say that you think children have ASD just because they do not make eye contact or socialize easily—they may just be shy. That being said, if you notice many of these behaviors and that the behaviors are significantly hampering a student's ability to succeed in school, you should voice your concerns to school personnel who are trained to identify these students, such as the teacher or a school psychologist.

Several social areas such as interpreting situations, making and keeping friends, generalizing, making transitions, and communicating effectively may be affected by Autism. We will discuss each of these.

Social Difficulties

A category of impairments or delays that is commonly seen with students with ASD is social difficulties. This can range from quirky, inappropriate social interactions to a complete disinterest or inability to engage in meaningful social interactions. For a student with more severe Autism, parents often struggle with the realization that they may not experience the typical loving interactions with their child that other parents experience. Two particular aspects of this result in behavioral issues for the classroom: lack of eye contact and struggling to interpret situations correctly.

Lack of Eye Contact

This may make the student appear insolent in Western culture ("Look at me when I'm talking to you!" is still a common request in classrooms). Alternatively, the student with ASD may use prolonged eye contact and have a flat stare (rather than the soft gaze of neuro-typical students) that can also seem insolent. These students commonly do not look at people who are talking to them but may look at the person's mouth, which is producing the words, instead of the person's eyes.

Interpreting Situations Correctly

Students with ASD may have difficulty understanding not only social situations but also situations that are dangerous. A student may walk into the street without taking proper care, for example.

> *Another example is a student who walks right up to another student who is acting aggressively and says something rude, not realizing that the aggressive student is likely to attack in response.*

Another aspect is that students with ASD may not understand jokes or why people are laughing. If the student unintentionally says something funny, he or she may not understand why other students are laughing, so the student may become upset. If the student is trying to be funny, he may tell the same joke over and over again, not understanding that most jokes stop being funny if they're repeated too often. And students with Autism may also repeatedly behave badly because it entertains other students, reinforcing the inappropriate behavior.

Friendships

Given the difficulty of not understanding social situations, students with ASD often have difficulty making friends. Those with more severe Autism may seem to have little or no interest in friends. They may ignore others, only engaging with them to get what they want; they may use people as tools.

> *An example of this is a child ignoring everyone in the classroom while he completes an activity until he needs something that the teacher is holding. The student then goes to the teacher and grabs the needed object. Once the student has the object, he returns to the same behavior of ignoring everyone else in the room.*

Students with milder Autism often want to have friends but lack the social skills necessary to persuade another child to be their friend. These students may have difficulty sharing toys or discussing other students' interests. Students with ASD can often be very blunt, brutally honest, or become verbally and physically aggressive when things don't go their way. Other students may find them annoying or a bit intimidating because of how difficult it is to get along with them. These students may not fully understand what a friend is. It is not uncommon for these students to say that they have many friends and list them off. But teachers and parents who know the child often realize that these "friends" are just people they have met in the hallway once or twice with limited interaction.

Students with ASD often struggle to understand the intentions or appropriateness of physical contact. Students may also struggle with understanding what another person's physical contact means. Some of these students find pats on the back from the teacher very uncomfortable or even threatening. They do not understand that the intention is to show love and/or appreciation. This can become a bigger issue when students reach puberty. Students may not understand the boundaries that should not be crossed concerning sexual desires and actions. Other students could be at risk if a student begins to act out sexually without an understanding of the implications of his or her behavior. Clare Sainsbury, an adult with high functioning Autism, titled her book *Martian in the Playground* because she says that as a child in school she felt like an alien, not understanding what was going on but knowing that she didn't understand and that everyone else did (you can find details of Sainsbury's book at the end of this chapter).

Generalizability

Something else that you might notice when working with students with ASD is that behaviors that are appropriate in one situation may carry over into another situation in which the behavior is not appropriate.

> *An example of this was a third grade boy who liked to read books on his father's lap at home. When he came to school, he wanted to read a book with a male volunteer in the class. He tried to climb on the volunteer's lap, making the volunteer very uncomfortable. Another common example is a boy discussing intimate, private matters about himself or his parents with every teacher or student he comes across.*

Communication Difficulties

Communication is another area in which students with ASD have delays or impairments. These communication disabilities (also referred to as speech and language disabilities) range from a total lack of verbal communication to voice and tone abnormalities as well as delayed speech. Students are likely to have difficulty understanding the subtleties of language such as sarcasm, idioms, jokes, exaggerations, overgeneralizations, and/or metaphors—features in common use that enrich our language—taking words very literally. Other students with ASD may repeat what others say instead of answering a question or performing the requested task. They do this to assist in processing the question.

Voice and tone abnormalities are common. You may notice a student who speaks in a monotone voice or a student who speaks in a high, squeaky voice.

Students may have difficulty responding to others when they are spoken to. They may not understand that it is socially important to respond. Some students respond by repeating what the person said—again, so that they can process the meaning of the words. Some students with ASD have difficulty referring to themselves and others using the correct pronouns. They may refer to themselves as "you" instead of "I" because whoever was talking to them referred to the student as "you." Students with ASD may also call themselves by their first names instead of "I." This can make it difficult for others to grasp the meaning of what the child is saying.

Children who take language very literally will often appear to be disobeying or defying an adult—even making fun of an adult—because they either take literally the nonliteral language that is so often used or because they may repeat something the adult has said in order to be able to process the language more easily.

Flexibility of Thinking or Imagination

A common issue for students with ASD is a need for a rigid pattern or schedule. This derives from an inflexibility of thinking, an impairment relating to imagination. Individuals with ASD crave "sameness" and find change very difficult to deal with. Thus when the normal schedule of events in the classroom is disrupted, these students will grow anxious or angry or may throw tantrums that will be difficult to stop.

Transitions

These students may have difficulty transitioning from one task to the other, particularly if they have not finished an activity—or they may insist on transitioning at a particular time, even though they have not finished an activity, as they know the timetable says it's time to change. Other students may demand that certain tasks be done in a certain order, including whole-class tasks, causing a lot of difficulty for the teachers and students.

One example of this rigidity occurred when a relatively high functioning student with ASD was told he couldn't have dessert because he hadn't finished his lunch. The student demanded that he must have dessert because everyone gets dessert after lunch every day. He began kicking and screaming that he was being treated unfairly. For days, every time lunch arrived he would become upset again just remembering that he wasn't given dessert several days before.

Another example happened on Halloween in the ASD unit at an elementary school. The students arrived in their costumes and seemed quite happy. But then the school had a costume parade, so instead of sitting in the usual semi-circle and singing songs to begin the day, students had to sit in the hallway and watch the parade. Since the students loved costumes so much, the teachers thought they would really love the parade. But many of the students reacted negatively to the change in schedule, some crying in the hall as the parade went by while others threw tantrums for over an hour. Trying to restore order by having singing time didn't seem to help.

Temple Grandin, a university professor with high functioning Autism sometimes referred to as Asperger Syndrome, relates how even as a successful adult with a professional career she lives in a constant state of anxiety because, for her, there is still so much that is unexpected about life. (Her book is listed at the end of the chapter, and if you search YouTube you will find a large number of video clips about her, including a movie about her life. Interestingly, these all detail not only the difficulties she encountered growing up but also the strengths associated with her Autism that have allowed her to be so successful.)

Narrow Interests

Another aspect of this inflexibility of thinking is for students to have a very narrow range of **interests**. Parents may comment that the student is obsessed with a TV show, a movie, or some type of activity, vehicle, color, or book.

> *One student we know of was completely consumed by pirates. He read the same pirate book every day and could talk for hours about famous pirates. Another seemed to live in a fantasy world with Sonic the Hedgehog and Harry Potter, believing they were her boyfriends. Another student would "dissect" every animal or bug he could find, including gummy bears and animal crackers. That same student also loved to tell you what letter came at the end of a word, which made it difficult when you asked him a question since he would only tell you the final letter of the answer.*

Sensory Stimulation

Another common feature of ASD is a need for sensory stimulation. Everybody engages in some level of sensory stimulation. You may notice people standing nervously in front of a classroom rocking on the balls of their feet or fiddling with an object in their hand. People may tap their feet when they get impatient or crack their knuckles. For students with ASD, these behaviors are often much more extreme and therefore disruptive. Examples include repeatedly making noises, biting themselves, or spinning in circles. They may "flap" their hands in front of their face or jump up and down. These behaviors appear to help regulate their emotions or allow them to cope with a difficult situation. Other times these behaviors are just fun. They can be loud, distracting, scary, or frankly annoying for other students and teachers in the class.

Hypersensitivity

Students with ASD are typically hypersensitive to noise, light, colors, and tastes. They may have a hard time tuning out background noise in order to focus on their teacher or other important sights and sounds. They may also find certain fabrics, foods, and textures to be either very appealing (to the point of obsession) or very aggravating, and they may be unable to tolerate cluttered walls or colorful displays. (Picture the classroom you work in—how difficult might it be as a learning environment for a student with ASD?) Alternatively, they can be hyposensitive, not seeming to notice the cold or not crying as you might expect if they fall and hurt themselves.

> *On a cold day when students are going out to recess, the student with ASD may refuse to put on a coat. Telling him, "But you'll be cold—and look the other children have their coats on" is unlikely to change his mind A) because he may not in fact feel the cold, and B) because he can't link other people's states of mind (in this case, feeling cold) with his own—he may assume that everyone feels the same as he does.*

Sleep Disorders

Finally, sleep disorders are common in children with ASD. Many parents find out quickly that children with ASD may stay up all night. These students often come to school tired, which may exacerbate the other difficulties associated with the condition.

The two most common purposes of inappropriate behaviors are attention and escape. We've expanded on these below, with some suggestions for simple strategies to prevent the behavior.

Attention

This is not likely to be the attention of approval, which so many needy students seek, as the social impairment of the student with Autism is likely to make them indifferent to an adult's approval. It is more likely to be attention in order to have access to some object or preferred activity.

Escape

Escape is generally a reaction to overstimulation. Individuals with ASD are often hypersensitive to light, noise, textures, and tastes. So their clothes, the normal noise levels of a classroom, the colorful displays on the classroom wall—can all be sources of distress from which they wish to escape.

Autism—Potential Solutions

Autism is now much more widely understood, and there is ample advice on how to best support students with ASD in school. If you have a specific assignment to work with an individual student, you should be provided with training for that role. But here are some strategies and approaches that you can use that may also be of help to other students who are not diagnosed with ASD.

Supports for Social Difficulties

- Teach students with ASD to make eye contact when teaching social skills. This is often paired with the social skill of initiating conversations or saying good morning to someone. If such things are taught as a type of rule or if . . . then situation, students will be more likely to accept it because they typically live by rules. "If someone says 'hello' to you, look at their eyes and say 'hello.'"
- Students who bite themselves can be given a plastic toy to bite instead. This may seem a bit inhumane, like a dog's chew toy, but it is better than a student biting his arm (or someone else's) until he bleeds. Other students may need to wear mittens or other items of clothing that reduce their ability to make noise or engage in a particular behavior.
- Social stories can also be used to teach children with ASD. A social story is a short story that describes a *social* situation and suggests appropriate responses. It is designed to help students understand and manage challenging social situations. Instructions on how to write a good social story can be found online

or in a variety of books, so you can write your own. But the critical feature of social stories is that they must relate directly to the situation for which the student needs support as the student will have difficulty generalizing principles to different situations.

- Don't make the mistake of punishing students for being disruptive when it is part of their condition; don't refer to the noises they make or their sensory stimulating actions as "silly"—they need them; don't take away a needed toy or article of clothing without discussing it with the student's main teacher first. The teacher will know what behaviors are being discouraged and which strategies are being used to discourage them.

Supports for Thinking and Imagination

- Because of a need for sameness, it is important to be considerate of students with ASD when you take them out of their normal classroom for tutoring or any other activity. Be sure to talk to the teacher before doing this so you can get a feel for how the student might react. If the student reacts to your arrival by getting very upset, it may be best to postpone your activity. Make sure the student is prepared for a change of activity. You can use a clock for this and give 10- and 5-minute warnings of the upcoming change. Unfortunately, schedules are often disrupted in schools by fire drills, assemblies, and other activities that may cause significant upheaval. Try to get advance notice of these events so you can prepare students' hours or days in advance, helping them to adjust and reducing their level of rigidity.
- Visual timetables are often used to help students know what to expect during the day, especially for nonverbal students. A picture on a time line can represent each class period. As the period ends, the picture can be put away; the next picture indicates to the student what he or she will be doing next.
- With students who are very interested in and knowledgeable about one or two things, use their interests to encourage them to participate in certain activities or to help develop their communication skills.
- Communicating with the parents of these students is essential. Ask how the child was the night before so you can know how much to demand of the student that day and can be better prepared for a possible rough day. Give parents information about how the child did that day.

For example, the parents of the student who struggled on Halloween in a previous example told the teacher that she had not slept well the night before because she only wanted to wear her princess costume, not sleep. The teacher was ready for the tantrums that came when the parade started because she knew the child would be easily irritated that day. The teacher let the parents know at the end of the day that the child had thrown a two-hour tantrum that day. The parents were then able to prepare themselves for the evening.

As you can see, in most cases students with Autism are not acting out because they choose to; the inappropriate behaviors are part of who they are. They can be taught more appropriate behaviors, but that requires great persistence and careful consideration of the student's needs, intolerances, fears, and capacities, and particularly their IEP goals. Interventions should be aimed at helping students in any area of schooling, social skills, language, or motor development. Many interventions and strategies have already been mentioned. You will find additional suggestions in the box below student's parents and teachers.

There are many strategies to help students with ASD learn and function in the classroom.
- Modeling is an important way to demonstrate to the student what needs to be done. This can help all students, but especially those who may have difficulties with verbal instruction. When modeling, the paraprofessional or teacher will perform the task for the student to see then ask the student to copy the same actions.
- Video modeling can be effective if given permission to record the students. When using video modeling, have the student perform the action. Then replay the video for the student so she can see herself doing the task correctly. Modeling can be used with academic, social, and communication skills.
- For students who are fascinated with characters from books, movies, TV shows, or video games (preferably the heroes, not the villains), parents and teachers can teach a student to behave like a favorite character. For example, does a hero treat others nicely? Does a hero share his or her toys? Does the villain share his or her toys? Are you acting like the hero or the villain?
- Make sure other students are not knowingly or innocently taking advantage of a student who may not understand the implications of what the other student is asking for. This could involve students making bad trades or performing actions that are rude.
- An intervention that can help calm students down is being wrapped up in a blanket or other object. This may sound strange, but some students will roll themselves in a blanket, creating a sort of calming burrito. Be sure the student is safe when doing this and discuss it with the teacher beforehand.
- Another common intervention is letting the student sit in a specialized swing that looks like a little cocoon at the end of a tether. These swings are often installed in special education units for students with ASD. The student climbs into the bottom part, is mostly closed in, and can then swing gently in the air. The teacher and other team members must have approval from the parents and must be sure to monitor the students when the swing is in use.
- Sometimes earphones are provided to help block out noises. Students may also have blankets or other objects they find soothing to hold.
- With nonverbal students or students with significant speech limitations or delays, it is not uncommon to see some type of simple sign language being taught. Other students receive help from assistive technology devices that produce language. This may involve buttons that the student can press in order to say words. Students may also receive speech and language services to improve their communication abilities, if possible.

Supports for Overstimulation

When a student tries to "escape" a situation where there is too much noise or other stimulation:

- Move the child to a quieter space.
- Allow the student to move around the school before the bell rings while the hallways are clear.
- Allow the student to work in an area of the classroom that is blocked off with screens and has plain walls (e.g., no bulletin boards).

Supports for Positive Behavior

We've addressed Positive Behavioral Interventions and Supports earlier, but Barry Morris, on an Autism-help website (see Bibliography at the end of this chapter) makes another important point in relation to PBIS and students with Autism:

> PBIS implies an understanding that people (including parents) do not control others, but seek to support others in their own behavior change processes. Most inappropriate behavior is prompted by difficulty in acquiring skills, so the child should always be treated with respect. There should always be a focus on humane changes in the child's life to learn better behavior, instead of using coercion or punishment to manage behavior.

This is a point we have already made in relation to behavior—that individuals choose how they behave; generally, no one "makes them do it." But notice that Morris goes further and reminds us of the principles behind this question of choice:

- Not only must individuals choose their own behavior, but others should not try to force that choice.
- This has to do with respect—we must respect other people's choices of how they behave.
- In addition, our purpose should be to support the individual in learning to make more appropriate choices as school and classroom rules are designed to provide a safe and pleasant learning environment for every student.

Understanding the individual and the unique needs of that person can assist paraprofessionals and teachers as they implement interventions and supports.

Emotional and Behavioral Disabilities (EBD)

Paraprofessionals who work with students with Emotional Disturbance and/or Behavioral Disabilities (EBD) encounter many situations involving student-displayed aggression and acting out behaviors. These behaviors can be directed at the teacher, other students, other adults in the classroom, or at the students themselves. Behaviors displayed may include violent actions such as hitting, spitting, biting, kicking, verbal and physical abuse, property destruction, and aggression.

EBD—The Behavioral Issues

The student who has been identified with emotional disturbance quite naturally will have behavioral difficulties. But as with ASD, these should be seen as a disability or difficulty rather than a total inability or lack of ability. The students with EBD *can learn how to behave appropriately,* but it will be much more difficult for them—and for you, as you work with them—because they will struggle. But think of it in terms of how you would approach a child who struggles to read or struggles with math because they don't have the necessary skills. You would:

- Provide additional support.
- Explain principles more than once and in as many different ways as needed so that the student can understand.

In short, you do what's necessary to find the approach that will enable students to access the necessary information and principles. We tend to sympathize with students who struggle with math, and we are therefore willing to persevere with them, finding a variety of ways to present information until we find the right approach to meet their needs.

Emotional Disturbance Defined

Emotional disturbance means a condition exhibiting one or more of the following characteristics over a long period of time and to a marked degree that adversely affects a child's educational performance:
- An inability to learn that cannot be explained by intellectual, sensory, or health factors.
- An inability to build or maintain satisfactory interpersonal relationships with peers and teachers.
- Inappropriate types of behavior or feelings under normal circumstances.
- A general pervasive mood of unhappiness or depression.
- A tendency to develop physical symptoms or fears associated with personal or school problems.

We talked earlier about the importance of the principle of choice in relation to behavior—students can be taught that they can choose consequences by choosing their behavior. But in the case of students with EBD, they are not simply choosing to misbehave but have genuine struggles with behavior and rules. They need the same type of perseverance and sympathy that we give the struggling student in math.

EBD—Potential Solutions

To meet the needs of students with challenging behavior associated with emotional issues, educators (teachers and paraprofessionals together) need to utilize evidence-based behavior management procedures, including social skills instruction, group instruction strategies, and faculty collaboration. Preservice and in-service training, on-site coaching for educators, and team teaching are also important. Perhaps the key aspect of behavior intervention design is a functional behavioral assessment (FuBA), which identifies student needs and helps schools allocate resources to meet those needs. Together, these approaches have been shown to improve outcomes for students with disabilities. Interventions can only be as effective as the person who implements them, and the relationship between the teacher and learner needs to be positive and trusting.

The functional behavioral assessment is usually conducted by teachers and/or school psychologists. It is a written assessment that leads to planning for improvement of the behaviors—often called a behavior intervention plan (BIP). As a paraprofessional, you may not be involved in the development of the FuBA but you should be involved in helping to improve the behavior. Ask your teacher(s) to share the FuBA and the BIP with you so that you will be thoroughly informed as you work with the student. We will refer to FuBAs again in Chapter 7.

Influence of School-Based Intervention

As we engage daily with students in the struggle to modify their behavior, we may sometimes ask ourselves whether we will ever really succeed. But the news is good. Research shows that, next to family, school provides one of the most socially significant influences on the child. Schools have become a powerful and influential setting for targeting at-risk students early in their academic career and implementing comprehensive interventions to remedy their problem behaviors and academic shortfalls, even before antisocial behavior patterns develop. This early intervention can decrease academic failure, rejection from peers and teachers, and delinquency and violence as the student gets older and moves into adulthood. Early intervention is key for preventing chronic behavior problems and lessening the impact of disabilities. Not lessening the disability, you notice, but lessening its effects on the student's behavior.

Attention-Deficit/Hyperactivity Disorder (ADHD)

A common disability now encountered in the schools is ADHD. In fact, paraprofessionals are often hired to help provide support for learning for students identified with ADHD.

The US Centers for Disease Control and Prevention (CDC) reports that the percentage of children diagnosed with ADHD has been steadily increasing in recent years—by as much as 5% per year. A 2011 survey of parents suggested that some 11% of 4- to 17-year-olds had been diagnosed with ADHD. That's a staggering 6.4 million children. Boys are more than twice as likely to be diagnosed as girls. The typical age of diagnosis is around 7, although younger children are identified if they are more severely affected. There has also been an increase in recent years in the number of children prescribed medication for ADHD, although as many as one-fifth of children diagnosed take no medication. ADHD has an associated financial cost, due to the increased likelihood of injury and accidents and therefore medical care and lost days of work on the part of family members. And as with the other conditions we have discussed, ADHD is not something from which a child necessarily recovers—it can be a lifelong condition, with up to 70% of children taking their symptoms with them into adulthood.

ADHD—The Behavioral Issues

Once this disability is understood, it becomes much easier to see its effect on learning. ADHD is a neuro-developmental disorder characterized by difficulty in the following areas: paying attention, impulsive action, and excess energy. There are three types of ADHD generally recognized:

1. Predominantly inattentive, where a child is easily distracted and most often has difficulty finishing thoughts, assignments, and instructions.
2. Predominantly hyperactive-impulsive, where a child has difficulty sitting still and is generally restless and fidgety.
3. Combined, where all of the above symptoms are present.

Educators must remember that the student is not necessarily trying to avoid classroom work; it may just be too difficult for them to focus on one task.

ADHD—Is School the Problem?

As a new teacher, one of the authors remembers being invited to accompany a class of sixth graders on a residential field trip. She thought this sounded like a fun idea and signed up for it. Colleagues tries to warn her off. "Do you know who's in that class? They're an awful group of kids. Most of the girls are OK, but at least half of the boys have been threatened with suspension. And you'll be camping with them in the middle of nowhere!" She was young and naïve and prepared to take the risk. She knew there'd be other members of staff with the group. Not knowing the kids at all, she had no way of knowing which ones to worry about. And indeed, once the residential week was under way, she didn't notice any boys who were causing trouble. There were a few girls who were homesick, but the boys were all helpful and engaged, willing to participate in any and every activity. Partway through the week, she thought she'd better check with one of the other teachers, in case she'd missed any important cues. In response to her question "So which of these boys are the ones who get into trouble in school?" the other teacher replied, "Most of them. Those two over there—the ones who just volunteered to clean up—they're both on their last warning. The principal wasn't going to allow them to come with us—he thought they didn't deserve a treat—but I stuck my neck out. Said I'd take responsibility, and I think he was glad to be rid of them for the week, so he let them go." That was an early and useful lesson for a new teacher—that classrooms just aren't the best learning environment for all kids.

ADHD—Potential Solutions

Fintan O'Regan, a behavioral expert from the UK, gives the following advice about students with ADHD:

- If students are looking for attention, just give it to them. Briefly and appropriately, and directing them back to their work as soon as possible.
- Accept that they have to shout out because if they don't, they'll forget what they wanted to say—their mind moves on too quickly, so they can't wait.
- They need a great deal of stimulation, so if we don't provide it for them they'll create it for themselves (hence the fidgeting, playing with a pencil, etc.). Why not give them a fidget toy? It actually helps their concentration because it settles their need for stimulation and allows them to concentrate on assigned tasks better.

To What Extent Can These Students' Behavior Be Modified? Do Rewards and Sanctions "Work" for These Students?

For an answer to this question we need to return to our definition of reward. Remember in Chapter 4 we defined a reward as something *designed to increase the likelihood of a behavior happening again/more often,* and in Chapter 5 we talked about a sanction being *a deterrent or de-motivator . . . something designed to decrease, discourage, or eliminate a behavior that is deemed inappropriate.*

What you would consider rewarding and motivating may not be motivating or rewarding to the next person and vice versa. Therefore the crucial point is to find out what constitutes a reward for *the individual child with the particular disability or special need* and incorporate that into your behavior management plans and strategies.

There are, however, some generalizations we can make about students with some of the conditions we have referred to in this chapter. The nearby box gives you an opportunity to reflect on some questions relating to this.

Reflect on the information we've covered in this chapter, focusing on behavior intervention and supports for students with disabilities. Ask yourself:
- Will the child with Autism consider praise or approval from an adult to be motivating? Your thoughts:

Likely answer: Probably not, because of the impairments in social interaction associated with ASD—difficulty relating to others, difficulty interpreting communication, and generally little regard for other people's approval.

- Will the child with ADHD be able to wait until the end of the day or class period before he is rewarded? Your thoughts:

Likely answer: Well no—he has a short attention span so the reward needs to be pretty much immediate. Remember we said that truly effective rewards have to be provided as close to the behavior as possible. For a child with ADHD, that may have to be instantly. And the definition of "as quickly as possible" also depends on the unique needs of the child receiving the reward. We remember this with age and automatically reward the younger child quickly while expecting the older child to be able to wait (delayed gratification). For the child with ADHD, the reward must be closely linked in time to the desired behavior. This is not because the child is young for his/her age but because the characteristics of ADHD are also characteristics of younger children. They persist with children with ADHD so our approach must follow suit.

Building Behavior and Social Skills

Jean Gross, a British expert in social and emotional learning, suggests that young people don't behave appropriately for one of three reasons:

- They can, but they don't choose to.
- They can't, because they don't know how.
- They know how and can, but they "lose it" when life gets too much for them.

"Knowing how" to behave, Gross suggests, is a question of having the necessary social and emotional skills. But balancing out this question of skills is the question of whether the rewards for misbehavior outweigh the rewards for behaving appropriately. She gives examples of each of these three patterns of student behavior.

1. The type of behavior we have all seen in young people—playing to the crowd. A student who we know is capable of behaving appropriately will often choose not to because, by misbehaving, he can get the attention of his classmates and make them laugh by acting the clown or just acting out, and he **values their attention more than the rewards the adults may be offering** for appropriate behavior.
2. The student who is **not motivated by any reward or sanction to behave in certain ways because he actually doesn't know how** to behave in those ways. Consider, for example, the student who hasn't learned to control his anger or doesn't know how to recognize his feelings (someone who has few or no emotional literacy skills). Rewards will only motivate students to do *what they can already do*. The student who can't read can't be bribed into reading—he needs to be taught so that he can develop that skill.

The same applies to the skills required for appropriate social behavior in classrooms.

3. The student who lashes out—verbally or physically—from time to time, even though the rest of the time she appears to be able to control her behavior. This could be due to the student having difficulties at home or in school but, again, **the rewards offered for appropriate behavior are outweighed by the emotions of the moment**.

Rewards will only motivate students to do *what they already know how to do*. No amount of praise or tangible reward will enable a student to demonstrate a skill he or she doesn't have. Think of an example in your own life. If you don't know how to change a tire or cook the perfect lobster, and if someone offered you a million dollars to change their tire or cook their lobster perfectly, you might be more motivated but you still wouldn't be able to do it. You'd have to acquire the skills first.

The British government department responsible for education has produced what are known as the SEAL materials (Social and Emotional Aspects of Learning). The box below gives an idea of the range of topics covered in the Early Years (Kindergarten). The SEAL materials can be downloaded from the National Archives.gov.UK website; you may be interested in exploring the suggestions and lesson plans provided there.

Social and Emotional Aspects of Learning (SEAL)
Outcomes for Early Years

New beginnings (belonging, self-awareness, managing my feelings, social skills, understanding rights and responsibilities)

Getting on and falling out (friendship, working together, managing feelings—anger, resolving conflict, understanding my feelings)

Saying no to bullying (don't give in to bullying, don't be a bully)

Going for goals (knowing myself, setting a realistic goal, planning to reach a goal, persistence)

Good to be me (knowing myself, understanding my feelings, managing my feelings, standing up for myself)

Relationships (understanding my feelings, managing my feelings, understanding the feelings of others, making choices)

Changes (knowing myself, understanding my feelings, understanding the feelings of others, making choices)

Take a moment to think about what strategies or programs you use in your work setting to help students develop social and emotional skills. These may be formal programs adopted by your school or district, or they may be less formal approaches or sessions your teacher incorporates into the school day. Write what these are and how they improve students' social and emotional outcomes.

Jean Gross also emphasizes the importance of embedding the teaching of social and emotional skills (through a program such as SEAL) as a whole-school approach. She recommends this for three reasons:

- Using a common program throughout the school helps to ensure a proactive approach as skills are taught to all students and the particularly needy students are identified and catered for early on. It also ensures follow-through as all staff become more aware of the need for this kind of curriculum—not just those who work with the youngest children. Remember our earlier discussion of consistency.
- A whole-school approach is more likely to ensure that all classrooms are supportive environments—with peers providing better support as they too become more emotionally literate and better able to empathize, offer friendship, handle conflict, etc.
- Staff members develop their own skills—personally as empathetic, good listeners who respect students' feelings and emotional needs, and professionally as educators who can teach these skills to their students as part of the more general curriculum.

Although Jean Gross works from the UK, she cites research in the USA that suggests that programs that teach social and emotional skills can raise student academic attainment by 11% on average, reminding us of the clear link between behavior and school success.

It is often the case that if a student is performing an unwanted behavior in the school setting and is taught the appropriate behavior for the situation, the unwanted behavior will decrease. In other situations, students require multiple types of interventions from a team that usually includes paraprofessionals. Paraprofessionals often play a major role in this tiered approach in which students who fail to respond to general, school-wide interventions are offered more intensive, personalized interventions.

PBIPs and Paraprofessionals

In Chapter 5 you read about school-wide positive behavioral intervention plans. Let's look at the plan from your perspective. Many paraprofessionals help to implement universal behavior plans. The plans focus on preventative and proactive measures. They include strategies that are quick to administer and inexpensive to implement but that prevent negative behaviors from developing. Behavior support plans implemented on a school-wide basis emphasize teaching, monitoring, and rewarding students rather than focusing on punitive measures. Because they maximize opportunities for students to be successful academically and behaviorally in the school setting, these interventions promote a positive school climate. They also teach classroom expectations and rules that are consistent across the school, so as to prevent students from becoming at-risk for school failure. At the same time, the interventions help educators identify students who are not responding to the universal supports.

Paraprofessionals involved with this level of intervention may be required to assist in making decisions and implementing strategies that will help students develop and learn. You can assist with teaching and modeling behavioral expectations, reteaching rules, writing up discipline referrals, passing out recognition slips, assisting with teaching materials, and giving verbal praise of appropriate behavior.

Group Interventions

Group interventions are highly efficient for some students considered at-risk, particularly as these students are most often taught in small groups rather than whole-class settings. However, even in these smaller groups some students do not respond quickly. Students who continue to struggle often come to school with many risk factors, including poverty, dysfunctional families, neighborhood deterioration, previous behavior problems, and possibly a learning disability. Sometimes as educators we may need to modify our academic and behavioral expectations to allow students with disabilities to succeed in a general education classroom. Some of these modifications take the form of individualized behavioral interventions.

Individual Interventions

Individual interventions are specific plans that facilitate student success in inclusive settings. Students with chronic behavior problems are given individualized plans and supports that are comprehensive and positive but that still allow access to group and universal support strategies. In other words, whether the student is in a small group or whole-class setting, he or she should not be isolated by the inappropriate behavior. Students should still have access to the incentives offered to the whole group or class. The amount of disruption that takes place in various settings and the frequency, duration, and intensity of the behavior help determine whether the student needs a comprehensive behavior plan, but as much as possible it should be implemented within a mainstream setting—or in the classroom with his or her peers (what IDEA refers to as the *Least Restrictive Environment*).

Based on assessment of student behavior, individualized interventions use intense, durable procedures to decrease problem behavior. These interventions should be written in the student's individualized education program (IEP) and should come into play only when the target behavior impedes school performance. The intensity of the intervention needs to match the intensity of the problem behavior being displayed by the student—remember the requirement for least restrictive intervention! As the student's problem behavior increases, the intensity of behavior needs and support also increase. And vice versa, as the behavior improves. Throughout the process, educators must carefully determine the intensity of the behavior and the warranted intervention.

Disability Not Inability

One of the important principles to remember with all disabilities is that the "D" stands for dis-ability, not inability. The capabilities you might expect from a child of a certain age may be present to some extent but not to the extent you would expect—or they may hardly be present at all or may not function in the expected way. We can liken a disability to someone who is farsighted or shortsighted. They're not *unable* to see; it's just that their vision doesn't quite function in the way you might expect—it's disordered or impaired. Fortunately, for most people this can be corrected with the simple piece of assistive technology: eyeglasses or contacts. Unfortunately, with most disabilities there is no such simple technological solution. Working with these students can be tiring but also very enjoyable and fulfilling. Don't shy away! Show them that you care and enjoy their company—even if they are unable to demonstrate in the usual way that they also enjoy yours.

Summary

You've learned about disabilities that have an effect on behavior. Students are not always misbehaving because they want to but rather because of a disability. You should now have greater understanding of the principles that help students learn.

Learning Outcomes

In this chapter you read definitions and information about some of the most frequently occurring special needs and their impact on behavior. You had a chance to apply your knowledge from earlier chapters of the clear link between behavior and learning. You should now be able to demonstrate your understanding of the following special education disabilities and the effect of the disability on behavior and learning: Specific Learning Disabilities, Autism, Emotional and Behavioral Disorders, Attention-Deficit/Hyperactivity Disorder.

You can state the strategies you will use to support the school and teacher in the school-wide intervention and behavior supports for working with students who have disabilities that affect their behavior.

Plan of Action

As a result of your reading and reflection on disabilities and the impact of these disabilities on behavior, it is now time to formulate or add to your plan of action.

- Now that I know more about specific disabilities, what will I do that I've not done before in relation to student behavior?
- What strategies and actions will I take to support positive behaviors in students with disabilities?

Looking Ahead

In Chapter 7, readers are asked to consider how some of the principles underlying these practices might be adopted in their work settings. Dive in and learn principles that you can apply in the classroom!

Bibliography

Ashbaker, B., & Morgan, J. (2012). *Paraprofessionals in the classroom: A survival guide.* Upper Saddle River, NJ: Allyn & Bacon.

Centers for Disease Control and Prevention. Data and statistics (ASD). (2014). Accessed at www.cdc.gov/ncbddd/autism/data.html. Published March 24, 2014, retrieved April 28, 2014.

Centers for Disease Control and Prevention. Facts about ADHD. (2014). Accessed at www.cdc.gov/ncbddd/adhd/. Published Feb. 21, 2014, retrieved April 28, 2014.

Centers for Disease Control and Prevention. Facts about ASD. (2014). Accessed at www.cdc.gov/ncbddd/autism/facts.html. Published March 20, 2014, retrieved April 28, 2014.

Grandin, T. (2006). *Thinking in pictures.* New York: Bloomsbury Publishing PLC.

Gross, J. (Nov. 2013). Addressing emotional and social needs. *Special, 13*(3), 359–365.

Hartwig, E. P., & Ruesch, G. M. (2000). Disciplining students in special education. *The Journal of Special Education, 33*(4), 240–247.

Hawken, L. S., & O'Neill, R. E. (2006). Including students with severe disabilities in all levels of school-wide positive behavior support. *Research and Practice for Persons with Severe Disabilities, 31*(1), 46–53.

Horner, R. H., Sugai, G., Todd, A. W., & Lewis-Palmer, T. (1999–2000). Elements of behavior support plans: A technical brief. *Exceptionality, 8*(3), 205–215.

International Site for Teaching Assistants and Paraeducators: Disabilities/Autism. Accessed at http://education.byu.edu/istap.

Lavoie, R. (1990). How difficult can this be? The FAT City Workshop. Available at: www.ricklavoie.com/videos.html.

Lewis, T. J., Hudson, S., Richter, M., & Johnson, N. (2004). Scientifically supported practices in emotional and behavioral disorders: A proposed approach and brief review of current practices. *Behavioral Disorders, 29*(3), 247–259.

Lewis, T. J., & Sugai, G. (1999). Effective behavior support: a systems approach to proactive school-wide management. *Focus on Exceptional Children, 31*(6), 1–24.

Morgan, J. (2007). *The teaching assistant's guide to managing behaviour.* London: Continuum Books.

Morris, B. (2008). Help with behavioral issues & learning life skills. Synapse.org.au. Retrieved from www.autism-help.org/behavioral-issues-autism-asperger.htm.

National Center for Learning Disabilities. (2014). Learning disabilities fast facts. Retrieved from www.ncld.org/types-learning-disabilities/what-is-ld/learning-disability-fast-facts.

National Institutes of Health & National Institute of Mental Health (2008). Attention Deficit Hyperactivity Disorder (ADHD). United States: National Institutes of Health. Accessed at www.nimh.nih.gov/health/publications/attention-deficit-hyperactivity-disorder/index.shtml.

O'Regan, F. (2013). SF3R 4 Behaviour. *Special, (13)*3, 36–37.

Pickett, A. L. (1986). Certified Partners. Four good reasons for certification of paraprofessionals. *American Educator, 10,* 31–47.

Sainsbury, C. (2009). *Martian in the playground: Understanding the schoolchild with Asperger's Syndrome.* Chicago, IL: Lucky Duck Books.

Smith, D. D., & Rivera, D. P. (1995). Discipline in special education and general education settings. *Focus on Exceptional Children, 27*(5), 1–15.

Sugai, G., & Horner, R. (2002). The evolution of discipline practices: School-wide positive behavior supports. *Child & Family Behavior Therapy, 24*(1–2), 23–50.

Sugai, G., & Horner, R. H. (2009). Responsiveness-to-intervention and school-wide positive behavior supports: Integration of multi-tiered system approaches. *Exceptionality, 17*(4), 223–237. doi:10.1080/09362830903235375.

Sugai, G., Sprague, J. R., Horner, R. H., & Walker, H. M. (2000). Preventing school violence: The use of office discipline referrals to assess and monitor school-wide discipline interventions. *Journal of Emotional and Behavioral Disorders, 8,* 94–101.

UK Department of Education. (May 2005). Social and emotional aspects of learning (SEAL): Improving behaviour, improving learning. Accessed at http://webarchive.nationalarchives.gov.uk/20110809101133/nsonline.org.uk/node/87009.

US Department of Education, Office of Special Education Programs. (2010). OSEP Center on Positive Behavioral Interventions and Supports (PBIS). Accessed at www.pbis.org.

Walker, H. M., Horner, R. H., Sugai, G., Bullis, M., Sprague, J. R., Bricker, D., & Kaufman, M. J. (1996). Integrated approaches to preventing antisocial behavior patterns among school-age children and youth. *Journal of Emotional and Behavioral Disorders, 4*(4), 194–209.

Chapter 7

Recent Developments in the Educational System

What You Will Learn

Learning Objectives:

In this chapter we look at some of the more recent developments in the education system that have been adopted in an effort to address broad behavioral issues. Several of these address the students' emotional needs, while the others such as Multi-Tier Systems of Support (MTSS) and Response to Intervention (RtI) call for a coordinated, team approach to meeting students' needs. You will be able to describe:

- The focus on the theory of learning styles as it relates to students with behavioral issues.
- How appropriate curriculum relates to acting out and withdrawal behaviors.
- RtI and MTSS in relation to your role.
- MTSS and how you can support the schools.

You will also be able to describe Restorative Practice, Circle Time, and P4C. In writing or orally, you can tell about your potential contribution in each of these programs. And you can tell or write examples of how each of these is used in the classroom.

Recent Developments

A number of approaches have come to be adopted in schools across the United States in recent years. Along with the employment of effective curriculum, learning styles are assessed to determine ways to teach students most effectively. And under the umbrella of MTSS, data collection, assessment, and analysis all assist in determining students' RtI. Additionally, new presentation techniques are being tried for student involvement in learning. These include Restorative Practice, Circle Time, and Philosophy for Children (P4C). We will provide an overview of each of these approaches and consider what they can contribute to positive behavior support and classroom management in terms of general principles and specific strategies that you may be able to adopt or add to your repertoire.

The Power of Appropriate Curriculum

As we have already stated earlier in this book, one of the most accessible behavior management tools in an educator's repertoire is the curriculum. Not just any curriculum, of course, but specifically a curriculum that is accessible to all students. In Chapter 3 we discussed the importance of ensuring that teaching content is interesting, relevant, and pitched at the right level of difficulty as a means of preventing the misbehavior generated by material that is dull, irrelevant, and too difficult, or too simple. Here we discuss the Common Core Standards and delivery of instruction with an eye toward identifying and matching the students' learning needs.

Common Core Standards

In the 1990s states began defining standards to identify what students were expected to learn at each grade level. They wrote curriculum and associated assessments designed to measure students' knowledge. Groups of leaders from corporations and government worked to reform education nationwide by raising academic standards and graduation requirements, thus holding schools more accountable for student learning.

Ready or Not: Creating a High School Diploma That Counts was a 2004 national report that claimed both employers and colleges were expecting much more of high school graduates than in the past. The report stated that the diploma had lost its value because graduates did not have the skills to compete successfully beyond high school. The report posits that the solution to this problem is a common set of rigorous standards. Combined with the increased efforts of states, the Common Core Standards were released for mathematics and English language arts in 2010. Financial incentives were available through federal government grant monies (named Race to the Top), and a majority of the states applied for the grant money and adopted the Common Core Standards.

As a paraprofessional you will have little—if any—say in the choice of the curriculum. But you can help support the implementation of curricular concepts and participate in the day-to-day measurement of student achievement. But you may well ask: If the curriculum is prescribed, how can it be accessible to all—even students with disabilities? The answer lies in both content and delivery. Paraprofessionals are often assigned to observe students to help determine the suitability of **content** (in terms of quantity and level of difficulty) and the appropriateness of the **delivery** in matching students' ability. When these are applied, the likeliness of better **engagement** in learning increases. We'll look at each of these in more detail.

Content

Even though the curriculum is prescribed, the teachers and the paraprofessionals have control over how that curriculum is presented to individual students—the scope (how much of it), and the pace (how quickly it is presented and the speed at which students are required to move through it). But the question that springs to mind is: *How much is enough?* How do we know how much of the curriculum is suitable for an individual student? This is a very individual consideration.

The rule of thumb is that the right amount is just enough to be challenging but not enough to overwhelm the student. It is delivered in steps that the student can manage without becoming bored or frustrated. The same is true of pace. *How fast is fast enough?* Well, it's fast enough for an individual student to keep up—not so fast that he panics, but not so slow that he loses interest. Each student will be different, so careful observation and data collection as a measurement become imperative.

We expect to broaden students' horizons and introduce them to new material and new ideas. However, students generally need to be able to make some connection with the curriculum content for it to have relevance and, therefore, greater attraction for them.

Where possible, direct links should be made with the curriculum content and the student's life and experiences. Research has shown that the most effective learning takes place when students can fit new material into the knowledge base of what they have already learned. But we can help bridge this for them—making explicit links that help them see how this fits in with their world. Learning for learning's sake is a fine notion, and not one to be totally dismissed, but students with special needs in particular need to see relevance in the curriculum.

Delivery

A wide variety of delivery methods are available to teachers, and the choice of delivery will make the curriculum more or less accessible to the student. We have already discussed the importance of factoring student **learning styles** into teaching and of using a variety of resources and teaching activities to accommodate visual, auditory, and kinesthetic modes (see Chapter 3).

Traditional schooling favored those with an auditory learning style, with information being delivered via lecture-type presentations. More recent methods have utilized media to supplement lectures with visuals, collaborative groups, and application activities—not only for the youngest students but throughout grade school, high school, and even college. Modern technology allows this to be done much more easily. The mode that is most often missing from "academic" subject teaching is the kinesthetic, which we tend to associate with vocational subjects (such as shop) or the arts (music, drama, etc.).

Different theorists have proposed a variety of ways to categorize learning styles. For example, in the 1980s David Kolb developed his theory of the following learning styles: Diverging, Assimilating, Converging, and Accommodating. These styles vary in the extent to which the individual relies on active engagement versus reflection and observation (essentially, doing versus watching) and focuses on the concrete (which Kolb links with feeling) versus the abstract (thinking). Here are some examples of how these learning styles may manifest in the classroom.

- *Diverging learners* like to gather information from concrete situations. They do well working in groups, although they learn through watching more than active participation. They may have many friends, show empathy for others, and have street smarts. Suitable tools for teaching them include the phone, audio conferencing, time and attention from the instructor, video conferencing, writing, computer conferencing, and e-mail or Facebook and other electronic social media.
- *Assimilating learners* are interested in ideas and abstract concepts. They prefer reading and lectures as teaching modalities and do best when able to listen to

information. Typical classroom lectures can be an advantage for this type of learner, whereas they are likely to find silent reading a much more difficult method for acquiring information. Kolb's idea of the Assimilating learner aligns well with the idea of auditory learning.

- *Converging learners* do well at solving problems and making decisions. They prefer to intake information through simulations, labs, and practical applications. They like to do—to draw, do jigsaw puzzles, and read maps, but also daydream. They can be taught through drawings and verbal and physical imagery. Tools include models, graphics, charts, photographs, drawings, 3-D modeling, video, videoconferencing, television, multimedia, and texts with pictures, charts, and graphs. These are visual-spatial learners—think of architects, designers, and sailors.
- *Accommodating learners* perform best with hands-on experience and prefer to work with others to complete tasks. These people learn best when bodily movement is involved, like making things and touching (tactile or kinesthetic/bodily learning). Learning is more likely to take place when the student carries out a physical activity rather than listening to a lecture or watching a demonstration. They can use the body effectively and have a keen sense of body awareness. They communicate well through body language and can be taught through physical activity, hands-on learning, acting, and role-playing. Tools include equipment and real objects. Professions could be a dancer or a surgeon.

At first, it may seem impossible to teach to all learning styles. However, as we move into using a mix of media or multimedia, it becomes easier. As we understand learning styles, it becomes apparent that multimedia appeals to learners and that a mix of media is more effective because it can meet many types of learning preferences. So, while it is not always possible to constantly match teaching with the learner's preferred learning style, it is important to note how the student learns best and, where possible, to match the teaching. Learners use more than one of these styles at different times so being aware of and teaching to multiple styles will help learners. The variety in teaching presentations may better help keep students' interest, as well.

Kolb's Learning Styles

- Divergent or Concrete—a person learns best working in groups and through interactions, but more as observers than participants. They like to gather information from concrete situations.
- Assimilating—a person learns best when able to listen to information (auditory learning). Silent reading, for example, is a much more difficult method for acquiring information than reading the same information aloud.
- Convergent—a person learns best in response to visual stimuli—pictures, graphs, video clips, and written information—or when lecture-type delivery is supplemented by such stimuli (visual-spatial learning).
- Accommodating—a person learns best when bodily movement is involved (also known as tactile/kinesthetic learning). Learning takes place by the student carrying out a physical activity rather than listening to a lecture or watching a demonstration.

Engagement

We discussed motivation in Chapter 2. Now we look at engagement. The two go together like peanut butter and jelly! If a student is motivated, she is more likely to be engaged in the learning activity. But engagement is an essential feature of student learning.

Engagement has variously been defined as "participating in the activities offered as part of the school program" (Gary Natriello, 1984) and "the time and energy students devote to educationally sound activities inside and outside of the classroom" (George Kuh, 2003). It seems obvious that if students aren't motivated to invest effort and time into participating in learning activities, they are unlikely to succeed in school. And conversely, it seems obvious that those students who are willing to participate and make the necessary effort are the ones most likely to be successful learners.

Keep in mind the discussion of human motivation from Chapter 2 and Maslow's Hierarchy of Needs. Maslow stated that humans are motivated by their unfulfilled needs, starting with the most basic needs. When these basic needs are not met, the person will struggle with the motivation to meet higher level needs.

Considerable research has been conducted into this topic, but interestingly a good deal of the discussion has also focused around what schools and colleges can do to promote student engagement. This is obviously our interest here: what we can do as educators to help students engage.

Heather Wolpert-Gawron asked her middle school students (220 of them) what helps to engage them in learning. You can find details of her suggestions in the box, but these are the 10 things her students told her.

1. Working with their peers.
2. Working with technology.
3. Connecting the real world with the work we do/project-based learning.
4. Clearly love what you do.
5. Get me out of my seat!
6. Bring in visuals.
7. Student choice.
8. Be human.
9. Mix it up.
10. Understand your clients—the kids.

Using the information from Heather Wolpert-Gawron on her blog on engagement, use the checklist to review activities with students:

CHECK	ACTIVITY	DESCRIPTION
1	Let them work with their peers.	Growing learners require and want interaction with other people. Teens find it most interesting and exciting when there is a little bit of talking involved. And discussions allow students to participate in their own learning.

CHECK	ACTIVITY	DESCRIPTION
2	Help them work with technology.	Learning by doing helps them focus. Technology helps them to be more engaged.
3	Connect the real world to the work we do/project-based learning.	It all boils down to relationships—relations between the text and the outside world. Interactions with real-life dilemmas and an opportunity to learn how to solve them helps students connect. Something challenging and not too easy can test you and stimulate your brain.
4	Clearly love what you do.	Let them know you are really passionate about teaching/learning. If you act like you want to be in the classroom with them, the students know. It's about passion! Show them learning is important.
5	Get me out of my seat!	Active learning provides for deeper learning. Movement and activities help brains engage.
6	Bring in visuals.	Pictures, cartoons, a few PowerPoint slides help to get and keep attention.
7	Student choice.	Provide more variety and choices in assignments. Make curriculum flexible for students who are more/less advanced.
8	Be human.	Help students have fun, but you have fun, too!
9	Mix it up!	Use a variety of activities, experiments, plays, etc.
10	Understand the kids.	Encourage them to voice their opinions. Make learning a partnership. Look at learning from their point of view.

Remember that every student engages differently. Find the best way to engage each one. Ask them. Get their input on how they learn.

Adapted from http://www.edutopia.org/blog/student-engagement-stories-heather-wolpert-gawron.

Interventions

When a student receives special help for a weak area of development—whether in the general classroom or out—it is called an intervention. In schools, children who need extra support are often provided with interventions through special education. Many people, when they hear the term "special education," think of a separate classroom for children who cannot succeed in the average general education classroom. In reality, many of the students who qualify to receive services through special education stay in the general education classroom for all or most of their instruction. Some are taken out of class for short periods of time for individualized instruction. Others meet with professionals in the school to receive individual or small-group specialized speech therapy, occupational therapy, or counseling, to name only a few.

Interventions come in many different types. Some are small, quick, and practically invisible to those around the student.

> *For example, this could be a small reward system to encourage or acknowledge participation and effort, or a simple number chart to facilitate mathematic calculations.*

Some interventions are used at a school-wide level, others at the classroom level; some are used with a small group of students, others one-on-one with an individual. Some interventions are considered more or less restrictive than others, ranging from giving praise (not restrictive) to physical handling when a student is acting aggressively and endangering himself or others (extremely restrictive).

Positive Behavior Interventions

You have already learned about Positive Behavioral Interventions and Supports (PBIS) in Chapter 5. Here we will discuss how interventions relate to the overall school philosophy and practice.

School administrators and school personnel have a philosophy regarding how interventions of all kinds should be used in the best interests of the students, the parents, and the school faculty. This philosophy should be expressed openly and made clear to staff, students, and other stakeholders, otherwise it can be assumed that there is general agreement on how behavior should be managed when in reality there may be little or no agreement. This in turn can lead to inconsistency and thence to conflict, with students receiving different messages or expectations (and therefore different rewards and sanctions) from different members of staff. This is a sure recipe for chaos (at best) and anarchy (at worst).

Ideally, when there are rule violations the **Least Restrictive Behavioral Interventions** (LRBI) are chosen for use with students. These interventions are put in place using a **Positive Behavioral Interventions and Supports (PBIS)** system. The PBIS triangle diagram, showing the three tiers of intervention, commonly represents these philosophies.

Here is an example of how this three-tier system of positive support operates for Utah schools, particularly in relation to reading.

Tier I—ALL Students, Core Classroom Instruction

Tier 1 represented by the base of the triangle in the diagram refers to core classroom instruction for **all** students utilizing scientifically based reading research to teach critical elements outlined in the Utah Core Curriculum. Most students will demonstrate proficiency with effective Tier 1 instruction, with many students exceeding this basic standard.

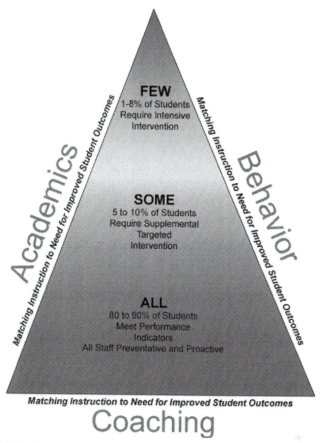

FEW
1-8% of Students
Require Intensive
Intervention

SOME
5 to 10% of Students
Require Supplemental
Targeted
Intervention

ALL
80 to 90% of Students
Meet Performance
Indicators
All Staff Preventative and Proactive

Matching Instruction to Need for Improved Student Outcomes

Coaching

Credit: Christopher Wells Barlow

Tier 2—SOME Students, Supplemental Targeted Instruction

Tier 2 provides supplemental targeted instruction in addition to Tier 1 and addresses the specific needs of students who do not make adequate reading progress in Tier 1. Tier 2 interventions should also be scientifically based and aligned with core classroom instruction. Approximately 5 to 10% of students will likely require Tier 2 instruction. The duration of this instruction varies based on student assessment and progress monitoring data, and it is generally provided by the classroom teacher.

Tier 3—FEW Students, Intensive Targeted Intervention

Tier 3 is designed to provide intensive, targeted intervention to the most at-risk students—those who have not responded adequately to the combination of Tier 1 and Tier 2 instruction. Students in this small group (1 to 8%) usually have severe learning difficulties (such as difficulties with the basics of learning to read) and require instruction that is more explicit, more intensive, and specifically designed to meet their individual needs. Because this intervention is extended over a longer period of time and its form varies based on student assessment and progress monitoring data, it is likely that you as the paraprofessional will be assigned to help sustain this intervention. Tier 3 intervention replaces Tier 2 instruction and is provided by a specialist—often with paraprofessional support.

Student Movement Through the Tiers

Student movement through the three tiers is a fluid process based on student assessment data and collaborative team decisions. At any time during this process, a student may be referred for consideration for a special education evaluation. Tutoring may be necessary in any of the tiers to provide extra practice and support to help students maintain benchmark progress.

Note that the diagram shows how lower tiers provide interventions that are not considered restrictive to the larger student population, while higher tiers provide more intensive and somewhat more restrictive interventions to smaller groups or individuals who need much more help to succeed in school. This is how that would ideally happen.

First, schools provide positive behavior supports that work at a school-wide or whole-classroom level for the vast majority of students in the school. Teachers and administrators use these effective educational practices every day with every student. This first tier of interventions is used to help all students perform better in academics as well as improve their emotional health. In the classroom, common Tier 1 interventions include:

- The lesson the teacher gives to the entire class.
- Class points for good behavior.
- Monitoring each student's progress in math, reading, and other subjects.

Some common school-wide programs include:

- Bullying prevention programs.
- Public posting of students' names for good grades and good behavior.
- Reading tests meant to measure all students' reading abilities.

Tests used to assess all students on a certain skill or ability are known as **screeners**. Screeners are an important part of identifying the need for more intensive interventions in order for students to succeed academically, socially, and emotionally. These screeners can be given by most, if not all, school faculty. They take little time and quickly identify students who are on track, need a little assistance, or are far behind. A common test that is used as a reading screener is the Dynamic Indicators of Basic Early Literacy Skills (DIBELS). DIBELS tests students on reading fluently, comprehending what they read, their ability to identify letters and sounds, and other essential skills for each grade level. Based on student scores, students' needs are easily and accurately identified for each tier of intervention. When a screener is not available, teachers monitor student progress and identify students who are succeeding, those who need a little more help, or those who need much more one-on-one assistance. In all of these cases, data is essential for making decisions.

Response to Intervention (Tier 1)

When data collected on a student leads school personnel to suspect a growing need for specialized help, a referral is made to collect more information on the student's successes and areas of difficulty. The student's **Response to Interventions (RtI)** at the Tier 1 level are measured. If Tier 1 supports are not sufficient to give the student the opportunity to succeed, then more supports are needed. Students could be struggling with reading scores or acting out in class despite the teacher providing plenty of rewards for good behavior and hard work, fun and interesting lessons, and using proper management styles. The student is not succeeding despite the fact that the majority of his peers are doing well.

Individualized Education Program

When the need for more specialized help is determined, the student is referred to members of the **Individual Education Program (IEP) team**. The IEP team makes decisions regarding student placement and interventions. The team usually consists of the student's general education teacher, a special education teacher, a school administrator, the student's parents, and other school specialists who can be of assistance. This may include the school psychologist, the speech and language pathologist, the occupational therapist, the physical therapist, or others with the training and skills relating to the student's particular difficulties. Paraprofessionals are ideally invited to at least part of the meeting to share observational data, or they may be asked by one of the teachers to provide observational data to be shared at the meeting.

When members of the IEP team review the data and assessments of a student, they determine whether a student qualifies for special services. Any special services that are decided on will be written up in an IEP. When determining interventions for each student who needs supplemental help in specific areas, it is important to remember that the least restrictive interventions should be used. This is true whether behavior, academics, or disabilities are being addressed. Interventions are considered more restrictive when students are being punished in any way, are removed from the general education setting, or are receiving different instruction from their same-grade peers. This IEP should then be shared with all school personnel who work with the child on a **need to know** basis. IEP's are confidential and should not be shared with anyone who does not work with the student. This is a legal requirement that applies to paraprofessionals too. It is an important note for paraprofessionals to make. Because you are in the classroom and work with students with special needs, you will likely have access to information that cannot be shared with others who do not work with the child. Be cautious! This is a law and you do not want to violate a legal requirement. The best approach is to assume that you must **not** share the information; check with a teacher or school administrator if you feel that the information should be shared with an individual and get permission first.

> Because you are in the classroom and work with students with special needs, you will likely have access to information that cannot be shared with others who do not work with the child. Be cautious! This is a law and you do not want to violate a legal requirement. Always consult a teacher or school administrator before sharing any information with anyone.

Response to Intervention (Tier 2)

Once it is determined that a student needs more than Tier 1 interventions, Tier 2 (SOME) interventions are typically implemented. These supplemental, targeted interventions can be used with an individual student or with small groups of students who have similar needs; they may be given to a group all at once or to each member individually. Tier 2 interventions look to increase structure and specificity. An example of a Tier 2 intervention would be a student, teacher, and school psychologist creating a behavior contract that gives the student rewards or **reinforcement** for meeting the expected behaviors in the contract. You, the paraprofessional, may be instrumental in implementing the plan and taking data on its success. Other Tier 2 interventions could include:

- Peer tutoring programs.
- Creating a video of students performing tasks so those having difficulty can watch and learn the behavior.
- Rewarding good behavior with tokens that can then be used like money to buy rewards or privileges.

Tier 2 interventions could also include more restrictive interventions such as time out or detention. But in general, using positive, rewarding interventions for good behavior is much more effective than punishing students after they have done something wrong.

Response to Intervention (Tier 3)

Once Tier 2 interventions have been implemented, some students may need even more help. As data is gathered on student progress, students who need more intensive and possibly more restrictive interventions are identified. Students can require Tier 3 interventions for multiple reasons. Students who have profound disabilities that impede their ability to learn at the pace required in the general education classroom—such as an intellectual disability—may need intensive help at a slower pace. Students with extreme behavior problems, such as aggression and violence, may also need to be instructed in an environment with much more structure than the general education class. They may also need teachers and paraprofessional staff who are trained to properly implement more restrictive Tier 3 interventions. These will quite likely be special education classrooms. They are often referred to as units, such as the severe unit, behavior unit, or Autism unit. Time out rooms, used for exclusionary time out, are often in the units. Some of the students with severe disabilities may need help using the bathroom, eating, or moving around the school. This type of classroom is often what people think about when they think of special education. But only a very small percentage of students served under special education are served in these settings.

Other Tier 3 (FEW) interventions can be implemented while the student remains in the general education classroom. In order to provide the least restrictive interventions, schools must keep students in the general education classroom as much as possible. (This is a legal requirement of the Individuals with Disabilities Education Act.) Students often go out of the general education classroom for short tutoring sessions in math, reading, speech therapy, counseling, etc. Other students may be able to behave well enough to be in the general education classroom but occasionally have extreme behaviors that require behavioral interventions. Many times a paraprofessional will accompany the student in the general classroom and will be available to provide behavior interventions when/ if the extreme acting-out behavior occurs. In rare cases it may require manual restraints. This involves holding the student to stop him from harming another student or himself. Only trained staff can perform this intervention, with as little force as possible, and only in extreme cases. (Note: if as a paraprofessional you are not trained—you must request and get training first before attempting to restrain a violent or aggressive student!)

If the behavior happens infrequently—once or twice in a week, twice in a month, or four times in a year—then the behavior is not considered an emergency, but it is a clear pattern of behavior and must be planned for in the student's IEP. The IEP team will observe and collect data to determine the function of the behavior and to plan appropriate interventions. You'll learn more about this on the following pages under the heading Functional Behavior Assessments (FuBA).

Whenever the most restrictive interventions are used, they must be closely supervised and data recorded. It is also important to remember that such intensive interventions should be followed by high rates of praise for appropriate behaviors throughout the day—in keeping with the school-wide positive support plan. These interventions may also cause students to cry, whine, scream, or fight with staff. People who are not aware of the situation may see these interventions as abusive or otherwise inappropriate. However, if you observe any teachers or staff clearly performing interventions in an abusive manner, report this immediately to a teacher, school psychologist, behavior specialist, or an administrator. The first priority of school personnel must always be the safety of the students.

The Data

State and national laws and policies require data to be gathered on student progress and achievement. Decisions on placement, the effectiveness of interventions, and the effectiveness of academic instruction are all determined by gathering data. **Progress monitoring** is used to track a student's gains and the associated effectiveness of the interventions being implemented. Many times school personnel work hard to help the students but have no tangible evidence of their hard work. There must be data to show that students, especially those in severe units where progress can be slow and hard to identify, are making gains. Paraprofessionals often observe and record these data—both for academic and behavior progress.

Functional Behavior Assessments

Functional Behavior Assessments (FuBAs or FBAs) are performed when problem behaviors arise that are affecting the ability of students to make academic progress or that cause physical or emotional harm. School psychologists and/or behavior specialists often perform these assessments. The goal of a FuBA is to understand when a behavior happens and why it continues to happen so that the negative behavior can be stopped and replaced by a positive behavior. When a FuBA is performed, the student is observed in the setting where the behavior occurs. The goal is to determine what happened right before the negative or target behavior to make it happen or to trigger it (antecedent). You learned about the ABCs of behavior in Chapter 2. The behavior (B) is then observed as well as the consequences (C) that the student receives immediately after performing the behavior. The consequences of a behavior either encourage the student to repeat the behavior or discourage the behavior.

All behaviors have a purpose, and different consequences may encourage different student behaviors. Research has shown that four basic things encourage, or **reinforce**, a behavior:

1. **Escape** from an undesired situation or task.
2. **Attention** from adults or peers.
3. **Obtaining** desired items or privileges.
4. **Sensory** stimulation.

School psychologists and the IEP team try to determine which of these four **functions** of behavior are reinforcing the negative behavior. Once the function is determined, a **behavior intervention plan** (BIP) is created.

Research has shown that four basic things encourage, or **reinforce**, a behavior:
- **Escape** from an undesired situation or task.
- **Attention** from adults or peers.
- **Obtaining** desired items or privileges.
- **Sensory** stimulation.

This plan identifies interventions that can replace the negative behavior with a positive behavior that fulfills the same reinforcing function. For example, a student might make inappropriate comments in class because the teacher and other students give her attention. The intervention will try to give the student attention for good behavior such as doing well on a test in order to fulfill the need for attention, making the inappropriate comments unnecessary.

The Support

Schools employ a variety of professionals who help students learn, and many of them specialize in helping students with disabilities. School psychologists help create behavior plans for students and assess intellectual abilities. Speech and language therapists/pathologists help students verbally communicate better. Physical therapists and occupational therapists help students with physical disabilities extend and develop their physical capacity and mobility. School counselors help students overcome emotional concerns and plan their future. Translators help students and their parents who speak other languages communicate with teachers and administrators. Each school district will have a variety of other professionals to help meet the needs of the students in their district. And as you already know, schools often employ paraprofessionals to provide more services for more students. You also know that paraprofessionals fill a wide variety of roles. Some help teachers grade papers, tutor students, or create projects for students. Others help special education teachers with students in special education units. Regardless of what role a paraprofessional is performing in a school, it is important to remember that all the children must be treated appropriately. The plans for the least restrictive interventions must be used. If you haven't been given this information, request it. But remember: praise, rewards, and other positive supports should be used over punishments.

Praise

One of the simplest evidenced-based practices that has been used successfully in schools to improve behavior and academics and that you can use as a paraprofessional is **praise**. Praise can be implemented within an MTSS or a School-Wide Positive Behavioral Interventions and Supports (SWPBIS) program, or you can choose to use it consistently and systematically within your own work setting. There are a variety of methods for using praise to reinforce appropriate behavior. Here we look at verbal praise and written praise.

Verbal Praise

Studies have found that the more teachers provide positive verbal praise, the more time students spend on task. This includes students at risk for behavior concerns. Verbal praise not only increases students' on-task behavior, it also has been shown to be socially valid among teachers. Teachers reported that after focusing on using verbal praise in their classroom, they noticed a positive change in their classroom environment. They felt comfortable providing those increased levels of praise, and the praise did not need to interfere with their teaching.

Written Praise

Written praise can take several different forms. An A+ on a paper is a short form of written praise. Likewise, short phrases such as, "Nice handwriting," "Good work," or "Well-written paper" can also be considered written praise.

A more extensive form of written praise is the **praise note** (see nearby box for an example). The purpose of praise notes is to reward and recognize students who follow the school-wide focus for behavior and academics. The praise note should make reference to the social skills and behavior plans that have been developed using the school-wide, data-based action plan. So comments might refer to such skills as (a) making good choices, (b) accepting responsibility, (c) showing appreciation, or (d) resolving differences.

Praise notes have been found to be an effective, proactive approach to influencing classroom behavior, particularly when the praise is contingent and specific.

Credit: Christopher Wells Barlow

Their use is more common among elementary and middle schools, but we see increased use in secondary settings with good results. In fact, one study found on-task behavior increased by 90% in some middle schools when praise notes were used consistently and appropriately. In another study, teachers wrote positive comments on post cards and sent them to the students by mail. Imagine receiving a postcard that says something great about what you did: you know your family may have read it, the postal carrier, and who knows who else may have seen it? That's a wonderful way to receive your praise!

Praise notes on a three-by-five note card:
- The student's name.
- Date.
- A check box next to the printed school expectation being followed.
- Teacher signature.
- Specific comment (e.g., Denzel did a great job resolving a conflict in the parking lot!).

Effective Praise

Studies have shown that to be the most effective the **praise must be specific.** You know this from your own experience. A statement from a dear friend, "You look nice today," doesn't mean as much as specific praise, "You look great in that shirt. The dark blue color complements your skin tone." That specific praise can make you feel good, but it is also likely to influence your choice of colors when you next dress for work or for going out with friends. Praise works that way with most students, too. Telling them what they did "right" increases the probability that they will do that specific thing more frequently. In fact, without the specific reference to what they did right, they may have no idea what they did to earn the praise, and they certainly won't know what to do if they like the praise and want more of it.

Praise is such a commonly used commodity that we can become quite careless in using it. Some studies have suggested that we also have to be careful of the focus of our praise. For example, we may say to a student, "You're really good at math!" And that may be a true statement, but it suggests a fixed characteristic of the student: good at math. This type of "personal" praise is fine as far as it goes and may make the student feel good. But what about the student who's not good at math? Is he or she to receive no praise? What the research suggests is that it's more helpful to praise something that the student has control over, such as effort, rather than what seems like a quality he or she is born with. So a praise statement such as, "You worked really hard on that math problem," is better because it highlights something the student has done and that he or she can do again—both in order to receive more praise and in order to increase his or her chances of successful learning. This is sometimes referred to as "process" praise rather than the "personal" praise described above. In classrooms where adults use process praise, students are more likely to be willing to engage with the learning process, even with more difficult tasks. Personal praise can be discouraging for students who are not good at something, because they see little point in making an effort if they're not "good at math" (or whichever other curriculum area they are currently working on).

Studies have also found that students who misbehave frequently are much less likely to receive praise than students who behave properly most of the time—even when they do things right! We can change that by being more positive with all students. Catch them doing what they should—and then praise them.

There are additional ways you can give written praise to the students. List a few of your ideas here—or some examples of written praise that you have seen from paraprofessional or teacher colleagues.

Multi-Tier Systems of Support (MTSS) Programs

An MTSS is a systemic, continuous-improvement framework in which data-based problem solving and decision making are practiced across all levels of the educational system. Its purpose is to ensure that **every** student receives the appropriate level of support to be successful. In practical terms, it should enable schools and districts to organize resources in such a way that every student's performance is accelerated, although this is possible only when academic standards and behavioral expectations are implemented with fidelity and sustained over time. One such system has been extensively developed in Kansas.

MTSS uses the principles of both RtI and PBIS (see box below), with the goal of offering a comprehensive and responsive framework for systemically addressing barriers to student learning. MTSS offers the potential to create systemic change, which results in improved academic and social outcomes for all learners. This is possible only if an integrated, system-wide approach is used to govern the use of resources, strategies, structures, and practice. Interventions available to students are typically categorized into three tiers.

Key Principles of MTSS

- Intervene early.
- Use a multi-tiered model of service delivery.
- Match instruction to the learners' needs.
- Use progress-monitoring data to change instruction within each tier.
- Use research-based interventions and instruction.
- Monitor student progress frequently.
- Employ practices to ensure that interventions are implemented consistently and correctly.
- Provide multiple levels of support for all learners (struggling through advanced).
- Focus on collaboration between general education and special education.
- Provide professional development that is aligned across school and district settings.

Benefits of MTSS

MTSS addresses the academic as well as social, emotional, and behavioral development of children from early childhood to graduation. The benefits derive from schools and districts engaging in aligning resources, promoting greater collaboration, and striving to serve students when they first struggle academically and behaviorally. This leads to:

- Gains in reading and math assessment scores for all students.
- A decrease in inappropriate referrals to special education, particularly for minority students.
- A decrease in office discipline referrals and suspensions.
- Improved collaboration between general and special education.

The Kansas State Department of Education (KSDE) reported the effects of using MTSS on K-12 student behavioral outcomes. This included a reduction in behavioral referrals from 1,151 in 2011–12 to 716 in 2012–13, with an estimated saving of 145 student hours and 181 hours for administrators.

MTSS Versus RtI

We have heard it said that MTSS and RtI are one in the same. This is not necessarily true. Basically, the difference between RtI and MTSS is that RtI is an integral part of MTSS, but MTSS is more cohesive and comprehensive in the goal of meeting the needs of all learners. Here is a brief explanation:

> *RtI is a school-based approach to providing support for students who are struggling, whether academically or behaviorally. Although it is not primarily or exclusively an approach designed to address behavior, it is a structured, team approach with a range of individuals contributing ideas to address a particular, identified need. RtI is used to help meet the guidelines mandated by No Child Left Behind 2002, but it was initially conceived as a prevention framework to provide early intervention to students at risk of reading failure.*

In Chapter 1 you learned about the Individuals with Disabilities Education Act (IDEA) of 2004, which compelled schools to incorporate a Response to Intervention that addressed the needs of students before they failed. RtI soon became a concept that reached beyond just reading; it moved to all academic content areas as well as behavior.

Restorative Practice

Restorative Practice has developed from the principles of Restorative Justice, an approach now widely adopted in the criminal justice system in a number of countries in the Western hemisphere. Restorative Justice was developed out of a concern for repeat offenders—criminals who, after serving a custodial sentence and leaving prison, would return to commit the same crimes for which they had previously been punished. Research showed that one of the important elements necessary for reformed behavior that was missing in these repeat offenders was any real remorse for their crimes. This appeared to be largely due to a lack of awareness of the effects of their crimes on the victims. They could reoffend because they remained detached from the people they targeted.

In 2008 the UK's Youth Justice Board published a report, *Restorative Justice,* that examined research carried out in the UK, USA, and Australia. It acknowledged that results differed according to types of crime, but overall the evidence showed worthwhile reductions in rearrests following the use of RJ with youth offenders. Importantly, there were also positive results for victims, with reductions in anger and vengeful thoughts toward the offender,

(Continued)

as well as greater confidence in the criminal justice system and higher levels of satisfaction with the process overall as compared with standard police and justice system processes.

Restorative Justice brings together the victim and the criminal/perpetrator to talk about the crime, face to face. The meeting is, of course, supervised. The victims participate only after counseling ensures that they will not be traumatized by meeting the offender. Both victim and perpetrator are allowed to tell their story—to describe the crime from their own perspective.

Restorative Practice uses the same model to deal with conflict in schools and other settings. When one student has offended another by his or her behavior—whether it be bullying, rudeness, or other types of conflict, the two students are brought together and both are given time to tell their own version of the event or incident, supervised by an adult. Students who engage in Restorative Practice are taught the ground rules before the conversation or conference takes place. For example, while one is talking, the other is not allowed to interrupt. There also is a set of particular questions that the facilitator asks—phrased in neutral terms and focusing on the effects of the behavior, particularly the emotions of the participants.

The International Institute for Restorative Practices (IIRP) makes the distinction between "adversarial" and "restorative" language. Instead of asking, "Who's to blame?" and "How shall we punish them?" (a traditional adversarial approach), restorative language and practice asks "Who's been harmed?" and "How can we put this right?"

Ideally, schools adopt Restorative Practice wholesale and all students are introduced to the process before incidents occur. Thus they know beforehand that if they behave in ways that are considered inappropriate and that affect particular individuals, they will be required to go through the process and confront the impact of their behavior on the other person. This is more than the simple, "Say you're sorry" or "Shake hands" that teachers and paraprofessionals often use in schools when one student has offended another by his or her behavior. Such actions are really just Band-Aids. They are least restrictive responses to inappropriate behavior in that they deal with the incidents quickly and allow everyone to return to teaching and learning. However, they may just represent a temporary truce as the underlying problem remains unresolved and is likely to result in further disturbances—at recess, after school, in the lunchroom.

One of the other elements of Restorative Practice that helps to establish it as part of the ethos of the school is the use of student facilitators. Students can be trained to conduct or supervise the exchanges between the offender and offended—it does not need to be an adult in every case. Obviously, for serious or physically threatening incidents, an adult would have to be present. However, for the more minor incidents, peer facilitation can be equally effective.

The principles underlying both the original legal setting and now the education setting involve:

- Increased awareness on the part of the individual who has behaved inappropriately of the effects of that behavior on others.
- Engagement with the person who has been affected so that the problem has a "face" and cannot be dismissed as something impersonal.
- A reframing of the offense as an offense against an individual (or group of individuals) as much as an offense against the state or organization (such as the school).

Although school staff must be trained to use Restorative Practices effectively, those who have embraced this philosophy school wide consider the rewards well worth it. Students take the principles on board and become more sensitive to the effects of their behavior on others. Many schools report significant decreases in the numbers of petty incidents, in particular, along with an improvement in the general atmosphere of the school. Students are seen to engage with the principles of Restorative Practice voluntarily, even without being compelled by a member of the staff. It is a collaborative process of peaceful resolution rather than coercion and forced behavior change by an authority figure. It's worth noting that Restorative Practice meetings need not be held for every small incident and, of course, it is specifically for use where inappropriate behavior has impacted another individual or group of individuals.

Write your thoughts here. You may also wish to take the opportunity to discuss these elements with your teacher to see where you might jointly improve behavior and the school's general ethos.

If you search the YouTube website with the keywords *Restorative Justice* or *Restorative Practice* you will find a great many fascinating accounts of how these practices have literally turned around the lives of those involved.

Consider the elements of Restorative Practice—offender and offended meeting to talk through the offense; the use of neutral prompts for this discussion through the presence of a facilitator (adult or peer); collaborative resolution and decision making rather than authoritative, forced behavior change. Identify events where you have seen any of these elements in operation in your school setting. Or if you have not, consider which of the elements you personally might adopt within your sphere of influence relating to student behavior.

Circle Time

This is a practice that has become much more widespread in schools in the last several years and is used in a variety of ways. In general, it provides a forum for a teacher and his or her students to discuss issues and concerns, including behavior, feelings, and social skills. It can be used simply to "check in" with students at the beginning of the day or as part of a more complex, structured approach such as P4C (see below). Circle time is literally what it says: time spent sitting in a circle (on chairs or on the floor if there is a carpeted area of the classroom) to facilitate discussion. The informal setting itself signals a change of format, but it also allows all participants to see each other and to hear comments made. It is also more suggestive of a democratic process with everyone equal, the adult sitting in the circle along with the students and facilitating rather than leading the discussion.

Philosophy for Children (P4C)

P4C is a very specific program developed with a clear set of procedures to promote thinking and discussion skills among students. As with the other approaches we discuss here, P4C has a set of ground rules for participants. And as with all procedures or systems, these need to be clearly explained and practiced by students so that they enable the discussion to take place without interruption.

One of the attractions of an approach such as P4C may be that it is new—almost like a new game, the students are perhaps more willing to engage and follow "new" rules that they might not otherwise obey in the classroom.

It also has a particular layout—chairs in a circle (approximately) without tables. This may differ from the regular classroom activities and helps to signal that students are engaged in a different activity and there are different expectations.

Students do not necessarily engage with the ground rules straight away. They may take time to accept and follow them, but P4C is a democratic process—many of the decisions (about the topic to be discussed, for example) are made by the students and decided by majority vote. So if there are students who refuse to abide by the decisions, then they are rejecting the decisions of the majority—the decisions of their peers rather than the teacher.

At the back of the book you will find some websites for further information on P4C and its application in the classroom.

Consider how some of the principles underlying these practices might be adopted in your work settings. This is an opportunity to "dream" what an ideal classroom could look like with application of these principles.

Write how you would enhance your classroom or school. You may wish to record your thoughts in the form of a mind map.

Summary

In this chapter you have looked at a variety of programs and strategies to address behavioral issues. MTSS are much broader than your role as a paraprofessional, but you can take an important role in the implementation. As a result of studying this chapter you can describe things you can do to support an MTSS or RtI system in your school. You can describe the focus on the theory of learning styles as it relates to students with behavioral issues and how appropriate curriculum relates to acting out and withdrawal behaviors.

Learning Outcomes

After completing this chapter you should now be able to describe:

* The focus on the theory of learning styles as it relates to students with behavioral issues.
* How appropriate curriculum relates to acting out and withdrawal behaviors.
* Response to Interventions (RtI) and Multi-Tier Systems of Support (MTSS).

You can discuss, either orally or in writing, the role that paraprofessionals can take in supporting students with behavioral problems through these programs:

- Restorative Practice.
- Circle Time.
- P4C.

Looking Ahead

In Chapter 8, readers will have opportunities to reflect on changes in philosophy and approach to behavior. You will see how the information gained throughout the text can relate to your responsibilities as a paraprofessional.

Bibliography

Batsche, G. (2005). Multi-tiered systems of support for inclusive schools. In J. McLeskey, N. L. Waldron, F. Spooner, B. Algozzine, (Eds.), *Handbook of effective inclusive schools: Research and practice*. New York: Routledge, Taylor & Francis.

Brophy, J. (1981). Teacher praise: A functional analysis. *Review of Educational Research, 51*(1), 5–32. doi:10.2307/1170249.

Circle time: The cooperative classroom. Accessed June 30, 2014. Accessed at www.circletime.co.uk/.

Duchaine, E. L., Jolivete, K., & Fredrick, L. D. (2011). The effect of teacher coaching with performance feedback on behavior-specific praise in inclusion classrooms. *Education and Treatment of Children, 34*, 209–227.

Dunn, R., & Dunn, K. (1978). *Teaching students through their individual learning styles: A practical approach*. Reston, VA: Reston Publishing Company.

Florida Problem-Solving/Response to Intervention Project. (2011). Continuous improvement: The problem-solving process. In the *Florida Department of Education guiding principles: Meeting the needs of all students*. Retrieved from www.floridarti.org/_docs/GTIPS.pdf.

Garner, H. (1999). *Intelligence reframed: Multiple intelligences for the 21st century*. New York: Basic Books.

Guskey, T. R., & Yoon, K. S. (2009). What works in professional development? *Phi Delta Kappan, 90*(7), 495–500.

Implementing the Common Core State Standards. Common Core State Standards Initiative. Accessed at www.corestandards.org/.

Irvin, L. K., Horner, R. H., Ingram, K., Todd, A. W., Sugai, G., Sampson, N. K., & Boland, J. B. (2006). Using office discipline referral data for decision making about student behavior in elementary and middle schools: An empirical evaluation of validity. *Journal of Positive Behavior Interventions, 8*(1), 10–23. doi:10.1177/10983007060080010301.

Kalis, T. M., Vannest, K. J., & Parker, R. (2007). Praise counts: Using self-monitoring to increase effective teaching practices. *Preventing School Failure, 51*(3), 20–27.

Kansas Multi-Tier System of Supports. (2010). School-wide behavior support within the Kansas MTSS framework. Retrieved from www.kansasmtss.org/briefs/School-wide_Behavioral_Support_within_MTSS.pdf.

Kolb, D. (1984). *Experiential learning: Experience as the source of learning and development*. Englewood Cliffs, NJ: Prentice-Hall.

Kuh, G. (2003). What we're learning about student engagement from NSSE. *Change*, March/April, 24–32.

Lewis, T. J., & Sugai, G. (1999). Safe schools: School-wide discipline practices. In L. M. Bullock & R. A. Gable (Eds.), Third CCBD mini-library series, *What works for children and youth with E/BD*. Arlington, VA: Council for Children with Behavioral Disorders.

Lloyd, G., & Munn, P. (Eds.). (1998). *Sharing good practice: Prevention and support for pupils with social, emotional and behavioural difficulties.* Edinburgh: Moray House Publications.

Luiselli, J. K., Putnam, R. F., Handler, M. W., & Feinberg, A. B. (2005). Whole-school positive behaviour support: Effects on student discipline problems and academic performance. *Educational Psychology, 25*(2–3), 183–198.

Maslow, A. H. (1943). A theory of human motivation. *Psychological Review, 50*(4), 370–96. Retrieved from http://psychclassics.yorku.ca/Maslow/motivation.htm.

Mosley, J. (1993). *Turn your school round.* Wisbech, Cambridgeshire: LDA.

Mosley, J., & Tew, M. (1999). *Quality circle time in the secondary school: A handbook of good practice.* London: David Fulton Publishers.

Natriello, G. (1984). Problems in the evaluation of students and student disengagement from secondary schools. *Journal of Research and Development in Education, 17,* 14–24.

Nelson, J.A.P., Young, B. J., Young, E. L., & Cox, G. (2009). Using teacher-written praise notes to promote a positive environment in a middle school. *Preventing School Failure, 54*(2), 119–125.

No Child Left Behind Act of 2001 (NCLB). 20 U.S.C. § 6319 (2008). Accessed at www2.ed.gov/policy/elsec/leg/esea02/index.html.

Osher, D., Bear, G. G., Sprague, J. R., & Doyle, W. (2010). How can we improve school discipline? *Educational Researcher, 39*(1), 48–58.

Office of Special Education Programs (OSEP). Technical assistance center: Positive behavior intervention supports (PBIS) (2014). Accessed at www.pbis.org/school/swpbis-for-beginners.

Ready or Not: Creating a High School Diploma That Counts. Achieve, Inc. December 10, 2004. Retrieved October 4, 2013. Accessed at www.achieve.org/ReadyorNot.

Sherman, L. W., & Strang, H., with Newbury-Birch, D. (2008). *Restorative Justice.* London: UK Youth Justice Board.

Sugai, G., Sprague, J. R., Horner, R. H., & Walker, H. M. (2000). Preventing school violence: The use of office discipline referrals to assess and monitor schoolwide discipline interventions. *Journal of Emotional and Behavioral Disorders, 8*(2), 94–101.

Swinson, J., & Harrop, A. (2005). An examination of the effects of a short course aimed at enabling teachers in infant, junior and secondary schools to alter the verbal feedback given to pupils. *Educational Studies, 31*(3), 115–129.

Swinson, J., & Knight, R. (2007). Teacher verbal feedback directed towards secondary pupils with challenging behavior and its relationship to their behavior. *Educational Psychology in Practice, 23*(3), 241–255.

The P4C Cooperative: Philosophy for Children. (May 13, 2014). Accessed at www.p4c.com.

Thornton, L. (2013). Teacher perceptions regarding positive behavior intervention support. *Dissertation Abstracts International,* Section A, 73.

Trickey, S. (2007). Promoting social and cognitive development in schools: An evaluation of thinking through philosophy. In The 13th International Conference on Thinking, Norrkoping, Sweden, June 17–21, 2007. Linkopings University Electronic Conference Proceedings. Accessed at www.ep.liu.se/ecp/021/vol1/026?ecp2107026.pdf.

Trickey, S., & Topping, K. J. (2004). Philosophy for children: A systematic review. *Research Papers in Education, 19*(3), 363–378.

Utah Parent Center. Information Sheet. RtI in Utah. Accessed at www.utahparentcenter.org/resources/response-to-intervention/rti-in-utah/.

Wolpert-Gawron, H. (June 17, 2014). Edutopia. Accessed at www.edutopia.org/users/heather-wolpert-gawron.

Chapter 8

Tying Things Up

What You Will Learn

Learning Outcomes:

The chapter will be a little different because you will be reviewing what you learned in earlier chapters. After a quick review you will be able to demonstrate, orally or in written form, your knowledge of the primary focus on behavior and learning—especially as it applies to students with disabilities. We consider the major themes that recur throughout the book, including Least Restrictive Behavioral Interventions (LRBI) and Positive Behavioral Interventions and Supports (PBIS) and how they apply to learning and behavior.

In this culminating chapter, you will also be able to dig a little deeper into the questions of motivation and choice because, as we discussed in Chapter 4, students choose how to behave, so we need to know how best to motivate them to make appropriate choices. We need to make them aware that they have choices. And as educators, surely one of our goals is to help develop self-determination in our students—the ability to make their own choices and take responsibility for their own behavior.

A Focus on Positive Behaviors

If you look back through the book, you'll notice how often we refer to the need for educators to focus on positive behavior. In the Introduction we stated:

> *The purpose of behavior management systems—whatever shape they take—is first to establish positive and appropriate behaviors ... the only way to successfully promote positive behavior is to focus on that positive behavior and use it to crowd out potential negative behaviors.*

And since that early statement we have used the word "positive" almost 200 times. We devoted the whole of Chapter 3 to Plan A: what can be done to promote positive behaviors so that they help to crowd out inappropriate behavior. So by now we hope the message has come through clearly. But we also hope it has made an impact on your classroom and personal life practices too. On the next page you will

Changing Practice: Focusing on the Positive

Take a moment to focus on what you do and how you have changed in terms of a greater focus on students' positive behavior as a result of studying the material in this book.

☐ Have you identified a particular student whose behavior has caused you concern? Have you have taken specific steps to focus on some of his/her positive behaviors rather than focusing only on the inappropriate behavior?

☐ Have you made deliberate attempts to recognize the positive behaviors that occur daily in your classroom, particularly those of students who always behave appropriately?

☐ Have you made any changes to the type of praise you offer to students, making it more specific—rather than using vague praise statements such as "Good job"— so that students know what they've done to deserve that praise?

☐ When you need to correct a student's behavior, are you now focusing on the behavior rather than criticizing the student?

☐ Are you focusing on "model" student behavior to encourage other students to behave similarly?

☐ Are you consistent in providing rewards to all students for positive behavior? (No extras for the student who typically misbehaves—once he/she behaves appropriately, the same reward is available as you give to other students.)

☐ Do you express your confidence in your students' ability to live up to the high behavioral expectations of the classroom?

What other things have you changed to increase your focus on positive behavior?

find a checklist to facilitate reflection on this aspect of behavior management. We have provided space for additional aspects of your practice you may have changed or that may have been enhanced.

In Chapter 3 we reported on the Rosenthal experiment, where students were told that they were very smart and those high expectations set for them led them to excel. This work became so famous that today it is called the *Pygmalion effect*, or the *Rosenthal effect*, and signifies that the greater the expectation placed upon people, the better they perform. (The Pygmalion effect is named after the Greek myth of Pygmalion—see nearby box.) Comprehensive School-Wide Positive Behavioral Interventions and Supports systems (SWPBIS) have high expectations for students as one of their defining characteristics. All school personnel are encouraged to build students' self-esteem and confidence. But let's not forget that teachers' and paraprofessionals' expectations, whether high or low, can lead to a self-fulfilling prophecy.

Pygmalion—High Aspirations Realized

According to Greek legend, Pygmalion was a sculptor who carved a statue so beautiful that he fell in love with it, bringing it gifts and worshiping it. He prayed to the goddess Aphrodite that the statue could be brought to life so that he could marry her. Aphrodite—impressed by his devotion, and the fact that the statue bore a remarkable resemblance to herself—granted his wish.

This myth suggests the possibility that the best and most beautiful things can be created—or brought to life—by a dedicated artist. The idea has been repeated in such stories as George Bernard Shaw's play *Pygmalion* (with the film interpretation *My Fair Lady*), where a refined and beautiful woman is brought to life or "created" from a street flower seller.

In the nearby textbox are some examples of the language you can use to show your high expectations of students. Remember that we teach and encourage behavior as deliberately as we teach academics.

Language Showing High Expectations of Students

- I'll let you try that next math problem on your own. You don't need me looking over your shoulder, do you? I'll check back in a few minutes.
- Wow, you did that really well. I bet you could do the next one too—it's just a little harder.
- Jake, you set a good example to the other students by getting your work finished last class period. Thank you.
- This one is hard, but I know you can do it, and the teacher and I can help you.
- You can do this. I've seen you do a math problem like this before and you got it right.
- You've been taught the behavior that I expect to see. I know you can do it.

There is an indelible link between expectations and motivation. It is evident when students show a desire to learn (intrinsic motivation) because it interests them or they recognize the importance of learning. Students are, of course, more motivated when they see the value of learning. And when they experience success, they are also more motivated. The importance, then, is to know that every learning opportunity—every lesson or activity—is a chance for students to experience success, enjoy learning, and become more motivated to learn.

Motivation

There may have been times when you've heard a teacher or a parent say, "Maria just isn't motivated." The lessons may be interesting, adequately paced, and geared to Maria's learning level. So what is it that causes her to be unmotivated? Let's examine motivation in more detail.

To be motivated is to be moved to do something. Motivation could be defined as a process of starting, directing, and maintaining physical and psychological activities. The term "motivation" is used to describe the process as well as the intensity and persistence of our actions, which means that different students have different amounts and different kinds of motivation.

> Motivation is literally the desire to do things. It's the difference between waking up before dawn to pound the pavement and lazing around the house all day. It's also the difference between completing a research paper and merely gazing about the classroom.

Because the act of being motivated is a difficult one to observe, researchers have developed theories about it. Some have described the sources of motivation as instinct, expectation, drive, and incentives. We feel that these are useful concepts, so let's discuss them briefly. You will have an opportunity to decide which, if any, of the theories you believe function as the source of motivation and how they relate to your students.

Instinct

In the early 1900s, Sigmund Freud, the Austrian founder of psychoanalysis, proposed that human drive, or motivation, arises from life and death instincts. He framed it as a subconscious reaction rather than a carefully thought out or considered action. However, this theory was somewhat discredited by later research, which found huge variations in behavior between individuals and across cultures. And of course, rarely are there actual life and death situations in the classroom, so you won't see that. However, daily or weekly you will see many variations in cultural "instincts." For example, the teacher or paraprofessional who uses competition for most activities will soon see that some students do not respond well to competition. The students may try to withdraw from the activity or may be found helping another student to do better, negating the supposed benefits of competition. This is particularly true of the Native American Navajo culture, for example, where it is considered inappropriate to put yourself forward or first—the interests of the tribe or family are given first priority.

The same type of issues may arise with the commonly used strategy of collaborative work, where some cultures would consider it inappropriate, or even a form of cheating, to be helped by another student or to share work and ideas.

Expectation

In the previous section of the chapter we discussed paraprofessionals and teachers having high expectations for student achievement. Now let's look at expectations from the students' perspective. "Expectation" refers to the idea that in the future it is likely you will get something—hopefully something you want. But remember that some of your students have very low or negative expectations because that is what life as they know it has taught them. Not surprisingly, theorists have hypothesized that motivation to reach a goal is likely to be greater if it is a goal you value and if it is highly likely that you will attain the goal (i.e., if you have high expectations).

You have no doubt seen this in your own life, but as a paraprofessional you also can see it in the students with whom you work. Some are capable and high achieving students who are motivated by the idea of gaining a high school diploma or a high score on the assessment for the Core Curriculum. And conversely, some students have low motivation because they expect that they cannot reach the goal. They believe it is too difficult a goal to reach—based on their previous experience and achievements—or it is not a goal they value.

Think of the high school student who says, "Why graduate? I can go to work now and make more money than my teacher is making. I don't see the value in high school and college. It's just more years of homework and tests that I hate anyway!" This may not be an attitude you approve of, but for some students this will actually be true—they may be much more motivated by the immediate certainty of earning money than by the less certain benefits of continuing study.

Effective Schools

This is a good point at which to remind ourselves of some of the characteristics of effective (and less effective) schools as identified from the research.
  Less effective schools:
- Provide ineffective instruction.
- Use punitive management techniques.
- Show a lack of appropriate social skills among staff and students.
- Have unclear expectations.
- Lack individualized instruction.
- Develop a pattern of students dropping out, absenteeism, suspension, and expulsion—and take insufficient action to combat these.
- Have poor academic offerings in reading, writing, and math.

Most effective schools:
- Have school-wide positive behavior support plans.
- Devote more time to learning than to behavioral issues.
- Protect the rights of students with disabilities.
- Have high expectations of all students and express those expectations frequently so that students know the teachers and paraprofessionals are rooting for them and believe in their capabilities.
- Use optimum interventions to address more than the aggressive behavior of specific students; interventions seem to create a local school environment that allows for the academic and social success of all students.

PBIS, LRBI, and Tiered Support

We introduced these concepts in the Introduction and discussed them more fully in Chapter 1. The importance of PBIS lies both in individual educator's classroom approaches and in the philosophy and ethos of the whole school. It links directly to what we have just been saying about focusing on positive aspects of behavior. However, it also reminds us that:

- We need to take deliberate steps to assist students in behaving appropriately (the *I* in PBIS standing for *Interventions,* the *S* for *Supports*—both things we need to plan for and put into place proactively).
- Students will need support both for maintaining positive behavior and for changing their behavior when it is inappropriate. Some students in particular come to us with a whole repertoire and history of poor behavior. This can be true even for our youngest students—by the time they enter kindergarten, they have already had as much as five years of "training" and encouragement for behaving in particular ways, and those ways may not match the ways of the school or of your classroom. They may in fact be in direct opposition to the standards set for a classroom where learning is a priority and educators are determined to not let inappropriate behavior get in the student's way.

As a paraprofessional, you can assist with teaching and modeling behavioral expectations, reteaching rules, writing up discipline referrals, passing out recognition slips, assisting with teaching materials, and giving verbal praise for appropriate behavior. All of these constitute appropriate, positive supports for student behavior. (US Department of Education, Office of Special Education Programs, OSEP Center on Positive Behavioral Interventions and Supports [PBIS], 2010).

Tiers of Intervention

Paraprofessionals often play a major role in a three-tiered approach to providing support for students who fail to respond to general, school-wide interventions and are therefore offered more intensive, personalized interventions.

Tier 1 is generally offered in the general education classroom, where accommodations and adaptations are made for students who need fairly minimal behavioral or learning supports.

The next level of individualized intervention (**Tier 2**) is offered when students have become at-risk due to peer relation problems, academic achievement, or environmental situations. Students receiving these interventions have been less responsive to the universal interventions within the school setting but do not display chronic, intense behavior problems. Ideally, these interventions quickly resolve problematic behavior. Paraprofessionals can assist with these interventions by monitoring group progress, providing social skills instruction, and developing relationships with the students being served.

The next level of intervention, called **Tier 3**, requires greater data collection, assessment, and behavior support planning. These interventions are comprehensive in nature and involve a team of individuals who are familiar with the individual student. The team may include administrators, community members, parents, and the student (when appropriate). Together, the team members create a plan to define what they will do to provide PBIS and how they will determine if the chosen interventions have been successful in supporting change in the student's behavior.

These Tier 3 interventions should focus on socialization and mental health, not simply behavioral repair. The interventions should address school, home, and community settings. The team should look across multiple life domains to address the needs of the student and his or her family members. When the behavior plan is coordinated in all environments, it will be more effective in bringing improvements and is likely to be resolved much more quickly.

Behavior and Learning

Throughout the text we've discussed the link between behavior and learning. In particular, in Chapter 3 we discussed the importance of effective instruction in helping students learn and avoid the boredom, frustration, and disengagement that lead to misbehavior. Let's remind ourselves of the essentials of effective instruction.

- Assessing student understanding:
  - To determine where to begin with the student.
  - To identify areas of strengths and needs.
- Determining instructional goals:
  - Making adaptations and accommodations (if needed).
  - Sharing those goals with students so that we journey toward them together.
- Delivery of instruction:
  - Pacing, using the Goldilocks Principle that speed of delivery and scope of content need to be 'just right' for each student.
  - Grouping of students, to allow them to learn together and from each other.
  - Giving plenty of opportunities for students to respond.
  - Quick and specific feedback, so that students know whether they've "got it right."

Establish Learning and Behavior Rules

In tandem with effective instructional strategies, the groundwork needs to completed for setting out clear behavioral expectations.

- Work with the students to develop rules and consequences (as a paraprofessional you can do this for your small groups).
- No more than four or five rules (even for secondary students).
- Clearly define rules and their associated consequences by having students discuss, "What if you do, what if you don't."
- Give choices for rewards (when tasks are accurately completed or rules followed).
- Give choices for sanctions (yes, even for sanctions—but let students know that if their behavior doesn't change with the selected sanction, you'll have to use another).
- Assure that the rules align with the teacher's classroom rules and those of the school.
- Regularly review rules.
- Praise/reward students for following the rules.
- Respond immediately to infractions and stick with the previously planned consequences.
- Make sure new students or transfers are aware of expectations, rules, and consequences.
- Use Circle Time for problem solving.
- Involve students in accepting responsibilities/leadership roles.
- Use peer-assisted learning group activities to help develop social/collaborative skills.
- With the teacher's support, use classroom meetings to generate options.

A 2005 report on behavior in schools in England and Wales was titled *Learning Behaviour.* This clever title was designed to focus attention on the fact that certain behavior is necessary if we're to see learning happen in the classroom—what we might refer to as learning-facilitating behavior. But it was also intended as a reminder that appropriate behavior can be learned—students are learning appropriate behaviors and, by extension, we are teaching them.

Incentive: Intrinsic and Extrinsic Motivators

Beyond instinct and expectation, what is it that motivates students to perform in the classroom? We have come to realize that our students—like ourselves—may need some type of incentive to learn and to behave in particular ways. Beginning in the 1970s, education research focused on two types of incentive or motivation, intrinsic and extrinsic, and we have already made reference to this is Chapter 4. Intrinsic refers to something internal, or motivation that comes from within a person, while extrinsic is something that comes from outside the person and is often (although not necessarily) tangible or concrete. An example of intrinsic motivation would be a person initiating an activity for its own sake because it sounds interesting, satisfying, and/or fun; an example of extrinsic motivation to initiate an activity might be the promise of a reward of some sort on completion.

> The student who works to improve his grades because he's been promised a new car if he gets straight A's is an example of extrinsic motivation. The student who works to improve his grades because he wants to do his very best and achieve his true potential is an example of intrinsic motivation.

Intrinsic Motivation or Drive

"Drive" is often defined in terms of biology—physical needs arise and we respond to them—or as Freud theorized, behavior may be motivated by inner psychological drives. Internal "drive" or intrinsic motivation operates at a more conscious level and refers to doing something that is enjoyable or inherently interesting just because it's interesting or enjoyable. It is part of a natural human need to seek out challenges and new possibilities. Researchers believe this type of motivational drive is necessary for learning to occur. You may have heard teachers say, "It's important that he learn for the sake of learning. He shouldn't need me to motivate him." This teacher is hopeful that she will have to do nothing more than present the course materials and students will simply learn because they know it is important to learn. And luckily for her, some students do! However, as individuals we are intrinsically motivated by some activities—but not by others. Diversity is one of the beauties of human nature. Some think mountain climbing is fun—while others would avoid it at all costs. A student may be motivated to read and study each chapter because she wants to learn more. A paraprofessional may study with the desire to acquire new knowledge that will assist challenging students with whom she works. These people are motivated. They are driven by intrinsic motivation.

Extrinsic Motivation and Incentives

Extrinsic motivation is often associated with tangible incentives or rewards. We discussed rewards extensively in Chapter 4, and you may wish to refer back to that chapter for examples of rewards or incentives for students to behave appropriately. On the next page you'll find a prompt for thinking about the incentives to offer to students in your school or classroom. We recommend that you respond to the prompt as a means of evaluating and—where necessary—changing this aspect of your classroom practice. But here's a reminder of the different nature of the incentives.

One example of incentive is a student who is highly motivated to complete all homework because of the letter grade (A) he may receive at the end of the term. But notice that in real terms, the A is not something physical or tangible. It cannot be eaten, or traded for an iPod. But it is something that is being given or granted to the student, rather than something intangible that comes from within. It therefore meets the definition of an extrinsic motivator rather than an intrinsic motivator.

Rewards such as money, prizes, or extra recess are external and tangible motivators and are important to most people. A paycheck is a great extrinsic motivator—a BIG paycheck is even better! However, in Chapter 4 we also made the point that typically the younger the students are, the more likely they are to need instant, tangible rewards. But even young children can be motivated by the reward of recognition from the teacher, the paraprofessional, or their parents—especially when it takes the form of that ever-popular intangible, praise. In the box below you will find a reminder of a variety of ways in which we can offer praise to students—even without using words.

Ways to Give Praise without Speaking

- Write a note praising the student for following a specific rule.
- Give the student a high five.
- Pat the student on the arm.
- Give the student a thumbs up.
- Write a note on a post card and mail it to the student at his home.
- Smile and wink.
- Smile.
- Nod as you make eye contact with the student.

For bigger rewards:
- Lunch with the paraprofessional or teacher.
- Walk together to an activity.
- Special privileges such as taking a note to the principal.

In reality, we all need both types of motivation—intrinsic and extrinsic. Very few of us can maintain our determination without external, tangible incentives of some kind, at least part of the time. We may promise ourselves something as significant as a vacation or something as simple as a quick catnap once we've accomplished a certain thing, depending on the magnitude of the task to be accomplished before the reward can be claimed. One colleague of the authors, who was himself an expert in behavior management, admitted to a weakness for making rude comments about other people's driving when he was on the road. So he kept a sticky note on the dashboard of his old car and awarded himself a point every time he encountered an example of poor driving *but managed to refrain from cursing the driver*. His motivation? He'd promised himself a Lexus—but only once he had gained 1,000 points!

Self-Determination Theory

In Chapter 4 we referred to psychologists Deci and Ryan, who explored the elements involved in self-determination—determining for yourself what you will do and achieve—as they relate to education settings. They suggested that people are driven by a need to gain knowledge and/or independence and that people have an

Evaluating Practice: Rewards and Incentives

Make a list of external motivators or incentives used *in the school* where you work. We have started you off with some that were discussed in the text.

- Grades

- Diploma

-

-

-

-

-

-

-

-

-

-

Now think about which of these *you personally can dispense or offer* to students. (Of course, these should be carefully coordinated with the teacher.) Put a check mark next to those.

Choose two of those you have checked and set goals to increase your usage of these rewards as a means of increasing student motivation to behave in appropriate ways in your classroom. Make sure the goals are SMART—specific, measurable, achievable, realistic, and with a time element attached to them.

inherent tendency toward self-fulfillment and agency. They proposed that self-determination theory encompassed three important concepts: *competence*, *connection* or *relatedness*, and *autonomy*. (You'll remember Maslow's Hierarchy of Needs from Chapter 2 and can see that these are related.) We will briefly discuss each of these, as they offer additional insights into student behaviors. First, we discuss competence.

Competence

As humans we feel the need to learn skills and master tasks. We want to have some control over outcomes and we want to experience the sense of achievement that comes with mastering a task. In fact, as adults this need to feel competent may make us reluctant to engage in new activities because new challenges can undermine our confidence. If you are studying this text as part of a college course, you may have experienced this type of situation as college study may have taken you out of your comfort zone and required you to engage in new endeavors in areas where you do not feel competent—such as writing assignments.

It has been shown that offering students unexpected positive feedback (e.g., identifying for them how competent they are) when they are doing a task increases their motivation to do it. In fact, specific and positive praise increased the intrinsic motivation and decreased extrinsic motivation for the task. (This applies to writing positive and specific praise notes as discussed in Chapter 7.)

Connection or Relatedness

As a natural human instinct, we want to interact and be connected. We need to feel that we belong. We want to experience the caring of others. Facebook, Twitter, and other social media use this concept and have done an incredible job of linking into this need and connecting people from around the world. Social media generally provide a useful avenue for all personality types to make connections with others—including those who are naturally reserved, or those who have a recognized disability such as ASD and find face-to-face interactions difficult (as discussed in Chapter 6). Social skills training groups, social narratives, and video modeling have also been used effectively to teach the needed skills. The methods and procedures for these programs are discussed at length in other sources. If you feel any of your students are in need of more specific training to develop the social skills that will allow them to better connect or relate to others, consult with your teacher for resources. Some students may need these more intensive interventions before they are introduced to the activities presented here.

Organizing to Support Group Connections

- Establish and clarify the goals or outcomes of the activities.
- Clarify rules for group members of listening and showing respect.
- Assign leadership roles and responsibilities of individuals within the group.
- Praise or reinforce students who abide by the goals and rules.
- Establish procedures for reporting outcomes to the whole class, e.g., written report, oral presentation, illustrations.

- Develop procedures for obtaining help, e.g., raise your hand if you need my help.
- Encourage collaboration among group members—reward evidence of collaboration, not just the end product.

Paraprofessionals support effective teachers and the students by reinforcing social skills instruction and helping to administer an array of positive behavior supports. Some students require multiple types of intervention, and the support for change comes from a team of educators and paraprofessionals. In fact, that may have been exactly the reason why you were hired as a paraprofessional.

Ideas to Build Social Support

- Encourage group activities.
- Celebrate student successes together with students.
- Advocate for caring relationships between teaching staff and students.
- Let each student, as well as the group, know they are behaving well.
- Sometimes ignoring inappropriate behavior works if you praise other group members for the behavior you want to see.
- Teach students to be supportive of each other in their comments and reactions rather than dismissing or making fun of each other's contributions to the group.

Autonomy

Situations that facilitate autonomy—as opposed to minimizing it—have a strong link to motivation. When students are offered choices and options—a degree of independence and freedom to choose—their participation is much more likely to increase. Some research suggests that the need for competence and autonomy is the very basis of intrinsic motivation and can diminish the need for extrinsic rewards. There seems to be a universal urge to be causal agents in our own lives. We want to be in harmony with ourselves. We want to have the agency to choose for ourselves. So intrinsic (internal) motivation—this drive to choose and be autonomous—has a much greater impact on student learning than extrinsic (external) motivation.

Autonomy—Choice by Another Name

When we discussed Plan A in Chapter 3, we also discussed the importance of teaching students that they have a choice in the way they behave and, therefore, choices in the consequences they enjoy. This is true whether their behavior is appropriate or inappropriate. In Chapter 5 we suggested that when there is a set sanction for a particular inappropriate behavior, students may not have a *choice of sanction,* but they can choose to engage in behavior that has no associated

Linking to Practice: From Theory to Action

As you review the principles of motivation, match the theoretical areas of motivation to the classroom and school activities.

1. Choosing an activity for free time: <u>Autonomy</u>

2. Working in a group with peers: _____

3. Winning a race that involves sharpened skills: _____

4. Receiving extra points: _____

5. Writing/Presenting a paper on your favorite topic: _____

6. Beating a deadline: _____

7. Facing the pressure of competition: _____

8. Catching a football pass: _____

9. Receiving detention: _____

10. Receiving 100% on a difficult test: _____

Make a note here of other instances you may have seen of these principles and underlying concepts among the students in the classrooms where you work.

sanctions—*they can choose to behave appropriately*. So student choice is not about the type of sanction imposed. That will already have been decided and recorded in the school-wide behavior support policy. The choice available to students is to choose to behave appropriately or not, and the rewards (incentives) and sanctions associated with particular behaviors are designed to guide and influence their choice.

Ways to Say "Good Job"

- That answer is exactly correct.
- I like the way you . . . [raised your hand before speaking].
- Congratulations!
- You did great work today.
- You make my job fun.
- I like having you in this class.
- You kept working when others were noisy. Good job!
- It's fun watching you learn.
- Way to go! You did [name behavior] right.

Influences on Behavior

In Chapter 2 we discussed influences on behavior, but this book is really all about what influences behavior. And in a sense, it's really all about you as a paraprofessional: how influential you already are, and how much more influential you can be as you seek to increase your knowledge and understanding of what drives and motivates students and their behavior. In Chapter 2 we also discussed the importance of building trust and respect with (and for) students because, above all else, they need to feel that you trust and respect them and that they can trust and respect you. This isn't just something warm and fuzzy that the good paraprofessional adds to her repertoire or uses to manipulate student behavior. It's at the very core of what you do for students. But because it's so critically important, it's also not easy. If you recall, in Chapter 2 we talked about the need for integrity on your part. Students need to know:

- That you will be honest with them.
- That you believe in them (think: high expectations).
- That they can rely on you (remember our discussion of the importance of consistency).
- That you have their best interests at heart—that you want them to succeed.

All of this must be underpinned by a sound understanding of what constitutes effective practice in managing behavior—students should also be able to feel they can trust and respect you because you have developed the competence needed to provide appropriate support in this area of your responsibilities. And of course, that's the very reason for this book, and presumably what motivated you to study it.

Last But Not Least

A principle that we hope has also been evident throughout the book is that of working under the direction of a professional educator. It's a legal principle, as we discussed in Chapter 1, but also makes sense on so many levels.

- Working as part of an instructional team boosts the impact of what either of you can accomplish individually.
- Consistency between you and your supervising teacher is supremely important because of the messages it gives to students—establishing your credibility and authority, confirming the stability of the rules and expectations, providing a more emotionally secure environment for students, and leading the focus back to learning at every turn.
- Keeping you safely within the bounds of what is appropriate and permitted as regards federal and state guidelines is imperative.

You may be more experienced than the professional educator you work with—this is often the case for paraprofessionals—but he or she is legally responsible for the learning environment you share and legally responsible for your work as well. If you can work willingly under the direction of a professional, you will have many opportunities to observe different ways of working, learn from that diversity, and become an ever more effective support for students and teachers alike.

Applying Theory to Practice: Case Studies

As a final exercise to draw together the different strands discussed throughout the book, we have provided on the next pages some prompts for you to apply the knowledge and understanding you have acquired through your study of this book. We offer two activities:

1. Case studies for three students, based on research conducted at Brigham Young University. For each of these, the student is briefly described and you are asked to respond to a series of questions about interventions you would use.
2. The opportunity to develop a case study on the behavior of a particular student you are familiar with. You will see that this requires you to reflect on the principles we have discussed and apply them to your own work setting in a very focused way.

For both of these activities we suggest you refer back to the relevant chapters to refresh your memory as necessary and, of course, consult your supervising teacher for clarification, support, and permission as required.

Activity 1: Three Case Studies: Amy, Juan, and Don

Below are case studies of Amy, Juan, and Don, who have all been identified as Emotionally Disturbed and who all display aggressive behaviors. Please answer all three questions after each case. Use techniques and procedures that you would normally use in your current classroom.

Amy

Characteristics: Amy is a fifth-grade student but is performing academically two years behind. She currently receives resource assistance in reading and math. Family stressors include an alcoholic grandmother, a blended family (stepfather), and a dysfunctional home life including marital conflict, lack of discipline, and poverty. Family members are loving toward Amy but two instances of sexual molestation have been confirmed.

Behavior: Amy displays aggressive behaviors towards her peers when she does not get her way or isn't given her choice of whom or what to play with. These behaviors include hitting and kicking. Incidences have typically occurred on the playground or during periods of free time but are now starting to be displayed during group instruction when Amy is paired with another student to complete assigned work.

1. Would you attempt to intervene with Amy? If so, how?

2. What would you consider to be the best strategy for dealing with Amy's behavior?

3. What would you consider to be indications of success in managing Amy's behavior?

Juan

Characteristics: Juan is a second grader whose teacher judges to have academically average performance in spelling, handwriting, social studies, and P.E. and below average academic performance in reading, language, math, science, and music. Juan was retained in first grade and has attended three different schools. Juan's mother is aware of his behavior problems and is supportive with school staff.

Behavior: Juan is continually verbally abusive. When speaking with teachers, he uses offensive, vulgar words and has threatened assault and aggression toward teachers if asked to do a task he does not like. He has been suspended for this behavior in the past.

1. Would you attempt to intervene with Juan? If so, how?

2. What would you consider to be the best strategy for dealing with Juan's behavior?

3. What would you consider to be indications of success in managing Juan's behavior?

Don

Characteristics: Don, a first grader, seems like a typical kid—tall, slender, and often disheveled. His mother and father both work while Don is at school. His mother is currently fighting a severe illness and is troubled with depression and fatigue. At school, interactions between teachers and classmates seem warm and inviting. Don can sit through story time (sometimes for long amounts of time) with few or no behavior problems.

Behavior: When given a simple request to turn in homework, asked to correct a mistake on his assignment, or given a mild rebuke, Don's behavior turns into disruption. He begins shouting obscenities, overturns desks, and vandalizes classroom property (displays, furniture, toys, etc.). Don shows temporary compliance at times and then begins his disruption again.

1. Would you attempt to intervene with Don? If so, how?

2. What would you consider to be the best strategy for dealing with Don's behavior?

3. What would you consider to be indications of success in managing Don's behavior?

Activity 2: Applying Theory to Practice: Your Own Case Study

Think of a student whose behavior is a cause of some concern. This may be a low-level disruption such as moving around the classroom at inappropriate times, or something more major such as violent outbursts. Imagine that you have to brief a new teacher or school psychologist about the student. We're going to guide you through the different sections of this report, but first let's establish some ground rules for professionalism:

- Keep this entirely anonymous (refer to the student by his/her first initial, or as Student X).
- As much as possible, stick to the facts—your impressions are important but first try to be objective.
- Keep comments appropriate by using appropriate and impersonal language (e.g., "There appear to be some difficulties at home," rather than, "The real problem is the parents!"—even if you think this is true).

You will see that there are a series of questions for each section. You do not have to answer each of these, one at a time. They are designed to prompt your thinking, so you may choose to write your thoughts first and then check back through the questions to see if there's anything you've not thought of.

Let's start with some notes about the **Student's background** (age, school history to date, family background, academic progress, attendance, relationship with peers, etc.). These can be notes—they don't have to be beautifully crafted sentences.

Now let's focus on the **Behavior of concern.**
Questions: What is it that the student does that's given rise to concern? How often does this happen? What seems to trigger the behavior? If necessary, and with the teacher's permission, you may wish to conduct a formal observation of the student in order to establish how often and under which circumstances the behavior occurs. (See Chapter 2 for notes about observable and measurable behaviors and about the ABCs of behavior.)

Now think about the **Consequences of the behavior.**
Questions: What do you and/or the teacher do when this behavior occurs? How does the student react to those consequences? Do they seem to have any effect? Is there perhaps only a short-term or temporary effect? Why do you think the behavior is persisting (here's an opportunity to be more subjective and speculate a little)?

Next we need to focus on the **Proactive measures taken** to try to prevent or lessen the behavior.
Questions: What steps have been taken to reduce the likelihood of this behavior happening? Have you been able to identify a positive, appropriate behavior you could encourage that would naturally eliminate the inappropriate behavior? Does the instruction the student is receiving appear to be at the right level for him or her? Have you discussed with the student why he or she is behaving in this way, how he or she feels about the current set of consequences, whether he or she understands how to behave appropriately, and whether he or she understands the benefits (positive consequences) of behaving appropriately?

And lastly, what **Conclusions** would you draw from this?
Questions: What seems to be the real issue with this student's behavior? Is it really as much of a problem as you thought, or is it perhaps worse? What do you now see as possible causes and/or solutions? Are there changes that need to be made to your interactions with the student? What do you think you need to do differently? Do you need to pursue this with your supervising teacher?

This type of exercise isn't automatically going to resolve all behavioral issues in the classroom, but it should advance your understanding of the situation and make you better prepared to support this student in appropriate ways because of an increased awareness of what's really happening and a close examination of the facts.

You could choose to complete this exercise orally, using the section headings and questions as prompts. In that case you might ask a colleague or another adult who is totally unconnected to the school (remember to keep everything completely anonymous) to listen to you as you talk this through—essentially thinking it through out loud. But don't allow yourself to get sidetracked. Ask your colleague to please not interrupt and allow you to just keep thinking and talking, and to keep any questions he or she may have until you have finished speaking.

Learning Outcomes

In earlier chapters you learned concepts that you have been able to apply here. Throughout the activities you have demonstrated your knowledge of the critical focus on behavior and learning. You have developed plans that apply to students with disabilities. You can demonstrate your knowledge of PBIS and tiered supports using LRBI and can explain how they apply to learning and behavior.

Summary

And so we come to the end of the chapters and hope that you have found useful information, greater understanding, and motivation as you have read and studied (or discussed) the different theories and strategies. What remains are the listings of further sources of relevant and useful information in the form of websites as well as a Glossary of important terms.

And lastly, we wish you well in your pursuit of excellence in your work. We believe in you as a paraprofessional—we believe that you already do much good work to support students and teachers and schools; we believe that you can enhance what you do as you carefully observe students and teachers and apply principles of effective practice.

Bibliography

Causton-Theoharis, J. N., & Malmgren, K. W. (2005). Increasing peer interactions for students with severe disabilities via paraprofessional training. *Council for Exceptional Children, 71*(4), 431–444.

Freeman, R., Eber, L., Anderson, C., Irvin, L., Horner, R., Bounds, M., & Dunlap, G. (2006). Building inclusive school cultures using school-wide positive behavior support: Designing effective individual support systems for students with significant disabilities. *Research & Practice for Persons with Severe Disabilities, 31*(1), 4–17.

Hall, L. J., McClannahan, L. E., & Krantz, P. J. (1995). Promoting independence in integrated classrooms by teaching aides to use activity schedules and decrease prompts. *Education and Training in Mental Retardation and Developmental Disabilities, 30,* 208–217.

Ryan, R. M., & Deci, E. L. (2000). Intrinsic and extrinsic motivations: Classic definitions and new directions. *Contemporary Educational Psychology, 25,* 54–67. doi:10.1006/ceps.1999.1020, available online at www.idealibrary.com on IDEAL.

Ryan, R. M., & Deci, E. L. (2000). Self-determination theory and the facilitation of intrinsic motivation, social development, and well-being. *American Psychologist, 55,* 68–78.

Skinner, B. F. (1953). *Science and human behavior.* New York: Macmillan.

Steer Report. (2005). *Learning behavior: The report of the practitioners' group on school behaviour and discipline.* London: Department for Education and Skills.

US Department of Education, Office of Special Education Programs, OSEP Center on Positive Behavioral Interventions and Supports, Effective Schoolwide Interventions. (2010). Positive behavior supports and the paraprofessional. Retrieved from OSEP Center website: www.pbis.org/school/tertiary_level/pbs_for_paraprofessionals.aspx.

Walker, H. M., Horner, R. H., Sugai, G., Bullis, M., Sprague, J. R., Bricker, D., & Kaufman, M. J. (1996). Integrated approaches to preventing antisocial behavior patterns among school-age children and youth. *Journal of Emotional and Behavioral Disorders, 4*(4), 194–209.

Glossary

ADHD (Attention-Deficit/Hyperactivity Disorder) This is a condition that is now recognized to be neurological in origin. Three different types have been recognized, depending on whether the main issue is poor attention or high levels of hyperactivity. Medication is used in the majority of cases to moderate the behavior of children with ADHD.

Asperger Syndrome A high-functioning form of Autism, generally with no associated cognitive disability but nevertheless including the classic triad of impairment (communication, social interaction, flexibility of thinking).

Autism (ASD, Autistic Spectrum Disorder) A wide range of conditions all characterized by impairments in the three areas of communication, social interaction, and imagination or flexibility of thinking. The highly respected *Diagnostic and Statistical Manual of Mental Disorders,* Fifth Edition (DSM-5) folds all subcategories (such as Kanner's, Asperger, etc.) into one umbrella diagnosis of Autism Spectrum Disorder (ASD). It is defined by two categories: impaired social communication and/or interaction and restricted and/or repetitive behaviors. Learning and behavioral issues occur because of frustration, uncertainty, an inability to interpret social cues, etc. A highly structured environment with minimal sensory distractions best suits the student with ASD.

Behavior In its purest sense, any action on the part of an individual, which may include "invisible" behaviors that can only be assumed to occur from observation (silent reading, paying attention, etc.), and emotional responses (worrying, thinking). However, for practical reasons, we generally deal with observable, measurable behaviors, which would include the symptoms of inner, invisible behaviors.

Behaviorism The science of the study of behavior. Originating with the work of Russian physiologist Ivan Pavlov and subsequently psychologists such as B. F. Skinner, a basic principle of behaviorism is that behavior is learned and can be shaped or modified according to the consequences that follow.

Circle Time A generic term for a variety of different activities, all of which involve gathering students in a circle (on the floor or seated on chairs) in order to address social and emotional issues. This may range from a simple check-in at the beginning of the school day to ascertain students' mood and attitudes to a full-scale Philosophy for Children (P4C) inquiry. See also P4C.

Cognitive behaviorism A more recent variation on behaviorism, based not only on the shaping of behavior through manipulation of consequences but also on recognizing the need to engage the student in considering his/her own behavior and the possible consequences. The principle of choice is important here—that students come to understand that they can choose a desirable consequence by behaving in an appropriate way and thereby come to take responsibility for their own behavior. See also Self-Determination.

Consistency   Recognized as a critical feature of any behavior management system. This includes consistency among members of staff, across settings for any one student, and school wide.

Construals   Construals are how individuals perceive, comprehend, and interpret the world around them. This influences the nature of individual experience, including cognition, emotion, and motivation.

Dyslexia   Difficulties associated with print and therefore reading. Students with dyslexia may also have difficulties with organization, short-term memory, and the language content of math.

Dyspraxia   Also known as Developmental Coordination Disorder. Refers to difficulties associated with movement and formerly considered as simply clumsiness. We now understand that this is a more far-reaching condition that includes organizational abilities, memory, and processing and affects both fine motor skills (e.g., writing) and gross motor skills (catching and throwing).

Individuals with Disabilities Education Act (IDEA)   Major US legislation relating to special education. Also refers to the need for paraprofessionals to be "appropriately trained and supervised."

Least Restrictive Behavioral Interventions (LRBI)   The idea that any intervention or response to a behavior should be minimal. This applies whether the behavior is positive or negative. First proposed in relation to students with disabilities but applied here to any student behavior, the LRBI approach helps to maintain a focus on teaching and learning in the classroom rather than allowing behavioral issues to distract and absorb unnecessary amounts of teaching/learning time.

Negative reinforcement   Providing a negative consequence to encourage a particular behavior. The student will work to avoid the potential negative consequence by behaving appropriately. See also Positive reinforcement.

No Child Left Behind   Federal legislation also referred to as the ESEA (Elementary and Secondary Education Act). Title I of the Act, which provides support for disadvantaged children, requires paraprofessionals who work in funded programs to meet specific requirements with regard to qualifications. It also requires them to work "under the direct supervision" of a professional.

PBIS (Positive Behavioral Interventions and Supports)   System of positive principles and strategies for managing behavior recommended by the Office of Special Education Programs (OSEP) of the US Department of Education. These are not necessarily new but have been gathered together from a variety of sources. Their common feature is that they have been shown—through systematic research—to be effective in managing behavior.

Philosophy for Children (P4C)   A program designed to develop students' abilities to reason, reflect, and think critically. Based on a Socratic approach, which facilitates learning through asking a series of questions, P4C is a democratic approach, where students determine the questions to be discussed, following the presentation of a prompt or stimulus (e.g., a video clip or a short story) by the teacher or facilitator of the P4C session. P4C has been widely used to allow students to discuss social and behavioral issues. See also SAPERE.

Positive reinforcement   Providing a positive consequence for a behavior in order to strengthen that behavior (akin to a reward). See also Negative reinforcement.

Psychodynamic approach The psychodynamic approach to behavior is based on the work of psychologists such as Sigmund Freud (father of psychoanalysis), who believed that human behavior is the outer manifestation of inner drives or urges. As an approach it is more relevant and appropriate for a therapeutic rather than a classroom setting.

Punishment A negative consequence. See also Sanction.

Reinforcement Strengthening a behavior by imposing particular consequences (which could be positive or negative). See Negative reinforcement and Positive reinforcement.

Restorative Justice An approach used in the criminal justice system in the USA and elsewhere to reduce reoffending/recidivism, where victim and perpetrator are brought together to talk about the crime or offense that has been committed, largely for the perpetrator or criminal to better understand the actual effects of the crime on the victim and therefore develop greater empathy. This approach has been shown to reduce reoffending as the perpetrator comes to see the full human cost of his/her actions rather than taking an impersonal view. It is generally acknowledged, however, that Restorative Justice may work better for certain groups of offenders than others. See also Restorative Practice.

Restorative Practice Adapted from Restorative Justice for use in schools and other noncriminal settings. Students who have behaved inappropriately toward other students are brought together with them to a conference facilitated by a trained adult. Discussion of the effects of the behavior is designed to reduce reoccurrence as the offending student realizes more particularly how his/her behavior has impacted the other student. Widely shown to reduce incidents of negative interactions between students. The facilitating adult is provided with a series of questions to ask, all of which avoid placing blame and focus rather on participants clearly stating what happened and what effects that may have had on those involved, including emotional effects.

Reward An object or consequence that is pleasing and/or motivating to the person receiving it. The use of rewards in behavior management is to increase the likelihood of a particular behavior recurring or to strengthen that behavior.

Sanction Something that is designed to reduce or eliminate a behavior. As with rewards, sanctions must be meaningful to the recipient in order to be effective as individual students will have different responses to different sanctions. Other necessary characteristics of effective sanctions include: timeliness, appropriate scope, and simplicity. See also Punishment.

SAPERE (Society for the Advancement of Philosophical Enquiry and Reflection in Education) Closely associated with Philosophy for Children (P4C) programs as used in schools in the USA and elsewhere.

SEAL (Social and Emotional Aspects of Learning) Materials developed in the United Kingdom for teaching social skills and emotional literacy. The materials are available for download (see website in the Useful Websites and Organizations section) and provide very specific help for educators in developing children's ability to recognize their own emotions, recognize the emotions of others, and learn to respond appropriately to those emotions in themselves and in others.

Self-determination The capacity to direct one's own life and actions by making appropriate choices.

Useful Websites and Organizations

This list of websites provides plenty of opportunities for you to pursue topics that are of particular interest to you in relation to behavior. We have included them here because they offer solid information and practical advice. Many of them offer further links—there's really no limit to the information available—so enjoy exploring and see where it takes you!

American Federation of Teachers (AFT) (www.aft.org) The American Federation of Teachers is one of the two main professional organizations for educators in the USA. It offers membership to paraprofessionals but also a range of free resources/information to nonmembers (see the section PSRP/School Support Staff).

Association for Positive Behavior Support (www.apbs.org) An international organization for promoting research-based strategies to increase quality of life and decrease problem behaviors. A search for Autism on this site will direct you to a range of resources and information.

Behavior4Learning (www.behavior2learn.co.uk) An archive of materials produced by the UK's Department for Education, including links to a whole series of YouTube clips relating to behavior.

Council for Exceptional Children (CEC) (www.cec.sped.org) Here you will find *Parability: The CEC Paraeducator Standards Workbook* that includes CEC Standards for Paraeducators, a Code of Ethics of Paraeducators, and two tools that can be used by district personnel, principals, trainers, and paraeducators to ensure that paraeducators meet the CEC Standards.

Dr. Mac's Behavior Management Site (www.behavioradvisor.com) Here you can sign up for regular updates and articles on various aspects of behavior management. Registration is free.

Dyspraxia USA (www.dyspraxiausa.org/) Provides information on symptoms and supports for students and adults with dyspraxia.

Effective Teaching (www.effectiveteaching.com) This is the website for Harry Wong. Under the "Resources" tab you'll find all the free resources in one place, including an e-newsletter with tips on managing behavior.

Fintan O'Regan (www.fintanoregan.com) A behavior consultant in the UK, Fintan O'Regan offers a variety of free resources and information via the "ADHD Plus" and "Parents Corner" tabs on this website.

International Institute for Restorative Practices (IIRP) (www.iirp.edu) Provides information on Restorative Practice and links to online resources.

International Site for Teaching Assistants and Paraprofessionals (ISTAP) (http://education.byu.edu/istap) Offers information relating to disabilities, practical classroom strategies, and links to other useful websites, with contributions from the USA, Canada, the United Kingdom, and Australia.

LDonline (www.ldonline.com) Website that provides extensive information on both Learning Difficulties (LD) and Attention-Deficit Hyperactive Disorder (ADHD). Also the source of information for the work of Dr. Richard LaVoie, expert in Learning Difficulties and presenter of the FAT City workshop.

National Association of School Psychologists (NASP) (www.nasponline.org) Offers free resources on a range of topics relating to behavior under the "Resource Library" tab, including teaching social skills, ADD/ADHD, and bullying.

National Autism Association (http://nationalautismassociation.org) This website provides extensive information on Autism, including contact information for local and state chapters of the organization.

National Education Association (NEA) (www.nea.org) One of the two main professional organizations for educators in the USA, NEA offers membership to paraprofessional staff (see the section Education Support Professionals under the "Our Members" tab) and a range of free resources/information. Look too for links to state affiliates.

National Resource Center for Paraeducators (NRCP) (www.nrcpara.org) This website offers resources for paraprofessionals as well as information on the annual international conference and links to state websites where further local information can be found.

Positive Behavioral Interventions and Supports (PBIS) (www.pbis.org) This website is the technical assistance center on PBIS established by the Office of Special Education Programs (OSEP) of the US Department of Education to provide "capacity-building information and technical assistance for identifying, adapting, and sustaining effective school-wide disciplinary practices." Aimed mainly at schools, the website contains a great deal of useful information, including video clips, checklists, and clear explanations of how to implement PBIS on a day-to-day basis with students.

SAPERE (Society for the Advancement of Philosophical Enquiry and Reflection in Education) (www.sapere.org.uk) Provides basic information about Philosophy for Children (P4C) and how it can be used to develop reasoning and reflection, presenting students with intellectual challenge but also social and emotional support.

SEAL (Social and Emotional Aspects of Learning) Resources available on the UK's National Archives website at: http://webarchive.nationalarchives.gov.uk/20110809101133/nsonline.org.uk/node/87009.

Smart Classroom Management (www.smartclassroommanagement.com) This is Michael Linsin's website, which offers practical advice on a whole range of behavioral issues. You can sign up for free updates or simply use the wealth of information that's already on the site.

University of Alabama Parenting Assistance Line (UA-PAL) (www.pal.ua.edu) Under the "Discipline and Guidance" tab you will find a huge number of resources for different aspects of behavior listed under five age ranges, from Infants to Adolescents.

Index

54506738R00127

Made in the USA
Lexington, KY
18 August 2016